THEATRE HISTORY STUDIES

Theatre History Studies is an official journal of the Mid-America Theatre Conference, Inc. (MATC). The conference encompasses the states of Illinois, Iowa, Nebraska, Kansas, Missouri, Minnesota, North Dakota, South Dakota, Wisconsin, Michigan, Indiana, and Ohio. While it is primarily a regional conference, its purposes are to unite persons and organizations within this region and elsewhere who have an interest in theatre and to promote the growth and development of all forms of theatre. Its primary areas of interest are represented by four symposia: History, Directing, Playwriting, and Pedagogy.

Theater in the Americas

A New Series from Southern Illinois University Press
ROBERT A. SCHANKE, SERIES EDITOR

QUERIES & SUBMISSIONS
Robert A. Schanke, Editor
498 Edgewood Lane
Pleasant Hill
IA 50219
E-mail: schanker@aol.com

The goal of the series is to publish a wide range of scholarship on theater and performance in the Americas, defining theater in its broadest terms and including subjects that encompass all of the Americas.

The series focuses on the performance and production of theater and theater artists and practitioners but welcomes studies of dramatic literature as well.

Meant to be inclusive, the series invites studies of traditional, experimental, and ethnic forms of theater; celebrations, festivals, and rituals that perform culture; and acts of civil disobedience that are performative in nature.

We hope to publish studies of theater and performance activities of all cultural groups within the Americas, including biographies of individuals, histories of theater companies, studies of cultural traditions, and collections of plays.

Southern Illinois University Press

P.O. Box 3697, Carbondale, Illinois 62902-3697 — www.siu.edu/-siupress

THEATRE HISTORY STUDIES

VOLUME XXIV

CONTENTS

2004

SPECIAL FEATURES

ARTICLES

BOOK REVIEWS

Front Cover: The Cherry Sisters, Effie and Addie, in the later years of their career, still wearing the same dresses and accessories. Photo courtesy of Orville and Jane Rennie Collection, State Historical Society of Iowa—Iowa City.

Theatre History Studies 24 (June 2004)

In Memory Of Albert Wertheim

(July 3, 1940 -April 16, 2003)

STACEY CONNELLY

At the 2004 Mid-America Theatre Association Conference in March, President Rhona Justice-Malloy opened the conference banquet by remembering our friend and long-time MATC member Albert Wertheim and requesting a minute of silence in his honor. The last time most of us saw him was at MATC's 2003 meeting in Indianapolis, where — even though he was gravely ill — he read a paper at the Theatre History Symposium. A month later, he passed away. He is greatly missed.

Born in New York City, Al was the only son of parents who had fled Nazi Germany. In 1961, he was elected to Phi Beta Kappa and took his A.B. degree from Columbia University with honors in English and German. He earned his M.A. and Ph.D. in English and American literature from Yale University and in 1965 taught for four years at Princeton. In 1969 he moved to Indiana University and became Professor of English, Theatre and Drama, and Comparative Literature, teaching Shakespeare, seventeenth-century drama, and modern British and American drama. Later in his career, he taught courses in dramatic literature from Australia, New Zealand, South Africa, and the Caribbean. Publishing widely in these areas, Al authored dozens of articles and two books: *The Dramatic Art of Athol Fugard: From South Africa to the World and Staging the War: American Drama and World War II.*

He served for many years on the executive boards of the American Society for Theatre Research and the Phoenix Theatre in Indianapolis, and as national president of the Eugene O'Neill Society. He was the recipient of awards from the National Endowment for the Humanities, the German Academic Exchange Service, the German Marshall Fund, The Folger Library, and the Newberry Library.

Whether he was guiding freshmen, graduates, or senior citizens through Indiana's continuing education program, Al's first love was teaching and his students knew it. He received seven awards for distinguished teaching, including the Herman Fredric Lieber Award, and was named 2002 Teacher of the Year Award by the Indiana Council for Continuing Education. As my professor and dissertation advisor, Al was indeed outstanding, but what I'll remember most is his warmth and the extraordinary effort he made to get to know his students personally—taking us on theatre excursions to Indianapolis and Louisville, having meals with us, shepherding us through daunting scholarly projects, and going to bat for us against all manner of institutional red tape. Once we were finally out and in academic positions of our own, he treated his former students as colleagues—with utmost respect and kindness. In honoring him at this year's conference, several of us thought fondly of the friendly dinners we had shared with him at past MATC meetings in St. Louis, Omaha, Chicago, and Kansas City. In the coming years, we'll continue to remember him and reflect with gratitude on his life as a scholar, teacher, and friend.

Stacey Connelly
Trinity University

Theatre History Studies 24 (June 2004)

Learning Eloquence: Theater is a Speech Act

MARTHA LAVEY

(This was the keynote address delivered at the MATC annual convention in Chicago, March 6, 2004.)

Thank you so much for having me. It's an honor to participate in your conference. Reading over the list of symposia, I am impressed by the breadth of your inquiry, of the inter-textual weave of history, pedagogy, and practice. It is heartening to observe how deeply your scholarly interests seek to embed the study and practice of theater within a larger cultural context.

I had the opportunity, recently, to work with designer Tom Lynch. Tom designed the set for our current production of OUR LADY OF 121st STREET and has worked with us at Steppenwolf on several previous productions. As you may know, Tom has a prominent design career – he works frequently on Broadway and throughout the country, designing both for theater and opera. Tom received his MFA from the Yale School of Drama and has had the opportunity to teach design, previously at Yale and currently in the MFA program at NYU. After telling me how much he enjoys teaching, Tom described the struggle he underwent in accepting his current teaching appointment. He feels torn, he said, about encouraging designers into a profession – through an arduous and expensive educational process – when the marketplace offers no guarantee of employment. He said, laughingly, but sincerely, "It got down to this: designing for the theater is better than killing. I know that much." We talked for some time about the value of educating eager and hopeful young people into the profession and arrived, finally, at a question that I think is germane to your work – and which figures very strongly in my own as a theater producer – and which I would articulate in this way: is theater a reliable, an insightful lens through which to survey the world? Is studying theater a valuable way to know the world? I guess it is a question about application: does what Tom teaches as a designer apply – effectively – to those of his students who may never practice design at the level at which he does? In my case, as a producer, I ask people to come and see plays. Does this activity apply to the rest of their lives? Does it support their being in the world? In Tom's equation, are we doing more good than harm?

The question – for all of us, I'm sure – became more urgent after September the 11th, 2001. The sense that our lives were in peril encouraged a collective and sober assessment of our actions. What is right livelihood? How am I spending myself in the world? Not incidentally, I think, the drama of this inquiry played itself out on Broadway. New York, devastated by the attacks, rallied behind its theaters, taking great sustenance in their reopening. Suddenly the old adage, "the show must go on," was imbued with a new resonance and depth. To play was an act of survival, a beacon of hope, a reaffirmation of a human collectivity and good. Actors admitted to a deep humility in the face of world events but returned to the theaters, finally, because as one said, "it is what we do."

I take it as instructive that at the moment of one of America's most profound cultural crises, theater found itself on the national stage. It mattered that their were plays. And why? For a host of reasons: because plays reflect our condition, because they divert us from the hardships of our condition, because they help us know ourselves, because they take us outside of ourselves, and because they ask us to gather together with others – with strangers – in the dark and breathe to the rhythm of others, on stage.

Whether an audience member in the theater or an actor on the stage, there is nothing virtual about the theatrical transaction. It is live, in real time, at a specific time and in a specific place. Nor are any of the other players in the theatrical collaboration – the directors, designers, dramaturgs, the casting directors, the marketers, the house and box office staffs, the production crews – a virtual presence. Everybody shows up and dedicates an enormous number of man and woman hours to getting the show on its feet and an audience in the house. In our furiously mediated world, the immediacy of theater, and the sheer people-intensive quality of its making and reception, is an anomaly and something of an antique. Which is the theater's beauty and its gift.

It seems to me that the very awkwardness of theatre – its ungainliness, its evanescence, its promiscuous relationship to both high and popular cultures – is its strength and its value. It is what makes instructing another generation into the practice and appreciation of theater a substantial and worthy undertaking. If we produce, by our teaching, accomplished theater artists, the logic and reward of our teaching is obvious. If, as Tom Lynch fears, we are training students for careers they may never achieve, we are, nevertheless, instructing people into the seriousness of play. We are asking people to work very hard, in cooperation with others, to create beauty and meaning that will, in the moment of its incarnation, announce its disappearance. Just like life. It is my conviction that a serious and thorough education in theater is an especially replete training in rigor, in the pursuit of a passion, in the crafting of what matters and what means. And that that is a portable education – that the training is fungible and can be applied to the learning and execution of a wide range of cultural activity.

And what is it, after all, of which we are in pursuit? What is the essence of the theatrical act? It is, to me, finally, a speech act, an utterance. The goal of the drama is eloquence and all of its theatrical conveyance aspires to make that eloquence elegant. We are storytellers, we are storytelling, and the energy of our craft is to refine our story and our telling to its most articulate condition. The drive toward refined articulation is, again, perhaps an anomaly, perhaps an antique pursuit in contemporary culture. In our world of instant messaging, in which telegraphic speech is the accepted standard and expectation, the intense focus theater provides on the production of the right word, the perfect silence, the metaphorical power of design and gesture – just the pure distillation of expressiveness – is an alternative education. We train our minds – as practitioners and appreciators of theater – to an interpretive act that seeks depth rather than speed and that is <u>collectively</u> rendered and received (rather than executed and received in isolation).

The creative and interpretive abilities that we cultivate in the theater are, finally, the constituitive abilities of citizenship. Theater asks us to be in the world – to be expressive, to develop empathy, to value the crafted and refined utterance as an expression of our human condition. To cultivate this expressiveness in our students, to cultivate an appreciation of this expressiveness in our audiences is to contribute to the body politic. It is, to return to this cultural moment, an urgent task. Much of the drama, playing itself out on the world stage, is centered on the question of free speech – on the contesting of who speaks, and when, and how. Developing, in our students and in our audiences, a sensitivity and discernment in the construction and interpretation of the speech act is to cultivate a nuanced expressiveness, a reception alive to texture, ambiguity, and feeling. These are not abilities encouraged by television, by the telegraphic discourse of e-mail, by any of the media that regard their audience as, first and foremost, a consumer.

What am I doing? Making a case, I guess, with Tom Lynch's reservations as a spur in mind, for the enduring value of what we do in our roles as teachers and practitioners of theater. Mine is an easy job, finally – theater has been a central human activity from the dawn of recorded history, it endures, vitally, to this day. But the inquiry into its value is not, I think, a frivolous one. You must ask yourselves, (I must ask myself), is what I am doing, in creating theater practitioners, in creating theater, taking students (taking audiences) more deeply into the world? Am I adding to the ability, in those I touch, to express and interpret information into meaning?

I return to the account of your symposia. My guess is that the topics engaged in this year's conference would not have appeared on the agenda even 20 years ago. The focus on historicity and cultural context – the inquiry into issues of race, gender, representational strategies, the attention given to community, the testing of power relations in mentoring relationships, the role of documentary in the creation of a politicized theater – all of these topics suggest a heightened awareness of the instrumentality of theater – as a site and source of personal and political action.

Little wonder that the study of our ancient art finds us, simultaneously, on the frontier of our culture's most contemporary concerns. The technology of the word – the communications industry – of which we are most surely a part is, I would argue, the central activity of contemporary culture. Our great contribution to this discourse is a slightly rebellious one. As much of the communication industry works toward the compression of information into smaller and faster infinitely negotiable units of transfer, we insist, in the construction and reception of the theatrical experience, that our practitioners and audiences take the time to create resonate speech. We support the metaphorical over the literal, we encourage silence into meaning, we demand the personal, contextual positioning of speech in the discernment of intention. And, as your symposia suggest, the cultivation of these "artistic" concerns is a political education. The credo, "the personal is political" (and its corollary, "the political is personal") could serve as the credo for theater itself. We imagine that the story of individual lives speaks authentically out of (and into) the larger concerns of our cultural life.

If my participation in the theater community of Chicago has any value as I address you, educators of our future theater practitioners, it may be this; Chicago remains a town in which it is possible to begin a career in the theater. Chicago is much more sophisticated a theater town today than it was when I began my career here. ("Career" would be an inflated description of what I was doing at the time. Really, I was just hacking around, doing what I loved, being in plays and working with performance artists, not getting paid (or getting paid very little), but making stuff.) But over that period of time, theater has become a very significant part of Chicago's identity. We are fortunate to have a mayor who values the arts – among which, importantly, the performing arts – in the quality of life of this city. Mayor Daley knows that having an active arts scene – and an arts education scene – is an important constituent in the entire ecology of what makes a city attractive to residents, to business, to visitors. And so, we have a city that supports over 200 theater companies from the very small, the very specialized in mission, the obscure, to among the most vital and recognized in the country (Chicago is, uniquely, home to three of the winners of the Tony's regional theater awards). Many of your students will look to Chicago as the place to begin their careers in the theater. I offer them all my encouragement. There is a community here. There are professional opportunities here that will put them in contact with practitioners of the highest order. And there is room here, there is space, for them to make their own mark.

I welcome your observations, remarks and questions about your own work and about mine. I salute your dedication and your passion in pursuing the rendering of our experience into speech. I salute your love affair with dialogue. Like you, I believe in the talking cure. Let's talk.

Martha Lavey is the Artistic Director at Steppenwolf Theatre, a position she has held since 1995. On stage at Steppenwolf her appearances include *I Never Sang For My Father, The House of Lily, Valparaiso, The Memory of Water, The Designated Mourner, Time of My Life, Clockwork Orange, Slavs!* and *Aunt Dan and Lemon*. Her awards include the Sarah Siddons Award and, on behalf of the Steppenwolf Theatre Company, the National Medal of Honor in 1998 for recognition of "outstanding contributions to the arts in the United States." She holds a doctorate in performance studies from Northwestern University.

Theatre History Studies 24 (June 2004)

Around the Moscow Art Theatre

THEATRE HISTORY CROSSWORD PUZZLE VIII

FELICIA HARDISON LONDRÉ

Constructed using Crossword Weaver

Note: Russian transliterations can vary; this puzzle consistently uses "i" instead of "y" in the spelling of names.

ACROSS

1. Stanislavski's right-hand man
10. Symbolist author of *Balaganchik (The Puppet Show)*
11. - leksandr N - ko - aievich Ost - ovski's *Snowmaiden* was staged at MAT in 1900

12. Stanislavski's servant
15. Initials of author of *A Month in the Country*, produced at MAT in 1909
16. - - per - aln - , a kind of theatre ended by the October Revolution
17. Actress/wife of Stanislavski
19. Color of the horse in Maiakovski poem on treating horses kindly
20. Initials of novelist esteemed by Chekhov; wrote *Oblomov* (1859)
21. Russian for a "ditch beyond"
22. Devilish play by Andreiev
25. Where Baba Yaga lives
28. "Kalinka" or "Stenka Razin"
30. Incomplete Russian title of Maiakovski play *The Bedbug: - - -p*
31. Greatest Russian stage director; executed under Stalin
34. Chekhov's wife Olga K - - pper
35. American analog of Young Pioneers (abbrev.)
36. Chekhov corresponded with this doctor from 1880s to 1904
39. Ludm - la Petrus - evskaya's *- in - ano* was produced by MAT in 1988
40. Stanislavski directed this dramatist's masterpiece in 1908; Maierhold in 1926
41. Traditional theatre in native land of Maierhold disciple Seki Sano
42. Wrote satirical novel on his behind-the-scenes observations at MAT in 1934
43. Ivan in Scottish

DOWN

1. Prolific literary director of post-Soviet Moscow Art Theatre
2. *P - tty - ou - geo - s* is one translation of the title of Gorki's *Meschanie*
3. Initials of long-remembered German Communist woman murdered in 1919
4. Bulgakov's NEP comedy is set in her apartment
5. Cyrillic acronym for People's Commissariat of Internal Trade
6. Alice Koonen's husband (incomplete): - - - - - v
7. Designed most of MAT's scenery from the beginning
8. Stanislavski's country house Liubimovka was on this river
9. Youngest of three sisters
13. Sophia - - - - itsova, author of 1985 memoirs about Stanislavski system
14. Eldest of three sisters
18. American source of support to study Moscow Art Theatre
21. Actress/wife of Maierhold
23. Chekhov's home town on the Sea of Azov
24. First name of Shvarts and Vakhtangov
26. Maierhold's former student whom he visited the night before his arrest
27. Where Stanislavski attended ballet and opera
29. - e - irovich-Danchenko
32. A Beatle
33. Summer cottage
36. To treat his tuberculosis, Chekhov drank fermented mare's milk, called - - - miss

37. Aleksandr K - - e - , leading St. Petersburg theatre critic, often ascerbic toward Maierhold
38. Olga Ba - - - nova, played title role in MAT's 19232 Musical Studio *Carmencita and the Soldier*
40. Aleksandr Sergeivich - ri - oiedov, author of *Wit Works Woe*

SOLUTION TO THE PUZZLE IS FOUND ON THE NEXT PAGE.

SOLUTION

S	U	L	E	R	Z	H	I	T	S	K	I
M	■	■	B	L	O	K	■	A	I	L	R
E	G	O	R	■	I	T	■	I	M	I	I
L	I	L	I	N	A	■	■	R	O	A	N
I	A	G	■	E	■	■	R	O	V	Z	A
A	N	A	T	H	E	M	A	■	■	M	■
N	■	■	A	■	V	■	I	Z	B	A	■
S	O	N	G	■	G	■	K	L	O	■	■
K	■	M	A	I	E	R	H	O	L	D	■
I	■	■	N	■	N	I	■	B	S	A	■
■	K	U	R	K	I	N	■	I	H	C	Z
G	O	G	O	L	■	G	■	N	O	H	■
B	U	L	G	A	K	O	V	■	I	A	N

Theatre History Studies 24 (June 2004)

Stanislavski's Champion: Sonia Moore and Her Crusade to Save the American Theatre

FELICIA HARDISON LONDRÉ

Sonia Moore (See fig. 1) was a zealot. She made it her single-minded purpose in life to save the American theatre. She knew only one way to do that: to win unequivocal acceptance of the Stanislavski system by every man, woman, and child performer or teacher of acting in America. This calling occupied every waking moment of her last thirty-five years on earth. No matter that she didn't discover her mission until she was nearly sixty; she believed that all the travails she endured under the Soviets had shaped her to that end.

"I am an obnoxious person," Sonia would say in her wonderful Russian accent, a determined smile on her face. "After all I have been through, I know I am still here because I have a purpose: to bring the American theatre closer to the day when training in Stanislavski's technique will be expected of every professional actor." She never could quite admit that in a pluralistic society there might be other teachers of acting who believed in the validity of their own systems. True, her unshakable certainty and idealism about what she needed to accomplish could be perceived by some as intolerance, but I loved her for caring so passionately about her work. When she tried to see herself in a larger context, she would speak in terms so touching that at my earliest opportunity I would write down what she had said. My random notes from the 1980s include these: "I have overlived everyone. I think God has forgotten about me. It's time for me to go to heaven, but I am worried who will continue with all I have to do." "I know a lot and I don't want to take it all away to heaven with me." "Look what happened to Stanislavski. People don't know how much he discovered in his last years. When I am in heaven, I still will be revising and revising."

Even in her nineties, Sonia Moore (1902-1995) was a striking figure: tall, slender, white-haired, with a glowing complexion. She wore her waist-length hair pulled tightly back from her face and tucked up into a braid in back, sometimes encircled by a turquoise chiffon scarf. Her usual platform outfit consisted of white pants under a flowing blue-green silk or cotton gauze blouse. In front of an audience, Sonia radiated vitality and conviction. Until her mid-eighties, she walked two miles a day; indeed it was a considerable trek from her Park Avenue apartment to her studio in a church rental space, as I learned when I accompanied her on foot. Later she reduced her walks to a mile. She became quite frail in her last couple of years, but even in 1994, during what would be my last days with her, at a theatre convention in Chicago, we strolled together from the Palmer House for several blocks along the lake shore.

When Sonia was not teaching classes, interviewing prospective students, or exercising, she husbanded the strength she needed for her work. She napped each

Figure 1. Sonia Moore. Courtesy of her daughter, Irene Moore Jaglom.

afternoon, ate sensibly (usually roasted chicken from the deli or Shun Lee's cashew chicken, and her own salads that combined lettuce, sliced banana, grapes, and raw broccoli), and at bedtime drank orange juice over ice with a double shot of Smirnoff's. She spent July and August each year at Sebasco Lodge in Maine, where she would catch up on her reading of Russian theatre books and periodicals. At some point she came to the realization that if Stanislavski's method of physical action allows one to control emotion for the stage, it should be possible to apply the system in life as well. So when she became angry or upset by the problems she often faced in running her actor training studio in a rented space, she would pause to think about "one certain star over Sebasco and the boats on the water," and then she would become calm. She felt that such applications of Stanislavski's psycho-physical connection had helped to keep her alive.

For thirteen consecutive years, from the ages of 79 to 91, Sonia presented her Stanislavski system lecture-demonstration at the annual convention of the leading academic theatre organization (American Theatre Association and its later incarnation, the Association for Theatre in Higher Education). When she died at age 92, she was already listed on the program for the summer of 1995. Year after year she also booked the Bruno Walter Auditorium in the Library of Performing Arts at Lincoln Center to give an admission-free open class. Until her last few years, she accepted all lecture and residency invitations at colleges and universities in the United States and Canada. For thirty years she ran the Sonia Moore Studio of Theatre. She founded the American Center for Stanislavski Theatre Art in 1964 and the American Stanislavski Theatre in 1971. She produced and directed off-Broadway. She published four books (which she constantly revised), articles (including the *Encyclopaedia Britannica* entry on Stanislavski), and two collections of materials she translated from the Russian, as she constantly kept abreast of the latest developments in the application of the Stanislavski system in Soviet theatre training.

My friendship with Sonia began in 1980 when she was brought to my university for a public lecture and three days of workshops in the Department of Theatre. At a dinner for her with others of the theatre faculty, I was able to claim only a few moments of conversation, as it was the acting teachers who naturally drew her attention. And initially I felt shy in the presence of the great lady with such a strong personality. But as a theatre historian researching Soviet productions of Shakespeare, I had a burning question: had she seen Nikolai Akimov's infamous 1932 production of *Hamlet* in Moscow? No, she had not attended it, but she had worked with most of the actors; indeed, "Vavochka" Vagrina, who played Ophelia, had been one of her best friends.

Luckily for me, the success of Sonia's 1980 workshops for our department led to her semester-long residency with us in the spring of 1981. I devised a strategy for claiming some of her time: I would write an essay about her for a reference work then in preparation. (The book, eventually published as *Notable Women in the American Theatre*, underwent several changes of editorship over the next few years, in the course of which my essay on Sonia was dropped; since other essays of mine were retained, I could not help wondering whether Sonia's intransigence about acting methods had miffed someone who exercised editorial control! My essay had at least served the purpose of bringing us together, and Sonia often circulated it with her press

Figure 2. Felicia Londré and Sonia Moore, Summer 1982. Courtesy of the author.

releases.) Our interview sessions segued into outings together. Sonia and I attended plays at various local theatres. She even sat through spring commencement exercises. When she returned to New York, we kept up a correspondence. When I received a fellowship to participate in a National Endowment for the Humanities summer 1982 Institute on Soviet and Polish Theatre, led by Alma Law and William Kuhlke at City University of New York Graduate Center, Sonia invited me to reside at her apartment during those eight weeks. (See fig. 2) From then until her death in 1995, every time I visited New York City, I stayed at 485 Park Avenue, even when she was off at her summer lodge in Maine. Best of all were the evenings when we would come in from the theatre, pour ourselves some orange juice and vodka, and talk about life. Through Sonia I came to appreciate firsthand the Russian "soul."

Talking about life was inseparable from talking about Sonia's work. It would begin the minute she opened her door to me when I arrived with suitcases for a weekend or a summer in New York; she couldn't wait for me to put down my bags before she would describe some new exercise she was developing in her studio classes. When we attended a play together, no sooner did the houselights come up for intermission than she would begin analyzing the performances in Stanislavskian terms. No sooner would the newest edition of her best-selling book *The Stanislavski System* see print than she would start badgering the publisher to prepare for yet another revised edition incorporating her more recent discoveries within the system. Over dinner in her apartment or at Shun Lee Palace, she would test me to see if I remembered the four steps that link thought and action in the unbreakable mind-body connection: wonder (a receptive state); evaluation (processing); physical response (possibly as subtle as an eye movement or nod of the head); speech (which might be intended to cover the honest physical response). Although I don't perform on stage and have not studied theory of acting, it was vitally important to Sonia that I understand the work she was doing.

Perhaps because she was perceived by many as prickly and uncompromising, Sonia Moore's passing was not sufficiently noted by the theatre community or memorialized to the extent that her contributions merited. My desire to write about her stems not from any delusion that I might help her posthumously to achieve her impossible dream, but from a sense that her life and its mission is a story that deserves to be told and that I probably know it as well as anyone outside Sonia's family and artistic associates. Most of what follows draws upon our conversations as well as the manuscript of her unpublished autobiography.

Born Sophie Evzarovna Shatzov on 4 December 1902 in Gomel, Russia, she was one of eleven children of Evser and Sophie (née Pasherstnik) Shatzov. Sonia's father was a successful importer whose wealth became a liability during the civil war that followed the 1917 October Revolution. The family's house at the corner of Aptechnaya and Rumiantsev in Gomel was the best in town, having running water in the bedroom washstands and bathrooms with sloping floors so that water let out of the tin bathtubs would drain into a central hole. Sonia's second-story room had a glass roof and an adjoining terrace. Two older sisters shared the mezzanine suite with their governess. At that time there were five children living at home, among whom Sonia was the fourth; her little brother Eza was eleven years younger. When the Red Army gained control of the town at the end of March 1919, members of the so-called *bourgeoisie* had all their possessions confiscated and were sent into exile. The servants were dispersed and the family moved to Kiev, where they were unknown.

Sonia's father refused to engage in profiteering as so many others were doing in those chaotic times. He had always taught his children never to lie, and indeed, the Sonia I knew was bluntly honest. (She laughed when I relayed Edmund Wilson's comments on Russian lying from his book *A Window on Russia*; yes, Wilson got it right, she said, but it didn't apply to her.) Luckily, Sonia's mother had left Gomel ahead of the Bolshevik takeover and had brought several trunks of finery which could be sold to sustain the family and two youths from Gomel who found hospitality with them in Kiev. The family's first house in Kiev stood on a small square, and from the window Sonia watched fearfully one day as White and Red Army soldiers entered from opposite sides of the square and slaughtered one another. It was the year in which Kiev passed through thirteen governments, including Germans, Poles, Petlura's Ukrainian Nationalists, and repeatedly the Bolsheviks. Ruthless bands of Cossacks often roamed the streets, robbing and murdering. Yet Sonia's father, ever optimistic, spent English pounds he had on deposit abroad to purchase from the Polish duke Radziwill a large apartment in the fashionable Passage on Kreschatik Street. For a time the duke retained a room there, which he shared with his mistress. After Radziwill returned to Poland, the room was occupied by a Chekist (secret police).

After graduation from the Gymnasia (secondary school), Sonia entered Kiev University to study biology, but finding herself drawn to the theatre, she also took classes at the drama studio of Kiev's Solovtzov Theatre. Defying her parents, she made a harrowing five-day train trip in a boxcar to visit Pavel, the boy she thought she loved, who had been arrested in Moscow. When she saw that he was already released from prison and safe with his family, she returned to Kiev, another journey fraught with danger. When her family emigrated to Riga, Latvia, Sonia insisted on remaining in Russia. She journeyed again to Moscow, married Pavel, and barely subsisted with him in their unheated one-room lodging. She entered Moscow University, but devoted herself entirely to theatre after winning admission in 1920 to the Moscow Art Theatre's Third Studio, directed by Stanislavski's greatest disciple, Evgeni Vakhtangov. Despite the fact that the Moscow Art Theatre and its studios used only actors with Moscow accents, Sonia's southern Russian upbringing surprisingly proved to be no barrier. Vakhtangov selected her on the basis of a highly competitive examination: 560 aspirants auditioned; Sonia was one of only fourteen admitted. Vakhtangov explained her miraculously-acquired Moscow accent as a gift from God.

During Sonia's three years with the Third Studio, she observed every rehearsal conducted by Vakhtangov. These were all-night sessions beginning at eleven o'clock, after the evening performance of whatever play Vakhtangov was acting in, and lasting until dawn; the daylight hours were taken up with classes. In *The Stanislavski System*, Sonia recalls that despite Vakhtangov's terminal illness (he died of cancer on 29 February 1922, the day after the opening of his landmark production of *Turandot*), his "sparkling, ironic humor, his sharp intelligence, artistic sense, limitless energy, and, above all, his hatred of all that was vulgar, commanded admiration and respect. . . . I shall never forget his rehearsals; never satisfied, he sometimes canceled in a second what had been achieved during long nights; continually searching for truth and force, he made each rehearsal new." Stanislavski was a frequent visitor at the Third Studio, but Sonia always later made it clear that she did not learn the system she taught from Stanislavski himself, since he had not yet discovered "the method of physical action" at that time. Eventually she moved into the cast of *Turandot* as a slave girl dancer, and occasionally performances were given on the Moscow Art Theatre stage.

At a party in March 1923, a cousin of Sonia's husband introduced her to a 22-year-old general in the Red Army, Lev Borisovich Helfand. The tall, handsome young man with a commanding presence was the son of a Ukrainian landowner. Idealism had spurred him to defy his father and join the Red Army at seventeen. There was an immediate mutual attraction, but Sonia resisted Helfand's attentions, even fleeing Moscow to visit her family in Riga, where they had reestablished an opulent lifestyle. At some point during the family's exile, Sonia's father obtained American visas, but never used them, so hopeful was he that the Soviet regime would collapse and the Shatzovs would be able to return to their homeland. As émigrés, however, they were "enemies of the Soviet state," and in the 1930s it would become dangerous for Sonia to visit them or even be known to have such relatives. Sonia's father died in Riga after a series of strokes in 1928, and the rest of the family--with the exception of Sonia, one older sister, and her older brother--perished in Nazi gas chambers during World War II.

Lev Borisovich Helfand (who would later call himself Leon Moore) followed Sonia to Riga; then she followed him to Berlin, ostensibly to visit her older brother, who was pursuing a career in film making there (though he presciently moved his family to London when Hitler rose to power). In spite of her love for Helfand and her longing to be with him, Sonia remained stubbornly loyal to her husband, so Helfand--back in Moscow--broke with her, and her letters to him were returned unopened. From 1923 to 1926 Sonia acted with the Russian Theatre in Berlin. Among the many Russian visitors to Berlin during those years was film maker Sergei Eisenstein. The impromptu movie he made of her seated in a wingback chair with spoons stuck through her braids is one of the possessions she most regretted having lost in the chaos of events in 1940.

In 1926, after three years of separation, Helfand sought Sonia out in Berlin and persuaded her to go to Paris with him. Having divorced Pavel, she married Lev Borisovich Helfand in Paris on 11 May 1926. Helfand had been assigned to Paris to learn French and gain experience in consular and diplomatic work; after six months, on the basis of an examination, he was appointed Vice Consul at the Soviet General Consulate in Paris. Meanwhile, Sonia earned a diploma in French at the Alliance Française (1927). When Helfand was promoted to Second Secretary, they moved into the Embassy and Sonia began learning how to function as a diplomat's wife. Their daughter Irina was born on 29 April 1928.

The Helfands were posted back to Moscow in February 1930. He served as assistant director of the Anglo-Roman Division in the Commissariat for Foreign Affairs. Sonia's friends in the theatre discouraged her from resuming that career, as the propaganda plays that then dominated the repertoire offered few good roles for women. Instead, she began teaching French to future diplomats at the Commissariat for Foreign Affairs, while also studying English and German. Sonia attended the theatre when she could, making a point of seeing everything directed by Meyerhold or Tairov, but she considered herself primarily a wife and mother. Her husband survived two *chistki* (party purges) and in 1935 was appointed First Secretary of the Soviet Embassy in

Italy.

Stationed in Rome during the worst of the Stalinist purges (dozens of their diplomatic and personal acquaintances were executed in 1936-38), the Helfands spent four years secretly preparing for a move to the United States. Anticipating a future need for income-producing skills, Sonia earned diplomas from the Instituto Interuniversitario Italiano (1938), Reale Conservatorio di Musica Santa Cecilia (1939), and Reale Accademia Filarmonica (1939). She studied art history, became a singing teacher, and ran the Intourist travel agency in Rome, saving all her earnings to help finance the defection. Sonia's Intourist job required annual return visits to Moscow to report to her superiors, and she always used such occasions for theatregoing. With her husband's promotion to Chargé d'Affaires at the Soviet Embassy in Italy, Sonia frequently hosted events for both Soviet and foreign visitors. Particularly thrilling to her was the visit of Alexander Tairov, director of Moscow's Kamerny Theatre. He asked Sonia to help him pick out a dress to take back to his wife, actress Alice Koonen, a friend of Sonia's. Tairov thought the black dress she chose was better for her than for Koonen, so Sonia kept it, even when it was "falling apart," for the rest of her life.

With the appointment of a new Soviet ambassador to Italy, the Helfands were to return to Moscow in June 1940. Their plan to defect to the United States was complicated by Italy's entrance into the war that month. The only air route from Rome involved stops in Spain and Portugal, both of which required transit visas that were difficult for a Soviet citizen to obtain without attracting the attention of Soviet authorities. The American ambassador William Phillips, who knew of Helfand's discreet opposition to Stalin's Non-Aggression Pact with Hitler and in whom Helfand confided his plan, readily obtained their American visas. In order to keep up the appearance that they were moving back to Moscow, the Helfands not only had to ship their belongings there, but also had to shop for Italian goods that any returning diplomat would have stocked up on. Sonia recalled that her inner panic while attempting to keep up a good front at the Embassy caused her to pack irrationally, so that family treasures were sent to Moscow, never to be seen again, while useless items were carried on the flight. The ruse involved the family's public departure from Rome by train, the stealthy return to Rome that night, and several hours of hiding in the apartment of an American correspondent until the time of the one daily flight from Rome to Lisbon via Barcelona and Madrid.

Virtually destitute upon their arrival in the United States at the end of July 1940, the Helfands' hopes were pinned on Sonia's ability to give singing lessons. They lived in a small cold-water flat on 113th Street in New York, and were told that her husband's best bet would be to learn to drive a taxi. The first one to help them was journalist Dorothy Thompson, who employed Helfand, his name now legally changed to Leon Moore, to assist with political research and writing. Soon he realized, as Sonia recalled, that with no more tools than "his brilliant mind" and a telephone it was possible to make money in a free country. He was one of the first to get into the business of coal exports, becoming a leading figure in the oil and coal industry.

Naturalized an American citizen in 1946, Sonia was always quite emotional about her gratitude to America, saying that only someone who had been through as much as she had could fully understand the value of our freedom. "I love this country," she told me in 1986. "I am in love with this country. Sometimes I still have to pinch myself to know I am here." She never had any desire to go back to Russia for a visit, not even after the collapse of the Soviet system in 1989: "I wake up in the night in cold fear of being back there." Indeed, she was upset when her daughter Irene visited the USSR in the course of her husband Jack Jaglom's business trip to Warsaw in the fall of 1986. And yet Sonia and Irene generously arranged for me to be invited to the March 1989 symposium in Moscow on "Stanislavski in a Changing World."

Sonia's happy 31-year marriage ended with Leon Moore's death from throat cancer in 1957. Devastated by grief, she dropped out of all social life and became "a zombie." Still heartbroken, she went to visit her brother in England. When he suffered a heart attack, she immediately threw away all her tranquilizers and took charge, regaining her own equilibrium in the course of overseeing his recovery. While she was there, a book on Stanislavski somehow appeared on her lap; she didn't know how it got there. She began reading about the acting techniques that Stanislavski had been developing at the time of his death in 1938.

Sonia Moore's commitment to making Stanislavski's final deductions understood by American theatre practitioners can be traced back to a letter she wrote to the *New York Times* Drama Mailbag (29 December 1957) in response to Arthur Gelb's interview with Anthony Perkins. Her letter pointing out misconceptions about Stanislavski's technique aroused considerable interest, and she was asked to write articles. Instead, she wrote her first book, *The Stanislavski Method* (1960), which later went through several revisions as *The Stanislavski System*. Because Sonia Moore's name was not then known in the American theatre, it was deemed advisable to include a foreword by an important figure. She got John Gielgud, while her editor got Joshua Logan. When her editor asked which one should be published, she replied: "Use both!"

Sonia's earliest understanding of Stanislavski's final deductions came from P.V. Simonov's book, *The Method of K.S. Stanislavski and the Physiology of Emotion*, which had not yet been translated into English. Simonov, a neurophysiologist, was the first to study Stanislavski from a scientific point of view, and he confirmed that the method of physical action is physiologically correct. According to Simonov, in Sonia's 1973 translation: "Stanislavski presents the thesis that in every physical action there is something psychological, and that the most complex psychological situations are expressed through physical actions. . . . In essence, Stanislavski's views exclude any possibility of subjective experience without physical expression." Stanislavski concluded that "direct reproduction of emotions is impossible," and that an actor could perform truthfully only by finding the physical behavior that would connect with the appropriate subconscious state.

Sonia subscribed to all the Soviet theatre periodicals and sent for a copy of every theatre book published in the USSR, where all training schools uniformly taught Stanislavski's method of physical action. She especially followed the work of Maria Knebel, a noted director, teacher and close disciple of Konstantin Stanislavski and Vladimir Nemirovich-Danchenko. After founding the Sonia Moore Studio in 1961, Sonia had little time for reading during the theatre season, so she would take accumulated cartons of reading materials to Sebasco Lodge in Maine for seven or eight weeks every summer. Just as important as her reading, however, were the discoveries she made through her studio classes. The exercises given in her subsequent books, *Training an Actor: The Stanislavski System in Class* (1968, revised in 1979) and its

1991 revision *Stanislavski Revealed: The Actor's Guide to Spontaneity on Stage*, were all developed through many sessions with students. The Sonia Moore Studio enrolled about 85 students a year.

In 1964 Sonia founded the American Center for Stanislavski Theatre Art, a nonprofit organization dedicated to promoting Stanislavski's teachings in America by sponsoring residencies, lecture-demonstrations, and seminars. Sonia Moore was president of ACSTA, and its board included such illustrious names as Norris Houghton, Joshua Logan, Patricia McIlrath (See fig. 3), Tom Ewell, Julie Harris, Maria Piscator, Dore Schary, and Faith Waterman. Sonia ran ACSTA from her Park Avenue apartment with an executive assistant coming in five days a week to answer the telephone and handle the paperwork. On the wall of the office were photographs of Leon Moore and Vsevelod Meyerhold. The office shared a bathroom with the library, which served as my room whenever I visited. In 1981, the library had been ravaged by a fire that started in a television set, so the apartment had been extensively remodeled before my first visit. The worst of it was the loss of some irreplaceable books and papers. Luckily, the wonderful Maliavin painting in that room was unharmed.

Leon Moore left Sonia a very wealthy widow. She lived comfortably yet frugally in her spacious fifth-floor apartment. Once she began her mission to instill the Stanislavski system in the American theatre, she poured her fortune into that. Nevertheless, I was dazzled the first time she opened the door to me, because the atmosphere of the public rooms was so evocative of "old Russia." Opposite the front door hung a tapestry. On the table in front of it was a huge assortment of family photos in silver frames, including one frame of 1930s Italian fascist design. The well-furnished dining room was never used during my visits, and only rarely did I enter the living room, although I remember one occasion when Sonia and I sat in there, according to the Russian custom, for a moment of silence before a journey. For our talks we usually sat at the kitchen table or in the library. Every time I visited, there seemed to be a different *au pair* girl occupying the servant's quarters; I would be introduced to the young woman and then almost never see her, not even throughout the summers when I lived in the apartment during Sonia's absence.

When Sonia left for her summer stay in Maine, she would follow the Russian custom of putting dustcovers over the furniture. Even the draperies and, of course, the chandeliers were fitted with muslin covers. The valuables would also be packed away, as they had been one time when I asked Sonia not long before she left for Maine if I could introduce Bill Kuhlke to her. Bill was working on a paper on Vakhtangov, and it would mean a lot to him to hear directly from her about Vakhtangov's rehearsal techniques. Sonia directed me to invite him for drinks at the apartment, followed by dinner at Shun Lee Palace. Then she realized that with all the silver packed away the entrance hall didn't look good enough for a guest. Unfortunately, the maid who had done that work came in only once a week, and Sonia didn't know where the things had been hidden. So she rummaged and found a few items to put out, then declared triumphantly: "We will have Potemkin village!" (The phrase originated when Catherine the Great decided to get to know something of her empire beyond the landscape between Moscow and St. Petersburg. General Potemkin traveled ahead of her and erected attractively-painted false fronts for the ramshackle villages she would see from

Figure 3. Sonia Moore and Patricia McIlrath, taken at the ATA convention in San Francisco, August 1984. Courtesy of the author.

her boat on the Volga. These were called Potemkin villages.)

In 1971 Sonia formed a repertory company composed of actors trained in her studio, and she served as its artistic director. Three productions comprised the first season of ACSTA 1 (later renamed American Stanislavski Theatre): *The Cherry Orchard, Desire Under the Elms,* and *Birdbath.* The company toured to underprivileged neighborhoods under the sponsorship of the Mayor's Office of Neighborhood Government. She revived *The Cherry Orchard* in each of the three following seasons while adding new productions. Critics responded warmly, as the following comments suggest. Emory Lewis (*New York Record* 26 May 1974) applauded the "fierce urgency" of *The Crucible* and said that "one is riveted to one's seat throughout the evening." Howard Thompson called the evening of one-act plays by Pirandello, Strindberg, and Baraka "a tingling refresher course in what theater is all about" (*New York Times* 26 February 1974); and of *Desire Under the Elms* he wrote of the "hard honesty and flexibly compact staging by Sonia Moore" (*New York Times* 12 April 1974): "Superior acting surmounts some garrulous O'Neill passages. . . . Herewith another credit for the ACSTA ensemble, geared to Stanislavski, whose artful, unified sensibility continues to give one of the steadiest theater glows in town." Ingvar Holm (*Dagens Nyheter*, Stockholm, 3 July 1972) called the company's work "among the very best that I saw in New York . . . in the casting, in the acting style, and in the entire tightness and milieu of the performance." In 1978-79 American Stanislavski Theatre followed its six-week New York run of *Long Day's Journey into Night* with a national tour of universities and colleges.

Before she founded her own company, Sonia had directed off-Broadway. *The Painted Days* by John Byrne at The Marquee Theatre (6 April 1961) was produced by Elliot Martin and featured Irene Moore in a leading role. (Sonia often commented appreciatively that her daughter is an excellent actress; then she would add wryly that as a teacher her daughter should do more to keep up with her mother's latest discoveries!) For the Irish Players, Sonia staged *Sharon's Grave* by John B. Keane (8 November 1961). Over the years, I happened to be in New York at the right time in the spring to see only two studio productions directed by Sonia: *The Lower Depths* in 1984 and *Anna Christie* in 1989. Although both seemed somewhat slow-paced to me, I savored the richness and subtlety of the acting. The performance of the role of Anna Christie was especially compelling in the way the actress so believably portrayed the character's slipping on and off of the mask of gentility over her coarseness.

By the 1980s Sonia was devoting more and more attention to giving presentations at professional conventions as well as schools. Among these were the Southeastern Theatre Conference (1974, 1975), the South Carolina Theatre Association (keynote address, 1981), the Celebration of Women in the Arts in Edmonton, Canada (1983), the National Educational Theatre Conference (1986, 1990), the Society of Stage Directors and Choreographers (1987), Kent Place School (commencement address, 1987), International Symposium on "Theatre USSR: Revolution and Tradition" at the University of South Carolina (keynote address, 1989). Beginning in 1982 she was on the program of every American Theatre Association/ Association for Theatre in Higher Education (ATHE) national conference through 1994. I had the pleasure of introducing her at the first two of those, New York in 1982 and Minneapolis in 1983; the 1982 session was especially memorable as it was held in a hotel ballroom that seemed filled to capacity. In subsequent years I thought it best to give others, especially actor-training specialists, the opportunity to be associated with her on the program. But I never failed to attend her session and relish the young people's amazement at the energy in Sonia Moore's commanding presence.

At the 1991 ATHE conference in Seattle, Sonia suddenly seemed more frail than before (she could no longer descend on escalators), but her conversation was as lively as ever. The last two ATHE conferences she attended were marked by unusual occurrences. In Philadelphia in 1993, I was present in her room as she negotiated with Anatoly Smeliansky of the Moscow Art Theatre studio school to become an associate of ACSTA or honorary faculty member for her studio; none of the three of us knew or would venture an idea of what sum would be appropriate as a retainer, which would allow the use of his name on the letterhead and a lecture or workshop at the studio during his more or less annual visits to New York; the issue remained unresolved. The next day I sat with Sonia for several hours until it was time for her to go to the airport, because she was departing the convention a day early to return to Sebasco. Somehow it didn't occur to me to want to get back into the flow of the convention, despite the languidness of our conversation. I was conscious of merely enjoying her presence and not wanting her to leave. Later I learned that at the airport she had become rather weak and had been given a wheelchair. Then an unidentified airport employee had wheeled her into a back room and threatened her, forcing her to give him all the cash she had if she wanted to get on the plane. The episode was terribly frightening to her, and it caused her physical setbacks in the following months.

Yet nothing could prevent Sonia Moore from getting on the program again for Chicago in 1994. Because of her trepidations stemming from the Philadelphia airport incident, I arranged my flights to arrive at O'Hare in time to meet her flight and to depart shortly after seeing her off. Little did I know that this conference would mark the last time I saw her. We dined together every evening at the Palmer House restaurant. Her presentation drew a good crowd and generated lively interest. On the day of departure, 31 July 1994, we arrived at O'Hare a couple of hours early, both of us having that kind of Type A-personality obsession with promptness. As we sat at her gate, I developed a craving for a Starbucks latte and when I saw at the same gate a young woman whom I recognized as having attended Sonia's session, I asked her to sit with Sonia while I ran down the concourse to the nearest Starbucks. The young woman was thrilled at the chance to chat with Sonia. When I returned no more than ten minutes later, the air between them was highly charged, as if they had been arguing. Sonia told me when we were alone together that this young woman could not understand that there is only one correct way to teach acting. To me Sonia was at her most lovable in her defiant certainty that she was right, even as she seemed to be somewhat abashedly thinking, "Oh, no, I've done it again." Later I came to think of that moment as an appropriate final memory of Sonia.

On 19 May 1995, Sonia Moore died at home after an illness of several months. She is survived by her daughter Irene Moore Jaglom and the two grandchildren she ardently doted upon, Leona Jaglom Hirsch and Drew Jaglom. Over the years, I sometimes heard Sonia Moore referred to as "a national treasure." In 1974 she was awarded the John F. Kennedy Library American Heritage Award. Although she was included in over twenty different biographical directories and topical "who's who"s, she expressed deep, genuine amazement and delight when she made it into the 44th edition of *Who's Who in America*: "This is really something. When you think . . . I am a refugee!" She was crediting the recognition not to herself, but to her country, the land of the free.

This essay won the 2003 National Amy & Eric Burger Essays on Theatre Competition ($2500), sponsored by the University of Wyoming

Felicia Hardison Londré is Curator's Professor of Theatre at the University of Missouri-Kansas City. She is Honorary Co-Founder and Vice President of the board of the Heart of America Shakespeare Festival. Upon receiving ATHE's 2001 Outstanding Teacher of Theatre in Higher Education Award, she honored the memory of her mentors Patricia McIlrath and Sonia Moore.

Theatre History Studies 24 (June 2004)

"Adieu, Adieu, Adieu. Remember Me": Konstantin Stanislavsky and Irina Rozanova

MARIA IGNATIEVA

In order to understand Shakespeare's true intentions, one must dig and uncover them underneath the dead letters, and thus restore his thoughts, his vision, his imagery, and his feelings, along with all subtexts buried in written text.[1]

In 1983, as a master's student at the Moscow State Institute for Theatrical Arts (GITIS), I completed my research paper for the seminar in Russian Theatre History: The paper was about Serafima Birman, the renowned Russian Soviet grotesque actress and the faithful student of Stanislavsky. The available documents of the First Studio and the Moscow Art Theatre-2 including Birman's letters, were given to me at the Moscow Art Theatre Museum. Are there words to describe that first touch of the precious historical materials? After working at the Art Museum for several weeks, I grew familiar with the handwriting of Birman and other actors from her circle.

On one of those days I stopped by the bookstore and noticed a book – a rare find, *The Moscow Art Theatre-2,* published in Moscow in 1925. (See Fig. 1) The ten rubles that it cost was one quarter of my monthly stipend, a lot of money, but I bought the book without even opening it. To my stunning surprise, the first thing I discovered in there was Serafima Birman's own handwriting, a rather long autograph. If there were omens for theatre historians that was the one! I immediately noticed an autograph of another actor, and another, and another – the whole book was signed by the most prominent actors of the Moscow Art Theatre-2.

Still not believing my luck, I started to carefully examine my book. All the autographs were signed on March 4, 1936, after the Moscow Art Theatre-2 was officially closed on February 28, 1936. This unique document witnessed one of the tragic days from the Stalinist Era. Sofia Giatsintova, the Moscow Art Theatre-2 actress, wrote:

> On the evening of February the 27th, as we gathered in the theatre, we heard on the radio that the 'so-called Moscow Art Theatre-2 is being liquidated. . . .' Strange were these weeks after. We were given two little rooms near the entrance to the theatre, where we were sitting days and nights without doing anything, and just looking through the windows at our scenery being taken away by trucks. We were not permitted inside the theatre, and only the make-up kits were returned to the us. . . .[2]

Figure 1. The cover of the book *The Moscow Art Theatre-2*. Courtesy of the author.

The autographs were signed for a young and obviously very talented female, as the writing stated. Her name was Irina, or Irochka, as most of them called her. The Moscow Art Theatre-2 had a theatre school, and this Irochka was a student in it. Serafima Birman wrote to her, "Irina! Eradicate the difference in you: one moment you are beautiful on stage, and the next one — you are ugly; work and technique will inevitably merge if the person is gifted."[3] Several autographs contained hints pointing at this time of trouble, and such was this one: "Dear Irochka, this *hurricane* touched you, too. . . ." Who was this "Irochka?" The one who, according to the autographs, had recently acted in scenes from *Joan of Arc*, who recited *Terek's Gifts*, Lermontov's romantic poem? Who was this girl in whose brilliant theatrical future all of them, who signed autographs, seemed to believe? Not knowing yet who she was, I already admired this Irina: the theatre had just been condemned, and despite this fact she was taking their autographs! Giatsintova wrote about others, "Some people who we thought were our friends, crossed the streets to the opposite sides to avoid encountering us. . . . It was then when we realized what it meant to be the 'so-called theatre. We felt like wretched outcasts. . . . We knew for sure: life was over, and only darkness was still ahead of us."[4]

With the help of a magnifying glass, I was able to finally understand Irina's last name: the book was signed for *Irina Rozanova*, the very Irina Rozanova who became one of the romantic legends of the Soviet Theatre, the same Irina who became a student of Stanislavsky's Opera-Dramatic Studio (founded in 1935) and rehearsed the leading role in *Hamlet* under Stanislavsky's tutelage. Only in 2003, when I finally was able to read the unpublished handwritten memoirs of Irina's close friend, Vladimir Fromgold, did the final details become clear and Irina's personality unveiled: her relations with Stanislavsky, her Hamlet and the circumstances of her untimely death. Irina Rozanova and her Hamlet provoke a battery of questions. What was Stanislavsky's late interpretation of Hamlet, the leading role and the play in general? How was the Stanislavsky System applied to rehearsals of Hamlet and to Irina's preparations personally? What happened to Irina after Stanislavsky's death and where did she disappear so suddenly? (There was a notion of a traffic accident in a book *Stanislavsky Rehearses* but no details).

In this essay, without taking the impossible task to answer all these questions in full, I'll outline a few.

After the closing of the Moscow Art Theatre-2, Irina became a student of the Opera-Dramatic Studio in 1936. Vladimir Fromgold, Irina's close friend, wrote:

> Irina came from a working class family, graduated from a technical college, and then worked at a factory. She lived with her mother, and they struggled financially. She was a student in the Moscow Art Theatre-2 School, and her master was there, Serafima Birman. When the Moscow Art Theatre-2 School was closed, Irina joined the Opera-Dramatic Studio. By that time she already thought she was an actress. She did not want to continue studying the Stanislavsky System, saying that she did not need it. She rebelled and thus was called to Stanislavsky. This was their conversation according to what Irina told me later:

Stanislavsky. So, what would you like to do?
Irina. Hamlet.
Stanislavsky. You want to play Ophelia, you mean?
Irina. No. I want to play Hamlet.

In about a week, there was a written circular posted on the callboard, which cast Irina as Hamlet and ordered Stanislavsky's assistants to start rehearsals.[5]

Another student wrote:

Once you saw her face, it was hard to forget: straight line of her nose with a short haircut, bangs covering a third of her forehead. . . . [A]dded masculinity to her face and strictness. One could imagine Hamlet's face exactly like it! . . . Her extraordinary personality was like a magnet. . . .[6]

The rehearsals started in February 1937. When Stanislavsky was in the Studio, he dedicated many hours to Irina, working on the super-objective of her role. Despite the fact that at the very beginning of the process Stanislavsky insisted that Rozanova would never play Hamlet, although it would be great acting school for her, he changed his mind later, and after a year of successful rehearsals started to envision the show.[7] At this time of the finalization of his System, he promoted the method of physical actions, repeatedly stating that feelings and emotions always change and thus were hard to fix, while the logic consequences of actions could be recreated, each and every time "pulling" the required emotions from an actor's subconscious. As was usual for his strategies in the thirties, Stanislavsky set off to work on *Hamlet* without using Shakespeare's dialogue. Fromgold wrote: "He did not want us to say the Shakespearian text but he did not ask us to replace it with our own words either. He wanted us to find action in every bit studying the text and be able to talk about it."[8]

It was not a new idea: even early in the 20th century Stanislavsky dreamed about "growing" an author's dialogues after the detailed analysis of an author's artistic logic and after actors' *becoming* characters from the chosen play. Alexander Blok wrote in 1912:

They rehearse Moliére (!) not knowing the text: having studied characters in details and the situations, the actors are asked to fill in the silences with their own words; Stanislavsky says that they have already almost recreated Moliére's text (Oh, I recognize him, the enthused man!)[9]

Highly idealistic as this idea seems today, it was very important to Stanislavsky and he never abandoned it. This time, Stanislavsky wanted to come even closer to this goal using the Method of Physical Actions. Stanislavsky asked Irina to find the uninterrupted development of Hamlet's physical actions in the play.

Stanislavsky. Here are your real circumstances: 'I was away for a long time. Then I came back, but everything had changed. Father died, mother married someone else. Mother became very different, coquettish, and gay.' What would you do in this case?

Irina. I would observe her carefully.

Stanislavsky. Aha, you have to write it down as a physical action: to observe her. How many physical actions are in this word "observe," one or many?

The whole group: Many!

Stanislavsky. So, the physical action "observe" consists of several sub-actions. The art of theatre cannot be "general." Art is always "concrete." What would you do to understand the real transformation that happened to your own mother? I am trying to shift you from the zone of acting to normal human life and reality. Please tell me what would *you* have done based on *your own* human experience in order for you to answer this question? What would happen inside you, in *your* soul?

Irina. This is a process of wondering. I don't understand what happened to Hamlet's mother.

Stanislavsky. There are no Hamlets, only you! You have to apply everything to yourself. Can you imagine that your neighbor is your mother?

Irina. May I imagine my real mother?

Stanislavsky. Let it be your real mother; you have to always start from your own emotional memory. . . . The first condition of art is this: as soon as I have the part, Hamlet for example, there is no Hamlet separately from me. It is you and your "I" in Hamlet's circumstances. You have to get the most out of your emotional memory.[10]

Irina Rozanova gave herself completely to the part: Hamlet filled her entire being and vice versa. Stanislavsky always encouraged his actresses to continue living in their characters' shoes outside theatre: such advice was given at different times of his career to Maria Andreyeva, Olga Knipper, Olga Gzovskaya, Maria Lilina, Alyssa Koonen. Together with Stanislavsky, Irina crawled through the labyrinths of her psycho-technique, analyzing the conscious and subconscious processes of creativity. Rozanova shared with Stanislavsky the details of her character studies, psychological and physical nuances. During one of the rehearsals she mentioned that she saw herself being Hamlet as if from the outside. Today, when Michael Chekhov's acting methodology is available, it is striking how close Irina came to Chekhov's personal acting experiences, one part of which was seeing himself playing his characters from the outside. But Stanislavsky compared her vision of herself as a character to those of Coquelin's and the presentational technique. Hence Stanislavsky corrected her potential move down the wrong road.

According to the book *Stanislavsky Rehearses* and Vladimir Fromgold's unpublished memoirs, at first one of the greatest obstacles for Irina was her initial scene with the Ghost. She was unable to envision the Ghost (played by Fromgold), a spiritual creature in a perfectly human appearance. Rozanova even asked Fromgold to go with her to a cemetery and to rehearse the scene there, at night. She wanted to feel the cemetery's real atmosphere but Fromgold was uncomfortable rehearsing among the graves. He continued:

> Stanislavsky loved Irina very much. Sometimes he looked at her with such kindness and love that she could hardly conceal her tears. She said that sometimes his eyes would become so deep that she even felt frightened. He worked with her delicately, carefully looking into her emotional changes during rehearsals. Irina was very talented, very emotional, and temperamental with a pure, passionate and open soul. All this made her life very difficult. She quarreled with the assistants and had confrontations with them; in turn, they often complained about her to Stanislavsky. He always took her side. . . .
>
> Following Stanislavsky's recommendations, Irina tried to transform every little details of Hamlet's thought into action. Gradually she became Hamlet to the extent that she fell on her back and fainted every time after her first meeting with the Ghost. Stanislavsky was very troubled by that: he told her that she needed to play 90% of Hamlet on technique, and only 10% on emotions otherwise she would die during the opening night.[11]

Another difficulty for Irina was to find the uninterrupted inner life of Hamlet in the given circumstances, which, according to her, she was unable to feel every time she lost the logic of his thinking. To help her, Stanislavsky suggested she speak the role out loud while sitting in a chair, with her hands under her knees to avoid excessive gesticulation. It certainly helped. Another student wrote:

> Rozanova unveiled the uninterrupted chain of events in Hamlet's life, his intentions and thoughts; in 2-3 hours, she barely reached the end of the first act within the given time period. It was a result of long and thorough preparations. Rozanova was telling Hamlet's story and living with her entire role while sitting. . . . I could hardly stand the suspense while following the events in the play. She did it in front of me, and as if under the surgeon's scalpel, this most difficult play was cut open, with all its tangled relations, conflicts and schemes. With my inner eyes, I envisioned the whole play, the characters' personalities, mise-en-scenes and even the scenery. My arms and legs were paralyzed with tension, and my jaw hurt me badly after my keeping teeth clinched. . . .[12]

Fromgold continued:

> In May 1938, during his last rehearsals, Stanislavsky was very pleased with Irina: he repeated that his experiment with *Hamlet* had reached fruition, and

he already envisioned the concept of the whole production.[13]

Not according to the *Chronicle of Stanislavsky's Life and Creativity*. The last rehearsal on *Hamlet* happened in June 1938, about a month before Stanislavsky's death, and it was a cold shower to all participants, including Irina. Why so? In May 1938, they still worked using the Method of Physical Actions and penetrating the inner life of the characters, without text. At the last rehearsal in June, Irina started to use the text and applied it to her thoroughly prepared and "lived through" character of Hamlet. As soon as Irina started to say Shakespeare's lines, she lost her confidence and the naturalness of living within her character. Stanislavsky criticized her rather harshly: he believed that Irina wouldn't be "broken" by his critic; on the contrary, it would encourage her to go farther. Nevertheless, the gap between her work on Hamlet without the text and with the Shakespearian text was tremendous. Stanislavsky noticed that she immediately started to use clichés and presentational techniques trying to conceal her insecurities and lack of knowledge about how to approach the text. He advised her and the whole group to learn how to recite great poetry, delivering the sense of every single verse and without violating the rhythm. The next stage of Irina's studies with Stanislavsky, we can speculate, would have emphasized her approach to poetry. Thus, Rozanova's organic creation of Hamlet without dialogue did not automatically merge with the Shakespearean text. In fact words disturbed Irina: her "homegrown" Hamlet did not need Shakespearian lines.

Because Stanislavsky shared with the students his general understanding of the play during his classes, it would be worthwhile to place his thoughts in both the context of the times and with his other interpretation of a Shakespeare tragedy from almost a decade earlier: *Othello*.

Having resumed his classes at the Opera-Dramatic Studio in 1937 after sickness, Stanislavsky offered *Hamlet* as ideal material for students. During rehearsals in 1938, Stanislavsky told Irina that Hamlet's meeting with the Ghost made him see the core of life and the quintessence of human evil. Stanislavsky envisioned Hamlet as a messiah; he spoke about an active Hamlet, not torn by reflection but as the one who took up the sword and started to cleanse the Earth from Evil.[14] Thus, his idea in *Hamlet* resembled that in *Othello*. It looks like the times orchestrated both interpretations, for in both we find the idea of ***cleansing the world*** matching the favorite political idea of the time in the Soviet Union. The idea of eradicating evil was not new for Stanislavsky in the era of Bolshevist following Stalinists repressions. While Stanislavsky's international recognition protected him and his closest circle (his wife and children) and kept them untouched, several of his own relatives were falsely accused of being "enemies of the people" and imprisoned, or sent to labor camps. Around 1930, Stanislavsky secretly informed his son, Igor (who was abroad for medical treatment) that his (Igor's) cousin died of scurvy and heart failure, and his cousin's wife had been sent to Siberia.[15]

"Cleansing" was the favorite idea of these evil times. Paradoxically, though his own extended family fell victim to these cleansings, Stanislavsky felt an urge "to cleanse the cleansers." Stanislavsky dreamt about "sanitization" of the Moscow Art Theatre from all parasites that sucked it from the inside. Vsevolod Meyerhold, whose theatre became another victim of cleansing, had tried to cleanse it from within before it was liquidated. The total confusion of "bad and good" cleansing overwhelmed the public mind. In the directorial plan of his *Othello*, Stanislavsky made Othello dream of cleansing the world, and while killing Desdemona, Othello helped to rid the world of evil. But where Othello performed "wrong cleansing," Hamlet was designated for good cleansing. Theatre and reality were utterly mixed in Stanislavsky's life at that time, and one episode deserves being described in particular because it involved two parties, both important in Irina's life. Before the liquidation of the Moscow Art Theatre-2, a group of its founders beseeched Stanislavsky to use his name and prevent the closing of the theatre.

Stanislavsky did not know mercy:

> For over two hours Stanislavsky talked about the betrayal of the principles that were founded by Sulerzhitsky at the First Studio. With the utmost frankness and sternness he reminded them about the organic nature of acting and about their loss of high ideals, their compromises in art, their tendency to succeed at any price. . . . He was pouring out his old offences. . . ."[16]

Stanislavsky did not sign the letter: he found out that the liquidation was decided and that nothing would have stopped it, and, according to V. Radomyslensky, was rather indifferent to its closing. Paradoxically, the end of the Moscow Art Theatre-2 came to him as an act of universal justice, which Theatre-2 brought upon itself. Stanislavsky's deep offense over the First Studio's "betrayal" in 1924 did not allow him to separate his hurt feelings from the government's violent intrusion into cultural life during Stalinism. But those were events about which Irina Rozanova had no knowledge at all.

The rehearsals of *Hamlet* were stopped upon Stanislavsky's death. Irina Rozanova, for whom Stanislavsky's determination to continue work on *Hamlet* was sacred, approached Mikhail Kedrov with a request to carry on.

> Kedrov became very uneasy about it, not refusing Irina but not going forward with it either. She was deeply offended. She, herself, gradually changed, too, as if life had been taken away from her all together with Hamlet, as if she had lost her creative nature and her spirits.[17]

Maria Petrovna Lilina and Zinaida Sergeyevna Sokolova, Stanislavsky's widow and sister, continued to work with Rozanova. Sokolova, truly faithful to her brother's wishes, tried to help her master her poetry reciting. Lilina appointed her to play Katerina in Ostrovsky's *Storm*. From time to time, Lilina asked Rozanova to play scenes from *Hamlet*.

Irina wrote to Vladimir Fromgold:

> September 1938. I had a strange dream as if KS (Stanislavsky-MI) was alive, talked to us lovingly, although we all went to visit his grave. Then when he saw me, he asked everyone to leave, placed his arm around my shoulders, seated me by his side, patted my hair, smiled at me and said: "Everything will be just fine. I am dead." Then he hugged me. Do you think I'll die soon? Oh, nonsense, but after this dream I was not myself for a long time.[18]

Then the war started. Because of her sick mother, Irina did not go to evacuation but stayed in Moscow, and performed for the army. Though she was dispirited, neither she, nor her work with Stanislavsky was forgotten. In 1943, she was invited by Ilya Sudakov to join the Moscow Maly Theatre, a very prestigious offer. In September 1943 a miracle happened. Nikolai Okhlopkov — the actor and director — in the past Meyerhold's actor from 1923 and until 1930, became the Artistic Director of the Theatre of the Revolution in Moscow. Upon his appointment, he immediately found Irina Rozanova and set a meeting with her in regards to her playing Hamlet in his future production.

> Irina was rejuvenated. She became the same Irina we had remembered from the Studio, inspired and enthusiastic. The meeting with Okhlopkov was supposed to happen next day. We went to the dorms where I lived. During the whole day and evening all she talked about was Hamlet. At 11 pm, we suddenly remembered about the curfew. It was 1943. I walked her to the subway, but halfway, she sent me back to the dorms. It was late. Later I found out that while crossing the street the same night, she ran in front of a trolleybus, not noticing the car driving behind it. Trying to escape the car, she moved back and was run over by the trolleybus. She died instantaneously. She was 25 years old, and officially she was a Maly Theatre actress.[19]

As for Nikolai Okhlopkov: he finally directed *Hamlet* at the Theatre of the Revolution in 1954, after Stalin died and *the Thaw* was about to begin. Ironically, the editors of *The Moscow Art Theatre Centennial Edition* in two volumes found no room for Irina Rozanova's short biography in the second volume, called *Names and Documents*. Irina *Aleksandrovna* Rozanova (her first, patronymic and last name) was not even mentioned in index of names, another actress, a contemporary one, Irina *Yurievna* Rozanova, was.

NOTES

*All quotations are my translation unless specified otherwise.

** I am very grateful for all support that I received from the staff of the Moscow Art Theatre Museum: its director Irina Korchevnikova, the Reading Room supervisor Maria Smoktunovskaya, and especially to Olga Radishcheva for her everlasting encouragement and help.

1. "Stanislavsky Works on *Othello*," in *Stanislavsky: Stat'i. Rechi. Besedi. Pisma.* [Stanislavsky: Essays. Speeches. Conversations. Letters.] Moskva, Iskusstvo, 1954, 571.
2. Giatsintova, Sofia. *S Pamiatiu Naediine (Alone with Memory)*, M, Iskusstvo, 1989, 358.
3. The Moscow Art Theatre-2, my personal book, bottom of page 1.
4. Giatsintova, Sofia, 358.
5. Fromgold, Vladimir, *Manuscript*, eight sheets, Moscow Art Theatre Museum, #21706

6. *Stanislavsky Repetiryet* [Stanislavsky Rehearses] Moscow, The Moscow Art Theatre Publishing House, 200, 485.
7. Ibid., 442.
8. Fromhold, *Manuscript.*
9. *The Chronicle of Stanislavsky's Life and Creativity*, volume 2, 349.
10. *Stanislavsky Rehearses*, 454-55.
11. Fromgold, *Manuscript.*
12. *Stanislavsky Rehearses*, 485-86.
13. Fromgold, *Manuscript.*
14. *Stanislavsky Rehearses*, 442.
15. Radishcheva, Olga *Stanislavsky and Nemirovich-Danchenko: Istoria Teatral'nykh Otnoshenii* [Stanislavsky and Nemirovich-Danchenko: History of Theatre Relations] volume3, 275.
16. *The Chronicle of Stanislavsky's Life and Creativity*, volume 4, 358.
17. Fromgold, *Manuscript*, 7.
18. Ibid., 7.
19. Ibid., 8.

Maria Ignatieva is an Assistant Professor in the Department of Theatre, Ohio State University-Lima. Before coming to America, she taught at the Moscow Art Theatre School-Studio. Ignatieva's portfolio includes publications on contemporary Russian theatre and theatre history, as well as presentations and lectures on Russian Theatre given in UK, Australia, Finland, Netherlands, Germany and Poland.

Theatre History Studies 24 (June 2004)

Re-Inflecting Femininity on the Czech *Fin-de-Siecle* Stage: An Analysis of Hana Kvapilová's Acting Style

IVETA JUSOVÁ

This essay focuses on the career of the most popular Czech turn-of-the-century actress, Hana Kvapilová (1860-1907). Kvapilová has been widely considered by her contemporaries and theatre historians both a "national actress" and a chief representative of Czech women's emancipation on the *fin-de-siècle* stage. She joined the Prague National Theatre in 1888, only five years after the opening of this most representative venue of the Czech nationalist movement. Although unpopular with the Theatre's Cooperative for her unconventional acting style distinguished by lack of extravagance, melodramatic gestures and "sexual animalism,"Kvapilová gradually became the favorite of Czech playwrights, and they frequently used their casting privileges to engage her in their plays. While at first Kvapilová's "amiable," "pleasant," and "modest" exterior (as she was described in contemporary reviews) simply seemed better suited for Czech plays' provincial settings than did the aristocratic beauty and dazzling wardrobes of her colleagues Hana Benoniová and Marie Laudová, soon the playwrights also came to perceive in Kvapilová a unique desire and talent to "give an expression to the Czech spirit [duch]."[1] Writing about Kvapilová's place in Czech culture, Bozena Viková-Kunetická (a turn-of-the-century nationalist playwright, novelist, and essayist)[2] expressed the pathos felt towards the actress by most of her contemporaries: "She was the purest expression of our nation, its innermost truth, its innermost sorrow and span. I doubt that this woman could have been a member of any other nation but ours."[3]

The Czech nineteenth-century nationalist discourse, within which Kvapilová became a chief icon, propounded spirituality, peacefulness, and sensibility as presumably constituting the "essence of Czechness."[4] Similar to other European nationalists at the time,[5] Czech writers tended to locate this "essence of Czechness" in the presumably autonomous "inner" domain and asserted the urgency of shielding this interiority of the nation from trends and developments in the Germanized economic sphere. While the Czech nationalism positioned men as active and forward-thrusting agents in national history, the task of being the repositories of the nation's "essence" fell on the women.[6]

Already one of the earliest myth-making projects of the Czech Revival, Jan Kollár's extremely influential cycle of sonnets *Slávy dcera* [*Sláva's Daughter* or *Glory's Daughter*],[7] posits the distinct roles of men and women in the Czech nation as follows: "Strong will, action, and courage suit men / humility, sensibility, and silence suit women / the former be the spirit / the latter be the soul."[8] The ideal Slavic woman is pictured in Kollár's "bible of Slavdom" as a virtuous, industrious, humble beauty, and as "a quiet lamb, the sins of this land redeeming."[9] Note that their prescribed role in the nationalist project typically constructs Czech women as silent and submissive, and Czech nationalism appears to stand (in Kollár as well as other Czech nationalists' narratives) on the institutionalization of gendered behavior. Indeed, *Slávy dcera* specifically opposes the notion of a "feminized man" and "masculinized woman," and mentions the elimination of traditional gender differences as a development potentially most harmful to the nation.[10]

Considering the centrality of traditional domestic womanhood in the Czech nationalist discourse, it is quite remarkable that Kvapilová — celebrated for her portrayal of conventional women characters in plays of Czech nationalism — has been also considered (both by her audience and theatre historians) a symbol of *fin-de-siècle* women's emancipation (for her roles in Ibsen and in Czech "modern"[11] plays featuring unconventional women).

Similar to many other European societies, the Czech *fin-de-siècle* was marked by a lively popular debate concerning women's rights. The Kollárian "quiet lamb" model of domestic woman remained central in Czech culture throughout much of the nineteenth century, working to channel women's subversive energy into family and nation building. Still, the growing economic crisis at the end of the nineteenth century (which reduced the numbers of Czech middle class fathers capable of providing for their daughters), combined with unfavorable demographic statistics suggesting a surplus of 200,000 women, supplied Czech women with license to begin putting forward claims for their rights.

Already in 1863, the first public high school for girls was opened in Prague, followed by a girls' school of commerce founded in 1871. "Minerva," the first "gymnasium" (grammar school) for girls in the monarchy, opened in 1890. By the 1890s, several liberal women's magazines (*Zenské listv* [*Women's Journal, Zensky' svet* [*Women's World*], *Zenská revue* [*Women's Revue*]) had been established. These magazines provided a platform for middleclass women's emancipatory efforts and championed Czech women's right for higher education, access to professions and public careers, and political equality with men.

The Czech theatre placed itself in the foreground of these debates, first with productions of woman-centered plays in translation (Ibsen[12] as well as now forgotten Russian realists A. I. Palm and Shpazhinsky) and later with woman-centered plays by domestic writers (Jaroslav Hilbert, Jaroslav Kvapil, M. A. Sim·cek, and F. X. Svoboda).[13] Kvapilová, through her sympathetic representations of female roles in these plays, came to be recognized and celebrated as the main advocate of women's rights on the Czech stage.[14] Indeed, having inspired numerous playwrights to create Czech contemporary women characters who would match her acting style and the type of womanhood she was perceived as embodying, Kvapilová, in fact, not only represented Czech women's emancipation on the stage but rather directly helped define the character and substance of Czech feminism for playwrights and audiences.

To her contemporaries, Kvapilová thus appeared as the embodiment of multiple and often contradictory symbols. Regarded as the most representative actress of the

Figure 1. Hana Kvapilová as Ellida in Ibsen's *Lady From the Sea* (1905). Courtesy of Národní muzeum, divadelní oddelení, Prague.

Figure 2. Hana Kvapilová as Ellida in Ibsen's *The Lady From the Sea* (1905). Courtesy of Národní muzeum, divadelní oddelení, Prague.

Czech nation and praised for her talent for expressing the "innermost truth of the Czech national character," she simultaneously epitomized Czech *fin-de-siècle* women's striving for emancipation. Furthermore, she also developed what was considered a "modern" acting style, distinguished by her focus on the psychological and spiritual "truth" of her roles.

In examining Kvapilová's acting style, the question of the extent to which her interest in the expression of inner feelings provided her with a resource for resolving contradictions (nationalist traditions vs. modern women's emancipation) otherwise unsettling to her contemporaries stands as a central matter of concern here. Optimistically, one might argue that her inward focus contributed to circumstances favorable for balancing her image as simultaneously modem (progressive) and national (traditional), as both emancipated and a quintessentially Czech woman. A closer look at her work and its influences, however, renders such an appraisal problematic on a number of counts.

Most Czech scholars have praised, idealized, and idolized Kvapilová. During her lifetime the actress did have to deal with political intrigues and sometimes harsh criticisms. One of the most painful of these was the 1903 vicious attack from the playwright Jaroslav Hilbert, whose 1896 play *Vina* [*Guilt*] Kvapilová had both inspired and popularized. But following her early death stemming from neglected diabetes and exhaustion, the actress became a sort of untouchable martyr for Czech drama scholarship. Kvapilová's predisposition to martyrdom and personal sacrifice may in fact have contributed significantly to her transformation into an ideal (because unthreatening) representative of Czech women's emancipation. Kvapilová earned her reputation as an emancipated woman for her rejection (and her stage representation of the rejection) of some traditions harmful to women, such as arranged marriages or women's confinement in the domestic space. At the same time, she was encouraged to embrace (and did embrace) what some scholars of Czech nationalism have labeled the "Czech cult of martyrdom" or "Czech masochistic nationalism,"[15] which in her case translated into a performance of self effacing and body-obliterating femininity. Analyzing her ethereal acting style and the roles that made her famous, the rest of this essay traces the process (in which she actively participated) through which Kvapilová was transformed into a symbol of appropriate Czech emancipated womanhood and later into a martyr figure by means of denying and effacing her corporeality.

Kvapilová's Psychological Acting Style

Kvapilová has been applauded by drama critics and scholars for an intellectual approach to her characters and intensive, detailed study of her parts. This method was perceived as intensely new, modern, by contemporary Czech critics. It clearly distinguished Kvapilová's style from the melodramatic acting style of the other popular Czech actresses at the time, Benoniová and Laudová, who (as contemporary reviews suggest) saw their work on the stage above all as an opportunity for a fashion show. Starting with reviews of her earliest work at Svanda's company[16] in Brno (the center of Moravia) and Smíchov (outskirts of Prague), Kvapilová's style was recognized as exceptionally reflective and self-conscious. Her later career was characterized by the prominent Czech *fin-de-siècle* critic Jindrich Vodák in terms of a "psychologist who analyzes, studies, and explores with the goal of seeing clearly the structure of the character's intellectual process."[17] And Frantisek Xaver Salda, perhaps the most influential critic of the Czech turn-of-the-century art generation, wrote of Kvapilová's roles: "Kvapilová knew her characters from all sides. Her knowledge of them went beyond the author's text — she completed and thought the script through to the end. She knew her character's childhood, youth, all that had happened prior to the first rise of the curtain."[18] Kvapilová, it appears, subscribed to the concept of character biography and saw her work on the stage in terms of an analyst. She viewed her work as an actress as consisting of collecting clues about her character's past, motivation, and intentions as inscribed into (or left out of) the script, and translating them for the spectators. A painstaking study of the role — based on a careful reading of the text directed toward filling in the gaps left ambiguous in the script — served as the foundation for Kvapilová's comprehension of the character's subconscious and for her inner identification with the role. Whereas the earlier generation of Czech performers (such as the actress of grand gestures Otylie Sklenárová-Malá) moved from one role to the next without significant changes (adapting the roles to their own disposition), Kvapilov· struggled to transfor m her "self" according to the requirements of the role, and did so by investigating the emotions of the character and adopting these for her own.

Doing so, Kvapilová sought to materialize the new concept of acting advanced by a group of young Czech theoreticians of theatre in response to the demands of recently imported Russian realist drama. In 1887, the National Theatre produced several realist plays by (now generally forgotten but at the time formative) Russian playwrights A. I. Palm, N. Y. Solovyov, I. V. Shpazhinsky, and A. N. Ostrovsky.[19] The production of these plays (hailed for their characters of "real" contemporary people presumably "true to life"[20]) was accompanied by the Czech playwright Vilém Mrstík's translation of Emile Zola's essay "On Theatre" (calling for a new realist drama), published in the January 1887 issue of the major Czech theatre journal, *Ceská Thalia*. In the same year, the theatre critic Pavel Durdík articulated his understanding of the "new theatre," naming as the basis of the modern actor's work his/her identification with the character. "The purpose of the dramatic artist," Durdík wrote, "is to make others feel what he himself feels and represents. This requires a great deal of painstaking intellectual work. The artist needs to thoroughly adopt the role, study and feel it to the slightest detail . . . embody [vtelit] it within himself. It is only this embodiment that turns an actor into an artist."[22] Finally, in 1889, *Ceská Thalia* reviewed and then serialized (in Bedrich Mares' translation) excerpts from William Archer's 1888 *Masks or Faces?* As the reviewer summarized it (perhaps not entirely accurately), Archer in his book rejected Diderot's earlier contention that an actor should avoid his/her absorption by the role, that feeling the passions an actor portrays on the stage would merely hamper the performance.[23] Most of the actors and actresses questioned by Archer agreed, the Czech reviewer underscored, that a genuine emotional identification with the character impresses the audience more deeply than mere imitation of outward behavior.[24]

As her own texts devoted to the subject of acting illustrate, a complete emotional conversion into the character was the goal of Kvapilová's creative process, and she became celebrated for her mastery of the psychological method. Her writings on this subject are preoccupied with the introspective method of her transformation into the character. For instance, in the manuscript fragment "Before a New Performance," Kvapilová describes an actress's creative process as a search for inspiration in developing a sort of inner model to be executed on the stage, as a production of a psychological and emotional environment from which the words and gestures of her character would flow naturally. The text is suggestive of influence (either direct or mediated through Archer's book) on the actress of Eduard von Hartmann's concept of psychological "autosuggestion"[25] as a way of attaining a deep concentration on the role:

> All day long, she would leaf through the pictures and touch the Chinese and Japanese toys with her fingers. She would test various paints, mixing them to achieve the pure opacity of ivory; she would try to deepen the eye's expression as required by the temperament of Joasien's being . . . and when she-after a long search-finally found the right perfume, she inhaled it with a sense of satisfaction. . . . (She would hide her soul from her colleagues, knowing she was a fool in their eyes and fearing the crudeness of their touches). Such seemingly trivial yet essential preoccupations filled the moments of rest during her study of a new role. Yet, even then, the foreign soul — the soul of the adopted being — hovered around her, forcing words to her lips, making her absent-minded and ridiculous to those around her, whose questions she now ignored.[26]

The passage produces a sense of the actress's work as magical, mysterious, and extraordinary by describing the actress's trance-like state and thus suggesting her exceptional ability to reach beyond the every-day reality of "ordinary" people. Still, the quote also gives away "the magic" of inspiration by representing it as reachable by outward mechanical methods. Kvapilová here describes conscious ways of controlling the actress' subconscious and making it perceive and feel with the character. The author also seems to distinguish in the passage between psychological acting (identification) and theatrical imitation. She expresses her allegiance with the former by discursively constituting her fictional actress-artist, the master of the psychological method, as a genius (misunderstood and therefore laughed at by her colleagues) and by portraying the other actors, presumably actor-imitators, as "crude."

In *Masks or Faces?* Archer allots much space to discussing the "paradox of dual consciousness," the perception (reported by numerous dramatic artists and first conceptualized by Diderot) of division of the actor's or actress's self from the character he or she impersonates on the stage at the moment.[27] Although Kvapilová shares with the English critic the concept of an artist's original "self" existing prior to the artist's transformation to another self required by the role, when describing her own acting, Kvapilová's texts rarely refer to "double consciousness" in terms of splitting or division. Much more frequently she describes what she perceives as the pleasurable moments of a total absorption — another indication of her prioritization of psychological acting.

Her notes on Sarah Bernhardt, whose work she observed during Bernhardt's Prague visits in 1888 and 1892, indicate that Kvapilová was aware of the concept of "multiple consciousness" (which Bernhardt evidently represented to her), but disapproved of it as somehow deceitful and dishonest and as presumably failing to achieve an adequate emotional response in the spectator. Although she admires the French diva's enterprising spirit,[28] bravura, and technical perfection, Kvapilová sighs after more moments "when Bernhardt would 'truly feel' rather than simply reproducing the role on the stage." "Often, I believe, she could boast . . . that in the most moving scene she could solve a difficult math problem."[29] While in the following passage describing her own acting Kvapilová speaks of a sense of multiplied feelings and doubled senses, she applies the terminology differently than Archer,[30] referring here to a total merging and harmony of two selves, rather than their split:

> It is peculiar how one's comprehension and feelings become multiplied at such times of intense creation, just as if these forcefully merged beings perceived simultaneously, with doubled, ten, senses. And on this festival of the soul, everything is immensely beautiful, everything is in a harmonious accord. . . . At moments like these, a tremendous, humble gratitude enters our heart, a great, immeasurable love, pacifying the life's confusions and softening its coarse touches.[31]

Although this statment is filled with a sense of exaltation presumably induced by the actress' total merging with the role, the expression "forcefully merged beings" also seems to indicate a presence of (repressed) anxieties on the part of the author. Some of Kvapilová's other published and manuscript writings testify more unequivocally to the personal sacrifices the actress perceived as required by the psychological method. Above all, the technique of identification seems to have produced in Kvapilová an unsettling perception, which she tried to suppress in her texts, of having to voluntarily surrender her identity, replacing it with the playwright's creation. In the essay from which the previous passage was quoted, "Zena v umení dramatickém [Woman in Dramatic Art]" (1903), Kvapilová also speaks of a "long journey of misgivings and suffering," which an actress-artist must undergo before "seizing the poet's image" (165). While at moments exalting total absorption on the stage as pleasurable, the metaphors she invokes to describe the process of embodying the author's image — the process of identifying with the character's self — suggest a distinct sense of her uneasiness with what would be later named by Stanislavsky "the psychotechnique":

> To merge with [the poet's] dream, to give life and pulsation of one's own blood to the being sketched by the poet, to live through the character's happiness and sorrow, to feel the beat of a strange heart in one's own bosom, to move through the depths of this foreign being who — throughout the study, throughout this struggle — has been slowly but surely strangling our own being, silencing our own thinking and feeling, breaking our will, only to sit squarely on the throne of our heart. To merge with the poet in this way equates to standing next to him, being to some extent his collaborator, protecting his lights and never letting them die, supplementing the beauty of his dream. (165-66)

A number of possible, in some ways contradictory, undertones can be discerned in this passage, so filled with metaphorical allusions to the interpretive process as a corporeal engagement of celebration and as an ordeal, almost at once joyful and violent. The celebratory beginning and ending of this section is interrupted by a disturbing scene of invasion, violation, and struggle — an encounter with the "foreigner" entailing "strangling," "silencing," and finally "breaking." The act of the actress's merging with the "poet's dream" (outwardly extolled in this passage) seems to require an annihilation of the actress's critical faculties, rather than encouraging her active and critical engagement with the role. In its extreme, the "poet's dream" appears leaning toward the parasitic, the "foreign being," a vampire of sorts threatening to draw off the life of the actress. To "protect the poet's lights" and prevent them from dying evidently demands a figurative death of the actress as an independent thinking being; in Kvapilová's perception, it seems to require emptying her self of all independent thought and will and lending her body to the poet's creation — hardly an empowering image.

In her texts, Kvapilová did distinguish between the trance-like states of total absorption and the more self-aware and critical moments in her creative process, but the feelings accompanying her more critical state of mind are described as ambivalently as are the emotions characteristic of the creative state. Rather than applying her critical faculties in the direction of assessing the ideology of the author's text and her performance of it, the actress seems to have turned the critical look at (and against) herself. A critique is thus substituted by an agonizing self-criticism, "a relentless dissection":

> Before the crucial battle of this evening she has already become an entirely borrowed, strange being — she now thought by this being's brain and felt by her heart. She has accepted for her own foreign passions, foreign virtues. Later, in a moment brightened by her own being, she analyzed her performance over and over again, subjecting it to a relentless dissection. Pain moved through her body and mind as fresh piercing misgivings filled her entire inner being.[32]

In all the above quoted texts, Kvapilová displays her self-perception as an exceptional actress-dramatic artist in Durdik's sense of the term — as an actress capable of embodying a role within herself, of transforming herself totally into the character. However, if the basis of the distinction between an "ordinary actress" and a "dramatic artist" starts with the actress's talent for introspection and conversion, this seems to translate in practice to a difference in a degree of self-sacrifice. Repeatedly invoking pain, Kvapilová's texts fetishize suffering and self effacement, implying masochism standing as an actress's (or, at least, this actress's) necessary prerequisite to success. What ultimately makes a dramatic actress exceptional — at least as inferred from Kvapilová's writing — seems to be her readiness to subject herself to emotional and physical suffering for the sake of the playwright's artistic vision.

The two promotional articles Kvapilová published in 1906 in order to prepare the Czech audience for Stanislavsky and Danchenko's company's visit in Berlin and Prague further illustrate her eager association of art with personal sacrifices. "They all forfeit their entire freedom," the actress writes with enthusiasm (suggesting her own identification with the Russian company's concept of creative work by switching between the third and first person pronouns), "honest art, as they understand it . . . means a loss of life; it is a voluntary exile, a spiritual solitude; it engages totally and forever our being; it leaves us with no leisure time or will for compromises."[33]

Having described her own experience of the opening nights in devout and pious terms as a "genuflection at the altar of beauty and art bareheaded," "the purest and highest tone in the melody of devotion," "an elevation, beautification, sacrifice,"[34] Kvapilová also enthusiastically identifies with Stanislavsky's statement of his company's artistic goal to "turn theatre into a temple, oneself into its celebrant; to make a religion of the acting vocation."[35] This manifesto best articulates Kvapilov·'s own understanding of dramatic acting as a vocation presumably endowed with the powers usually attributed to a religious sacrifice — the potential to bring a redemption for the artist and through her a redemption for the audiences. Given the popular perception of pious spirituality as the main feature of the Czech national character, such a concept of theatre makes it a particularly suitable art form for embodying, expressing, and celebrating the spirit of the Czech nation.

Although Hana's father was a bohemian rebel and it was he who supported Hana's decision to become a professional actress, her mother and paternal grandmother's devout Catholicism seems to have had a more lasting effect on Kvapilová than she herself wished for, as she would complain to her friend and decadent author Ruzena Svobodová later in her life.[36] It was no doubt also this influence that predetermined to a great extent the actress's pietistic perception of her work and perhaps — considering the emphasis placed in Catholicism on Virgin Mary's suffering — also her own fetishization of pain. After all, it is the pain and grief Mary undergoes that seem to warrant a veneration of her in Catholic liturgy. And it is her specifically female sorrow that makes her (because she is presumably understanding of their own pain and suffering as women) into an attractive and powerful icon for women. Such a symbol of suffering femininity, with which Czech women were encouraged to identify, would channel women's discontent into an idealized masochism, encouraging the already mentioned "cult of martyrdom" and providing for the amount of masochism in the stage career of Kvapilová.

Kvapilová's Catholic upbringing might be also at the core of the many similarities (highlighted throughout the rest of this essay) that seem to have existed between her own approach to acting and that of her famous Italian contemporary Eleonora Duse — also a Catholic.[37] Both of these national actresses (each quite dedicated to expressing the greatness of her respective nation) associated art with suffering.[38] Although Duse was still an actress who tried to adapt her roles to her own personality[39] whereas Kvapilová worked to adapt herself to her roles, they shared a particular type of psychological acting that was perceived as highly interior, piously spiritual and non-corporeal, and that was lauded for its subtlety. And both Kvapilová and Duse — the most celebrated Ibsen actresses on their respective nation's stage — became famous for their rendering of Ibsen's Ellida Wangel, a role described by James Agate as "a godsend to a great actress whose *forte* is not so much doing as suffering that which fate has done to her."[40]

The Ethereal Aspect of Kvapilová's Acting Style

The internalized suffering and anxiety characteristic of Kvapilová's creative process would become also the hallmark of the characters most associated with the actress. Although she created and cherished numerous parts in Shakespeare's comedies, the roles with which she has become identified (in dramas by Hilbert, Kvapil, Ibsen, and Chekhov) are those of either intellectually and emotionally agonized or at least patiently suffering women. Kvapilová's preoccupation with expressing the spirituality of her women characters and with gaining the audience's empathy for them underwrote her sympathetic rendering of these women as tragic and amiable.

Most of her Czech critics have commented approvingly that even the most controversial characters (who would, as they argued, become demonic and ominous femme fatales in the hands of other actresses) were represented by Kvapilová as sympathetic, compassionate women searching for harmony. For instance, Arne Novák notes admiringly about Kvapilová's rendering of Ibsen's women: "She deliberately softened, even suppressed, that in Ibsen's women which was Nordic-like predatory, unscrupulous, demoniac — curbing their wild, elemental fire smoldering underneath their hard coldness. . . . Where it was impossible to avoid such features without harming the poet's work, she domesticated them and translated them into the minor key."[41] Frantisek Cerny', Kvapilová's most recent biographer, interprets the actress's tendency to idealize her characters and express their desire for a "better world" as indicative of her active engagement with the playwright's work and as potentially subversive: "A woman in her interpretation would be not only what she is in reality, but what she might become under more favorable circumstances. . . . The conflict between reality and the individual's potential, impossible to be fulfilled in the present society, would generally produce an accusatory impression."[42]

Perhaps in some cases Kvapilová' s sympathetic rendering of unfavorably portrayed women characters might be interpreted as resulting from the actress's critique of the playwright's representation of women, and viewed as having a subversive potential. Still, the tendency among Czech scholars to interpret enthusiastically as transgressive the actress's "softening" of her character's' controversial attributes seems ideologically suspect, particularly where it is accompanied by the critics' praise of Kvapilová's "poetic," "ethereal," "non-corporeal" acting. From a feminist perspective, the political efficacy of such an acting style (its ability to expose and critique the traditional roles expected from women) seems questionable, particularly since this style in practice facilitated a painful suppression of the actress's body on the stage — a subordination of a woman's body to an expression of desire attributed with redemptive powers.

The praise Kvapilová earned from Czech critics and theatre scholars for her analytical, psychological approach to her roles is matched by their tribute to the actress's unique ability to create the illusion of a spiritual, de-materialized presence. Kvapilová has been lauded for inventing an acting style ideally matching the endeavors of Czech *fin-de-siècle* avant-garde playwrights and directors (Kvapil, Svoboda, Hilbert) intent on reaching beyond the naturalist realism of Stroupeznicky', Preissová, or brothers Mrstíks and ushering first a new era of psychological realism and later of impressionism on the Czech stage. Referring to her famous 1905 impressionist rendering of Ellida Wangel, (See Figs. 1 and 2) Viková-Kunetická wrote: "Her soft, silky figure . . . ceased to be a physical being and became a wave. . . . There were moments when nothing was left of her but her wide-open eyes and the vibration of her presence. . . . Everything around her appeared too hard, too still, too physical in comparison."[43] Based on contemporary reviews of the production, Cerny' describes Kvapilová's *Princezna Pampeliska* [*Princess Dandelion*] in (her husband) Kvapil' s 1897 dramatic tale as a "poetic, web-like, de-materialized, ephemeral being woven from grace and poetry and surrounded by magical charm and gentle radiance."[44] Even the early feminist Pavla Buzková praised Kvapilová for inspiring her husband, the famous poet and director,[45] to write the role of fragile and un-earthly

Pampeliska, which inaugurated Czech dramatic impressionism: "No other of our actresses has inspired in our poets an image of a being so incorporeal and so belonging to other worlds."[46] Buzková continues ecstatically: "The more sophisticated and spiritually refined spectators ascended with her to other, purer worlds. All souls who could free themselves from the sphere of the material were grateful to her — in theatre and in the nation" (156). Buzková's notes perhaps best express the desire and trend among Czech scholars to attribute transcendental potential to K vapilová' s spiritual acting. Perceived as capable of transcending the material, the actress embodied a promise to guide her audiences and (as Buzková's statement suggests) the nation in general to a better, more spiritual, and thus presumably more Czech, "elsewhere."

Kvapilová's published notes on the work of Duse, Modrzejewska, and Hennings — in which she aspires to discursively constitute the spiritual acting style as characteristic of artists from "small nations" (appearing to mean rather nations struggling for political sovereignty) — suggest both Kvapilová' s own enthusiasm for the non-corporeal style and also her tendency to perceive an appropriateness of an acting style as to some extent determined by the requirements of specific national cultures. Of Duse, Kvapilová wrote: "Watching her act, you will notice how her physicality disappears from one act to the next."[47] Her later article on Betty Hennings, following the actress's 1904 guest performance in Prague, compares the Danish interpreter of Ibsen to the Polish actress Helena Modrzejewska (who had visited Prague in 1891), overtly speculating about links between their acting styles and their nationality. "Hennings," Kvapilová remarks, "comes from a small nation, just like Modrzejewska, and thus she speaks through her heart and soul in a concise way and with a multiplied force just as Modrzejewska did. . . . Her art . . . is sanctified by the actress' deep heart-felt inward immersion."[48] Kvapilová's rhetoric concerning the art of the actresses from "small nations" suggests the author's assumption that the quality of "spiritual depth" in acting is contingent upon experience of prolonged personal sacrifices for the sake of a broader community — an experience which Kvapilová seems to have ascribed to members (specifically women) of repressed nations.

Not surprisingly, Kvapilová's observations on the art of spiritual acting indicate its interconnectedness with a suppression of women characters' sexuality, or rather its sublimation in the actresses' performances to a "higher" level. "It is the sophistication of every human passion, the ennoblement of even the lowest instincts," that makes Modrzejewska an actress poet, according to Kvapilová.[49] Similarly, Duse's ability to eliminate the "crude animal passion" and "purify her woman in love by spiritualizing her" seems to be the underlying feature of her art of ethereal acting: "Her art is seraphic-like, pure, as if not from this world, chaste. . . . There is no trace here of female animal-ness."[50]

Seeking to personify the pure and presumably transcendent Desire, as she became both willing and expected to, Kvapilová found herself likewise faced with the task of constantly suppressing her sexuality and body and battling her own corporeality on the stage — a particularly cruel task for a woman with a leaning toward plumpness and suffering from diabetes at the turn of the 20th century. Subscribing to the cult of redemptive spirituality, Kvapilová seems to have become locked into a self-damaging cycle. Although she was (and still is) celebrated for her presumed ability to express women's desire for freedom, Kvapilová's goal to communicate desire through her incorporeal acting style led to her becoming a rather conventional model of women's self-restraint and self-effacement. Rather than using her body to critique traditional women's roles and perform new and more empowering models of behavior for women in the audience, Kvapilová' s mastery of the spiritual acting style was likely to reaffirm the traditional masochistic feminine ideal, particularly since many of the plays written for the actress involved self-annihilation of the "modern woman" (meaning a woman attempting to transgress traditional femininity).

Vina [*Guilt*], the perhaps most celebrated Czech "modern play" created specifically for Kvapilová by Jaroslav Hilbert (a Czech follower of Ibsen), consciously employed efforts at emulating the Ibsenite dramaturgy as well as the Norwegian playwright's censure of bourgeois morals. Similar to Ibsen's plays, the tragedy of Hilbert's drama had happened prior to the rise of the curtain, and the audiences were encouraged to interpret the heroine's secret from the clues she provided. Mína's secret is her seduction, seven years prior to the play's action, by a student, Uhlír — an event for which she (despite her outward contempt for traditional morality and her present happy relationship with a poet Stána) feels inescapably guilty. When Uhlír reappears in her life, confident that his past action gives him the right to claim her for his wife, Mína promises her hand to him only to later take her own life by jumping out of the window.

While Uhlír is the main villain in the play and his insolence makes him particularly repugnant to the audience, the major part of the blame for Mína's "sin" and her death is placed on her mother, Mrs. Maráková, who is portrayed in the play as apathetic, cold, and detached. In contrast to Mrs. Maráková's obsession with her son (Mína's older brother), her mother's neglect and indifference towards Mína is portrayed as the cause of Mína's suffering. On several occasions, the daughter explicitly blames this maternal neglect for her past naivete which presumably led to her transgression. "Mother does not love me," she tells Stána, "she feels nothing for me, nothing. . . . the responsibility for the sins of my youth falls on her!"[51]

The theme of an "unnatural mother" who withdraws all expressions of fondness and even interest from her daughter appears to have dominated the audience's impression of the play. Cerny' quotes Karel Masek, Kvapilová's contemporary, as remarking: "Especially women were swept away by the play, identifying in many aspects with the maternally neglected character of Mína."[52] Such identification, while pointedly exposing the patriarchal tradition of the Czech parental preference for the sons to the point of neglecting the daughters, was likely disempowering to the women in the audience since the character with whom they were encouraged to empathize turns masochistic and, in the end, self-destructive. What else other than masochistic might we call Mína's decision to marry the man who had seduced her and for whom she has no affection, as she explains her decision to Stána as follows: "You, I have loved and will always love, but it is his wife that I will become. . . . I must marry him because with him the life's sorrows and hardships will be the harder" (93).

The unusual dramaturgy (for the Czech stage), the urban bourgeois drawing-room setting, the subject matter of a middle class "fallen woman," and the relatively complex characters turned the 1896 premiere of the play into a celebrated manifestation of the new acting style and a “great event of modernity."[53] Appreciating the play's psychological realism as a new development in Czech drama and applauding

Kvapilová' s dazzling identification with the character, [54] the critics failed to notice that the inauguration of the Czech modern drama was redeemed in a conventionally misogynist way — by a woman character's self-annihilation. Furthermore, by blaming the mother for Mína's downfall without pointing out the social enforcement behind the mother's behavior, the patriarchy is let off the hook rather than becoming (like in Ibsen's social dramas) the focus of the narrative's censure. And while Hilbert's play ostensibly dismisses the bourgeois morality which dictates that Mína feel ashamed for having been seduced, it ultimately — by confirming the power of this sense of guilt — reaffirms it.

Princezna Pampeliska [*Princess Dandelion*], a dramatic fairy tale written for Kvapilová by her husband in 1897, was another modern play aspiring to critique contemporary Czech society by portraying a woman character too ideal to survive the society's corruption. A kind but incompetent king of a poor, small country decides to remedy his poverty by marrying his daughter Pampeliska off to a mighty prince of Hispania. She refuses the prince and runs away with a poor cottager, the "silly Honza" (a popular fairy-tale character). Their travels occasion the narrative's unflattering critique of a variety of (what are portrayed in the play as) Czech characteristics and traditions, such as mediocrity, kowtowing to the powerful, acceptance of the status quo, timidity, as well as the tradition of arranged marriages for money. By the time the season in the narrative changes to winter, the princess (much like dandelions in nature) withers, is lifted by a whirl of wind, and transformed into a snowstorm. Similar to the woman character in *Vina*, Pampeliska, pure and innocent, cannot survive in the present world and dies, with her body being literally blown off from the stage — a symbolic ending particularly befitting the ethereal, non-corporeal acting style developed by Kvapilová.

Perhaps as much as a critique of the weaknesses the playwright detected in the broader *fin-de-siècle* Czech national community, *Princezna Pampeliska* might be also interpreted as Kvapil's critical commentary on behind-the-scenes intrigues against his wife, which were gaining strength in the 1890s and did not cease until the actress's death in 1907. The National Theatre management valued the farce, opera, and melodrama over the drama and used all means available to marginalize Kvapilová and her male colleague Eduard Vojan, who both represented what was generally recognized as serious dramatic acting. The role of Pampeliska, too fragile and poetic to survive in the world of intrigue — which is how the actress herself has been portrayed in relation to her adversaries — became a demonstration of everything the actress represented on the stage and in the national culture. To this day, according to Cerny', the role "merges in our consciousness with [Kvapilová's] personal and artistic character."[55]

The play is often represented as not only having been inspired by Kvapilová's life to that point but also as having anticipated the actress's future fate. Similar to Pampeliska's end, Kvapilová's own death is generally attributed by her biographers to the exhausting battles against political intrigues which worsened the actress's already fragile health. And similar to the characters of Pampeliska and Mína in Kvapil's and Hilbert's dramas, the accounts of Kvapilová's career usually represent the actress as a martyr who suffered death in the service of the truth. Kvapilová's struggle to endorse the new acting style on the stage of the National Theatre — recognized generally as part of a broader national striving of Czech artists to demonstrate the high level and modernity of Czech *fin-de-siècle* culture and perceived as causing the actress's premature death — made her particularly suitable for becoming stylized into a Czech national hero. Unfortunately, while enabling the perception of them as national heroines, the martyrdom shared by the fictional characters of Pampeliska and Mína with Kvapilová as the character of her biographers' accounts, also restricted their stories into the traditional narratives of masochistic femininity since it required the women's suffering and ultimate annihilation.[56]

The reviews of Kvapilová's roles suggest that the actress was for the most part successful at transforming herself and creating the impression of lightness, fresh youth, and ethereality, with which she remained associated until her death in her late forties. Cerny', for instance, makes a typical remark that in spite of her (presumed) heaviness, as soon as she entered the stage, Kvapilová "became suddenly beautiful." He quotes her contemporaries who argued that in the role of Pampeliska, "she managed to create an illusion of a fragile flower," and as Goethe's Marguerite (1906), she was "a true little girl",[57] despite her expressed anxiety that the critics would mock her for lacking a suitable exterior required by the role. Still, comments like these seem to confirm the actress's success at suppressing her body and age too eagerly, thus inadvertently indicating that her physicality (and history) did re-assert itself on the stage (if against the actress's wishes), ideally telling to the audiences a subversive tale of the cruelty inscribed into the expectations placed on women in Czech turn-of-the-century culture. And if Kvapilová's too corporeal body (in her and some critics' eyes) did not counteract and subvert the actress's striving for its annihilation on the stage clearly enough for *fin-de-siècle* audiences, the actress's letters — filled with expressions of misgivings about her appearance — expose to us just how difficult and harmful the constant rejection and learned loathing of her own physicality was to the actress's self-esteem and health. As Cerny' summed it up, Kvapilová worried her entire productive life that "she was not beautiful enough, often assuming that her presumed lack of beauty professionally harmed her." At the time of her creative zenith (in the late 1890s and 1900s), she "literally suffered for her appearance because she got substantially heavier."[58]

Kvapilová's correspondence with her friend Ruzena Svobodová is perhaps the best source of the actress's expressions of agonizing doubts about her body and appearance. In one of her last letters to Svobodová, written during particularly intense rehearsals for Chekhov's *The Three Sisters*, Kvapilová despairs: "I am unhappy. I imagined [Masha] tall, slim, proud, and yet soft and nervous. . . . My whole physical being is hideous and paltry; it spoils everything for me."[60] Buzková, who published the letters, points out the increasing emphasis in Ruzena's correspondence to Kvapilová on her friend's appearance, ascribing it correctly to the actress's decreasing self-esteem and her growing preoccupation, even obsession, with her image. "My little girl," writes the eight years' younger Svobodová to Kvapilová, effectively infantilizing the actress, "you were so beautiful the day before yesterday; so slender, neat, and combed down, just like you used to be years ago. I thought I would die. You looked like a first love."[61]

If Kvapilová subscribed to the cult of youth and spiritual non-corporeality, Svobodová's (certainly well meant) advice only further encouraged such an ideal in the actress. Asking her if she has been following her advice and going for daily three-hour walks, Svobodová reminds her friend that the new generation of the early twentieth century "has an utter disgust for fat [tlusté] people." "It is enough for a person to be fat today," Svobodová continues, "for them to condemn everything about him and ignore all the better qualities. You, my dear Hanicka, must collect yourself together, you must resolve not to kill your great art of youth in this way. You play a heroine, but a heroine must be all wind. . . . It's just that nobody believes fat people's suffering."[62] Kvapilová's art is here once again equated with her ability to communicate youth and vulnerability: in order for her performed suffering to be believable, the actress needs to maintain an appropriate (slender) image.[63]

Kvapilová's anxieties over aging and losing her girlish figure were not uncommon among nineteenth-century actresses in general, working as they were in the medium notoriously favoring the young woman character. To a great extent, these anxieties were also determined by the circumstances of, and especially the position of women in, Czech *fin-de-siècle* theatre. Historians of the National Theatre all comment on the hostile competition among the National Theatre's leading actresses at the *fin de siècle*. In fact, the rivalry was so pronounced that the Theatre historians generally use the pairs of leading actresses-adversaries as period markers: Thus the rivalry between Marie Pospísilová (the "representative" type) and Marie Bittnerová (the realist-drama type), which characterized the developments at the National Theatre in the 1880s, was supplanted in the 1890s by the next pair of rivaling leading women actresses, Hana Benoniová (the representative of passionate, "dark," and superficial womanhood mostly in French drama) and Hana Kvapilová (the representative of kind, compassionate, suffering, and "deep" heroines mostly in Czech plays). Importantly, each of these pairs consisted of one actress whose character was represented as unblemished and exemplary, whose sexuality was safely confined to the marital bed, and who portrayed women roles of a corresponding virtuous character (Bittnerová and Kvapilová), and her direct opposite — an actress notorious for her scandalous sexual escapades and generally "unscrupulous behavior" most of whose roles on the Czech stage matched her presumed profile (Pospísilová and Benoniová). This division of actresses and roles into quintessentially good and evil, and the barrier of hostility between them sustained by the National Theatre's management's practices, worked well to reaffirm expectations concerning the traditional stark distinction between women-saints and whores and between virtuous Czechness and morally suspect foreign-nes. The division reinforced the rule of normative obedience as a condition of Czech womanhood and effectively censured any expression of female defiance or disobedience on the Czech stage.

The fact that the National Theatre was for many decades the only Czech theatre of its kind (no other Czech company approached the National's reputation or offered competitive salaries) and that it was controlled by men (all members of management and artistic directors were men) did not make matters easier and, instead, contributed to the vicious rivalry among the actresses. Rather than reconciling them, the management seems to have encouraged and manipulated the animosity. The artistic directors and playwrights often used individual actresses as tokens in their political and artistic battles, thus adding to the unproductive and unhealthy atmosphere of hostility and back-stage intrigues of which Kvapilová frequently complained. The case of Marie Pospisílová, who was forced to leave the National Theatre after defying Frantisek Subert's[64] authority, worked as a warning example, effectively precluding future actresses (including Kvapilová) from asserting control over the circumstances of their work.

After leaving the National Theatre in 1884, Pospisílová won success after success as the leading actress of Prague's German Estates Theatre, Deutscher Theater in Berlin, Berliner Theater, even the Court Theatre in Vienna (the principal Austrian stage at the *fin de siécle)* and became (under a germanized name of Maria Pospischil) one of the leading European actresses. Despite her dazzling international triumphs, she was, however, not accepted back at the National Theatre even after her triumphantly successful guest performance series there in 1894. Her success on prominent European stages (in the roles of Medea, Lady Macbeth, Iphigenia, Sappho, and others) notwithstanding, she has been treated in Czech scholarly discourse only marginally, often being portrayed as a national renegade and callous egoist who after all only got what she deserved. While some of her contemporaries described Pospisilová favorably as an actress who possessed "enormous diligence, iron perseverance, invincible defiance, a true talent and love for art",[65] she has been overall viewed through the eyes of her opponents as "excessively ambitious and passionate, merciless towards women and cruel to men, calculating and unpredictable," as a woman who"had an illegitimate child with [the actor] Vojan, destroyed Subert . . . drove mad the greatest heroines the Czech nation ever possessed only to shamelessly betray the nation later . . . simply a devil."[66]

The case of Pospisílová suggests that there was no place on the first Czech stage for aggressively assertive women like herself. For actresses like Kvapilová, who desired above anything else to work on a Czech stage, Pospisilová's example likely served as a warning that even the best and most popular Czech actresses possessed less power over their own circumstances than their male management did. It also served as a lesson, as it was designed to, [67] that too much assertiveness — particularly when combined with a presumed disloyalty to the nation (or perhaps in itself constituting behavior perceived as disloyal to the nation?) — would not be tolerated in women working at *the fin de siécle* on the main Czech national stage.

NOTES

1. Pavla Buzková, *Prítelkyne: Hana Kvapilová a Ruzena Svobodová ve svy'ch dopisech [Friends: Correspondence of Hana Kvapilová and Ruzena Svobodová]* (Prague: Topicova edice, 1939) 38. All translations of Czech texts quoted in this essay are mine.

2. Bozena Viková-Kunetická is also an important figure in the history of the Czech women's emancipation movement. She was elected the chairwoman of the Czech Woman's National Liberal Party. As their representative, she was elected in 1912 to the Bohemian Diet but was prevented by the conservative and German majority in the Diet from taking up her seat. See Jan Voborník:, *Bozena Viková-Kunetická* (Prague: Ceská akademie ved a umení, 1934) and Robert B. Pynsent, "The Liberation of Woman and Nation: Czech Nationalism and Women Writers of the Fin de Siécle," *The Literature of Nationalism: Essays on East European Identity,* ed. Robert B. Pynsent (New York: St. Martin's Press, 1996) 83-155.

3. Bozena Viková-Kunetická, "Hana Kvapilová," *Vyznání: Reci a studie [Confessions: Speeches and Studies]* (1907; Prague: Unie, 1919) 208.

4. The idea that every nation has an "essence" and specific "char acter" originated from the eighteenth century German philosopher Johann Herder, whose *Outlines of a*

Philosophy of the History of Man was extremely influential among the nineteenth-century writers of Czech nationalism. Following Herder, Czech authors (starting with the earliest myth-makers Frantisek Kollár and Pavel Josef Safarik) emphasized tolerance, peacefulness, piousness, and industry as constituting the "essence" of the Slavic, and more specifically Czech, national character.

5. For instance, in their response to the English derogatory stereotype of the simianized Paddy, the authors of the Irish literary revival represented spirituality as a genuinely Celtic characteristic and idealized the Irish peasant "as the romantic and heroic bearer of the torch of idealism in a grossly materialist modern commercial world." G. J. Watson, *Irish Identity and the Literary Revival: Synge, Yeats, Joyce and O'Casey.* 2nd ed., (Washington: Catholic University of America Press, 1994) 64. The presumably genuine Irish peasant's spirituality was commonly invoked in the turn-of-the-century Celticist writing to portray Irish culture as culturally superior to English culture, which was identified with materialism, industrialization, and lack of spirituality. Also see Partha Chatterjee's examination of anti-colonial strategies in nineteenth-century India. Chatterjee has observed that as part of their emancipatory struggle, the Indian people created a sovereign domain within the reality of colonialism by dividing the world of social practices and institutions into the material and spiritual spheres, locating the essence of national identity within the spiritual domain, and striving to maintain this domain's independence. While British economic and political supremacy had to be acknowledged, the autonomy of the Indian national character was still sustained, in this concept of nation, as long as the spiritual domain remained separated from the material sphere and unaffected by British cultural values. Partha Chatterjee, *The Nation and Its Fragments: Colonial and Postcolonial Histories* (Princeton, NJ: Princeton UP, 1993).

6. In this respect, Czech nineteenth-century nationalist discourse was far from unusual. As Anne McClintock has articulated it, women are typically positioned in nationalisms as "the atavistic and authentic body of national tradition (inert, backward-looking, and natural)," while men "represent the progressive agent of national modernity (forward-thrusting, potent and historic)." *Imperial Leather: Race, Gender, and Sexuality in the Colonial Context* (New York: Routledge, 1995) 357. Also see Nira Yuval-Davis's study of the positionings of women in nationalist discourses, *Gender & Nation* (London: Sage, 1997). Yuval-Davis has pointed out that constructing the nation's women as symbols of national "essence" is typical of nationalist narratives (116).

7. *Slávy dcera* was published in several revised editions between 1821-1852.

8. "Muzi vule, cin a smelost slusí / Zene prosba, cit a mlcení / Ten bud více duchem, tato dusí." Jan Kollár, *Slávy dcera* (Prague: Kober, 1868) 46, sonnet no. 75.

9. "Ona pak jest tichy' beránek, ktery' snímá kraju techto hríchy." Kollár 46.

10. "Vrivobytí lidském zádná zmena / Horsí není jako v pohlaví/ Kdyz se ona outlá rozpraví/ Povah v nem a charakteru stena;// Zensky muz se tak, jak muzská zena/ Cti a stestí svého pozbaví:/ Toho tam se málem zohavi/ Této mnohem clovecenství cena." Kollár 46.

11. When Czech critics and scholars of the turn-of-the-century theatre use the term "modern" drama (or "modern" theatre), they tend to refer to the turn-of-the-century Czech playwrights' and performers' efforts to create a theatre that would tackle the problems faced by contemporary men and (particularly) women. The term extends over various acting and writing styles, including realism of the 1880s, psychological realism of the 1890s, and impressionism of the 1900s.

12. Ibsen's characters Kvapilová created during her career in Svanda's theatre company in 1887 include: Petra in *The Enemv of the People*, Rebecca in *Rosmersholm*, and Nora in *A Doll's House.* On the stage of the National Theatre, Kvapilová created the following roles in Ibsen's plays: 1891 — Petra, *An Enemy of the People*; 1897 — Fanny, *John Gabriel Borkman*; 1899 — Rebecca, *Rosmersholm*; 1901 and 1906 — Nora, *A Doll's House*; 1905 — Ellida, *The Lady from the Sea.*

13. As I will point out later in this essay, the National Theatre's interest in producing woman-centered drama remained unmatched by any perceivable interest on the part of the management in the rights of actresses.

14. Having herself rejected a matched marriage and becoming a (relatively financially successful) professional woman, Kvapilová herself could be seen as representing a turn-of-the-century emancipated woman. She did eventually marry — the playwright and later director of the National Theatre Jaroslav Kvapil — but remained childless. While not politically active in the Czech women's movement, Kvapilová was acquainted with one of its chief representatives, Bozena Viková-Kunetická. Frantisek Cerny, the actress's biographer, also notes that Kvapilová signed the 1890 Czech artists' petition for the right of Czech women to attend philosophical and medical university programs.

15. Robert Pynsent provides a useful overview of various scholars' comments on the Czech "martyr complex" (which he links with the broader myth of the suffering Slavs) in *Questions of Identity: Czech and Slovak Ideas of Nationality and Personality* (Budapest: Central European University Press, 1994) 190-210. Pynsent cites Tomás Garrigue Masaryk as one of the earliest scholars who noted the "martyr complex" (191). The other Czech writers who have commented either on the Czech or more generally on the Slavic "mythic masochism" include (the decadent writer) Arnost Prochazka, (the current Czech scholar) Vladimir Macura, as well as Václav Havel.

16. Svanda's was the second most prominent Czech theatre company at the time. Many of Ibsen's plays (including *A Doll's House*) were first introduced to the Czech audience by Svanda's theatre.

17. Jindrich Vodák, *Tri herecké podobizny* [*Three Actors' Portraits*] (Prague: Melantrich, 1953) 50.

18. Frantisek Xaver Salda, "Hana Kvapilová," *Duse a dílo: Podobizny a medailony* (Prague: Unie, 1918) 267.

19. See Frantisek Xaver Salda, *O nasí moderní kulture divadelne dramatické* [*Concerning Our Modem Dramatic Culture*] (Prague: O. Girgal, 1937) 23.

20. See Frantisek Cerny', *Hana Kvapilová: Zivot a dílo* [*Hana Kvapilová: Her Life and Work*] (Prague: Orbis, 1963) 84.

21. The Czech terms "vtelit" (verb) and "vtelení" (noun) — used by Durdik (and other Czech theatre critics) — have their exact equivalents in the English words "to embody" and the "embodiment," which I am using in my translation. The Czech verb "vtelit" consists of the preposition "v" (meaning "in") and the noun "telo" (meaning "body").

22. Pavel Durdík, qtd. in Cerny' 69.

23. As Joseph Roach has underscored, while most of the contemporary performers questioned by Archer did indeed denounce Diderot's acting methods as presumably insincere, Archer "ultimately accepted Diderot's answer on their behalf. Archer's attempt to refute the *Paradoxe* ends with his appropriation in the name of Victorian science of most of its contents, especially the idea of double consciousness." *The*

Player's Passion: Studies in the Science of Acting (Ann Arbor: University of Michigan Press, 1993) 162.

24. -er, "Zanglickího divadla [From English Theatre]," *Ceská Thalia* 3 (1889): 182.

25. As Joseph Roach has pointed out, Eduard von Hartmann's 1862 *Philosophy of the Unconscious* "dominated the discussions of the Berlin intelligentsia" throughout the 1870s (179). The influence of Berlin on the Czech stage (starting in the later part of the 19th century) has been noted by such scholars as F. X. Salda. See his*O nasí moderní kulture divadelne dramatické* [On Our Modem Dramatic Culture] (Prague: O. Girgal, 1937) 24.

26. Kvapilová, "Pred novy'm vy'konem," *Literární pozustalost Hany Kvapilové* [*Collected Letters of Hana Kvapilová*], ed. Jaroslav Kvapil (Prague: Sole & Simácek, 1946) 208.

27. William Archer, *Masks or Faces?*, *The Paradox of Acting! and Masks or Faces?*, ed. Eric Bentley (New York: Hill & Wang, 1957) 184.

28. Finding herself often financially mistreated (when compared with the National Theatre's other actresses and actors) by the National's management, Kvapilová must have been drawn to the independent aspect of Bernhardt's career. While Bernhardt's career as an independent artist had many financial ups and downs, her 1891 - 1893 tour is believed to have brought her a net gain of 3.5 million francs. See John Stokes, "Sarah Bernhardt," *Bernhardt, Terry, Duse: The Actress in Her Time*, eds. John Stokes, Michael Booth, Susan Bassnett (Cambridge: Cambridge University Press) 22.

29. Kvapilová, "Zena v umení dramatickém," *Literární pozustalost* 178. First published in *Zensky' svet* [*Women's World*] in 1903.

30. Joseph Roach reminds us that Archer does cite some examples of actors "whose powers of concentration allowed them to maintain an intense absorption in their roles" (179). If Kvapilová had been among the performers questioned by Archer, she would have probably figured in this group.

31. Kvapilová, "Zena v umení dramatickém" 166. All subsequent references to this essay will refer to this edition and will be given parenthetically in the text.

32. Kvapilová, "Pred novy'm vy'konem" 209.

33. Kvapilová, "*Moskevstí herci* [*Moscow Actors*]," *Literární pozustalost* 191. Two articles by Kvapilová on Moscow Theatre were published in *Zlatá Praha* and *Cesky' svet* in 1906. Jaroslav Kvapil's impression of Stanislavky's art in 1906 was similar to Kvapilová's:"[Stanislavsky] spoke piously of his artistic mission, as a priest does about religion. . . . His life is a genuine self-sacrifice." Jaroslav Kvapil, fragments from *Of What I Know* [*O Cem Já Vím*] reprinted in English translation in *K. Stanislavsky*. 1863 1963: *Man and Actor, Stanislavsky and the World Theatre, Stanislavsky's Letters*, trans. Vic Schneierson (Moscow: Progress Publishers, 1963) 163. In his 1901 letter to the Russian actor Alexander Borodulin, Stanislavsky writes: "Love of the stage has sprung up in you. Start by making sacrifices to it, because serving art means making selfless sacrifices. . . . Together with me and all my comrades, prepare yourself to follow a thorny, difficult and harrowing path. . . ." Stanislavsky's letter to Alexander Borodulin reprinted in English translation in *K. Stanislavsky*. 1863-1963 236-237.

34. Kvapilová, "Zena v umení dramatickém" 166.

35. Kvapilová, "Moskevstí herci" 198.

36. "Thinking back on my childhood and youth, I find roots of evil. I was inoculated with humbleness and modesty; I was told at home and at school that life was only a

preparation for death." Kvapilová's letter to Svobodová (1905), qtd. in Buzková, *Prítelkyne* 188.
37. Kvapilová met Duse during the Italian actress's visit at the National Theatre in 1892.
38. Susan Bassnett notes about Duse: "Pain and the representation of pain had been for so long a quintessential part of her life and work that she could not imagine any other state of being." "Eleonora Duse," *Bernhardt, Terry, Duse: The Actress in Her Time* 166.
39. Bassnett 170. Cerny also noticed this distinction between Duse and Kvapilová (138).
40. Quoted in Bassnett 168.
41. Arne Novák, *Podobizny zen* [Portraits of Women] (Prague: Fr. Borovy', 1918) 204.
42. Cerny' 40.
43. Viková-Kunetická 205-6.
44. Cerny' 178.
45. Hana Kubesová married Jaroslav Kvapil, then a burgeoning young (he was eight years younger than Hana) poet, in 1894. As a playwright and (starting in 1900) the artistic director of the National Theatre, Kvapil was a major exponent of impressionism on the Czech stage.
46. Buzková 157.
47. Kvapilová, "Zena v umení dramatickém" 170.
48. Kvapilová, "Betty Henningsová," *Literární pozustalost* 182. First published in *Zensky' svet* in 1904.
49. Kvapilová, "Zena v umení dramatickém" 169.
50. Ibid., 171.
51. Jaroslav Hilbert, *Vina* [*Guilt*] (Prague: Bursík & Kohout, 1906) 29. All subsequent references to this play will refer to this edition and will be given parenthetically in the text.
52. Karel Masek, *Tri léta s Mánesem* [*Three Years with Manes*], qtd. in Cerny' 174.
53. Quoted in Otokar Fischer, *Cinohra Národního divadla do roku 1900* [*Drama at the National Theatre until 1900*] (Prague: Cs. spisovatel, 1983) 291.
54. Sípek, rev. of *Vina*, *Svetozor* (May 22, 1896), qtd. in Cerny' 173.
55. Cerny' 176.
56. Another unconventional woman character, Olga Rubesová, in a play written in 1902 for Kvapilová by F. X. Svoboda, also ends up committing suicide. A daughter of upper-class parents, Olga refuses to participate in the conventional man-hunting tradition, deciding, instead, to dedicate her life to writing. Significantly, she shrinks not only from the company of her conventional parents and suitors, but also from a group of emancipated women, or rather their caricatures, who invite her to become the chair of their organization. The feminists are portrayed in the play unsympathetically as stereotypes; they are unattractive looking and wear tasteless clothes and hair-does. They are represented as differing little from Olga's frivolous, coquettish younger sister — they all desire, in Olga's perception, above anything else to get married and do what is in their powers to attract suitable men. Olga herself is beautiful, sophisticated, and unusually insightful, of course — the genius whose talent cannot be appreciated by her contemporaries. She wishes to be left alone, working on her novel, but then she suffers because of a lack of companionship. Nobody seems to understand Olga, and unable

to find satisfaction in the present world, she jumps out of the window.
57. Cerny' 262.
58. Cerny' 262.
59. The decadent author and Niezschean enthusiast Ruzena Svobodová was the wife of the successful *fin-de siécle* playwright F. X. Svoboda.
60. Kvapilová's letter to Svobodová (1906), qtd. in Buzková, *Prítelkyne* 262.
61. Svobodová's letter to Kvapilová (1905), qtd. in Buzková 185.
62. Svobodová's letter to Kvapilová (1905), qtd. in Buzková 187.
63. That Kvapilová married a man eight years her junior did not make aging easier. While the marriage was for the most part happy, there were times when Hana was made to painfully realize the difference in age. In a short story, "Jako by kámen do vody zahodil," published under a pseudonym in 1895, about Anna, an opera singer (a character based on herself) married to a younger man, Kvapilová expressed the insecurity she herself experienced. Going to a dinner party where her husband encounters Helena, his beautiful young acquaintance, and feeling the ridicule in flirtatious Helena's eyes measuring her up, Anna finds herself beginning to doubt the sensibility of her marriage. Matters get more painful for Anna when at the dinner she finds herself seated, by Helena's arrangement, with the senior members of the company, while her husband obediently accompanies Helena to the other end of the room occupied by the youth. "Jako by kámen do vody zahodil," *Literární pozustalost* 53-84. First published in Svetozor in 1895.
64. Frantisek Adolf Subert was the Director of the National Theatre from 1883 to 1900.
65. Ladecky' quoted in Arnost Kraus, "Marie Pospísilové vy'klad Fausta [Marie Pospísilová's Comments on Faust]," (Prague: Goethuv sboník, 1932) 346-60.
66. A summary of the predominant characterizations of Pospísilová at the *fin de siècle* taken from Adolf Branald, "Úklady a láska [Intrigues and Love]," *My od divadla: Zivoty hercu* [*We Theatre Folks: Lives of Actors*] (Prague: Panorama, 1983) 72-112.
67. The author of "Úklady a láska" points out that many *fin-de-siècle* critics, such as Jan Herben, who found Pospísilová's behavior (especially her acceptance of an engagement at German theatres) abhorrent, called for "an exemplary punishment for her breach of national discipline." Others, like Salda and Vojan, asked, "Where was she supposed to go when we only have one stage for her and from there we banished her?" Branald 111.

Iveta Jusová is a Visiting Assistant Professor of English and Women's Studies at Wittenberg University, Ohio. She has published articles on British and Czech nineteenth century women writers and actresses and is working on a book on the New Woman movement.

Theatre History Studies 24 (June 2004)

"New Negro" Performance in Art and Life: Fredi Washington and the Theatrical Columns of *The People's Voice*, 1943-47

CHERYL BLACK

"Don't forget the whites judge the entire Negro race by our performances both on and OFF the stage!"

—Fredi Washington, *The People's Voice*

In February 1942, two months after the United States entered World War II, New York City Councilman Adam Clayton Powell Jr. launched a propaganda crusade for freedom and justice at home.[1] Like other civil rights leaders at the time, Powell seized the opportunity to link the struggle for racial equality in the U.S. with the fight against fascism in Europe: "we are against Hitler abroad and just as strongly against Hitlerism at home."[2] The organ of Powell's political crusade was *The People's Voice*, a militant "New Paper for the New Negro."[3]

In using the press to carry on this crusade, Powell was joining a fight already in progress. According to historian E. Franklin Frazier, the Negro Press was the "major influence in mobilizing Negroes in the struggle for their rights during World War II." Convinced that full participation in the war, including combat duty in all branches of the armed services, would help insure full rights of citizenship after the war, the Negro Press was also a major influence in mobilizing Negro support for the war. The country's most widely read African-American newspaper, the *Pittsburgh Courier*, introduced the "Double V" campaign for victory at home and victory abroad. This campaign, which combined wholehearted support for the war with persistent protest of racial injustices at home, was immediately embraced by "nearly every newspaper and pulpit," and the Double V symbol appeared everywhere on buttons, stickers, and pins.[4]

Although *The People's Voice* was part of this larger effort, it was, in several

******

This essay is part of a larger study on women artists/activists during the Harlem Renaissance/New Negro era, partially funded by grants from the University of Missouri Research Board and by the National Endowment for the Humanities.

Figure 1. Actress Fredi Washington (2nd from right) with actors Canada Lee (2nd from left) and Frederic March (3rd from left), singer Dorothy Maynor (far left) and Judge Hubert T. Delany (far right), participating in a Race Relations Sunday Broadcast, 1943. Courtesy Fredi Washington Photograph Collection, Photographs and Prints Division, Schomberg Center for Research in Black Culture, New York Public Library, Astor, Lenox and Tilden Foundations.

respects, extraordinary. A significant factor was the leadership of Adam Clayton Powell, Jr, whose activist ministry as head of the Abyssinian Baptist Church, including the successful employment of pickets, strikes, and boycotts to end discrimination in employment, housing, and use of public services, had made him an influential political figure even before his election to the New York City Council.According to *Chicago Defender* editor Chuck Stone, Powell's editorials "clearly anticipated" the "Black Power" militancy of the 1960s: "For tough, uncompromising militancy, brilliant editorial writing and exciting layout, [*The People's Voice*] has rarely been matched." The radical new weekly offered "strong competition" to Harlem's well-established and relatively conservative *Amsterdam News*.[5] One scholar has described the *News* as "essentially conservative" compared to the *Voice*, and has also perceived a significant distinction in the *Voice*'s tendency to treat race relations "within the larger context of a [class-and ideology-based]' people's movement' composed of labor and the political left, both white and Negro."[6] Recognizing no differences between races but those caused by differing economic and social circumstances, the goal of the *Voice* was complete integration of the African-American community into the larger community of first class American citizenship.

Despite its uncompromising demands, the *Voice* advocated only legal means of creating this new social identity. Therefore, representation and performance were crucial components of the crusade. Centuries of racial segregation had insured that white America's perceptions of African-American identity were based almost entirely on virtual, racist representations—the infamous tom, coon, and mammy stereotypes of stage and screen. In this context, theatrical performance, as well as private and political acts by African-American theatrical performers (as among the community's most celebrated and visible citizens) were crucially important. Among the most militant, eloquent and influential of the *Voice's* performance arbiters was actress Fredi Washington, who joined the *Voice's* staff as a public relations representative in spring 1942, becoming theatrical editor the following year. (See fig. 1)

Although the two theatrical columnists who preceded her, Nell Dodson and Joe Bostic, had established the theatrical columns as militant propaganda for "New Negro" representation in art and life, and a number of other writers contributed theatrical columns throughout the paper's years of operation, most had little knowledge or experience of the theatrical profession.[7] Washington, on the other hand, was a theatrical insider with twenty years experience on stage and screen appearing with such stars as Paul Robeson, Duke Ellington, Ethel Waters, Louise Beavers, and Bill Robinson. Washington had garnered international attention in 1934 for her powerful performance as Peola Johnson, a young woman who "passed" as white, in the celebrated and controversial film, *Imitation of Life*. As a founder of the Negro Actors Guild in 1937, she had earned a reputation as an activist and spokesperson on behalf of African-American theatrical performers. Moreover, Washington had the moral authority of one who had left her performing career at its height rather than accept objectionable roles or work in objectionable circumstances.[8]

As journalist Marvel Cooke, who served as the *Voice*'s assistant managing editor during Washington's tenure, later claimed, "no black paper up to that time had ever had a columnist who was as well versed in her field, or his field, as Fredi was . . . she was important. Her name was important to the paper, and her copy, the things that she was presenting about difficulties blacks were having in the theatre, was important."[9] This study looks at how Washington, thru the medium of her *People's Voice* columns, attempted to arbitrate the wide spectrum of private, political, or cultural performances of, by, or about African-Americans in order to forge a new social identity for African-Americans and to effect a new social order.

Even before she assumed the duties of theatrical editorship, Washington most certainly shared her experiences and opinions with the paper's theatrical columnists—one of the earliest articles (unsigned) regarding racial discrimination in the theatre drew specifically from Washington's experiences as an actor "too light" for Negro roles.[10] Pressure from the NAACP was beginning to bring attention to such issues, even in the mainstream press. Major figures in the industry were adding their voices to the protests, and even Hollywood studio executives were promising better roles and better working conditions. Washington seemed genuinely encouraged by these developments, but also adamant that African-American performers themselves join the fight. In her first column, in April 1943, she tackled the perennially thorny issue of "Uncle Tom" roles, placing the responsibility for eradicating Uncle Tomism in life and art squarely on the shoulders of the actors:

> ... until those of us in the theatre realize the full impact and responsibility of our position as public and race-relations ambassadors (and we're just that—don't forget the whites judge the entire Negro race by our performances both on and OFF the stage!) there is no pressure group in the country who can solve this problem or stamp out all of the evils hidden behind the scenes. Let us of the theatre learn the real and fundamental importance of our unique position and make it pay dividends.[11]

Like most of her *People's Voice* colleagues, Washington seemed to view white Americans as more ignorant than inherently evil, and African-Americans as primarily responsible for educating them: "It is therefore our duty to enlighten and set straight any misconception of the Negro held by those who are entrusted with the responsibility of setting down portrayals of us." Washington insisted that actors were not powerless to effect changes. She cautioned them to read contracts before signing and to demand script changes, a privilege she claimed to have been granted in several instances. Finally she insisted that it was better to take a job outside the theatre than a "part which causes you to lose your pride and birthright." Washington especially challenged top-ranking stars to "use their power for the good of all" and flatly dismissed economic need as an excuse to take degrading roles: "Do what I'm doing. Get a job outside the theatre.... You won't be paid Equity minimum [but] you'll have your SELF-RESPECT."[12]

Washington consistently stressed the social significance of the theatre and its connection to all aspects of life: "... the theatre and its people are very much a part of the war, church, politics and society in general."[13] In keeping with the "Double V" platform, Washington linked the war against Hitler with the civil rights struggle and identified the "New Negro" as, first of all, a loyal citizen committed to the war abroad. Washington encouraged participation in the war effort as servicemen and servicewomen, nurses, workers in defense industries, or volunteers in service organizations, setting an example by joining the American Women's Volunteer Service (AWVS) herself. Washington strongly encouraged young men to enlist in the armed services, proudly publishing a photograph of her handsome nephew in uniform. She urged the race's top celebrities to volunteer for USO shows and hospital tours and promoted dramatic performances aiding the war effort, such as Paul Robeson's address to the *Labor for Victory* rally at Yankee stadium in May 1943 and Carlton Moss' documentary, *The Negro Soldier*, released to the general public in 1944. Produced by the Frank Capra Army Unit to promote racial unity and win African-American support for the war, *The Negro Soldier* was criticized by some *People's Voice* readers as misrepresenting the reality of life for Negro soldiers. Washington reported these accusations in her column, but continued to defend the film for its "dignified" presentation of Negroes. In addition to its depiction of Negro soldiers as heroes, she was especially pleased that "those who have been chosen to represent the Negro civilian population are good, clean wholesome types."[14]

The "New Negro" was of course equally committed to the struggle against "domestic fascism" (Jim Crowism) at home. Washington exhorted all theatrical performers "to see with clarity his or her relation to this fight."[15] Recommended political activism began with exercising the basic rights of citizenship: voter registration, political campaigning, union activism, formation of citizens' committees, and participation in related organizations such as the Hollywood Entertainment Industry Emergency Committee, the Theatre Chapter of the American Veterans Committee, and the Cultural Division of the National Negro Congress, all formed to combat racial discrimination in the arts. Political activism for Washington specifically excluded violence and extralegal acts as counterproductive. In criticizing the wave of riots that erupted in 1943, Washington focused on their devastating economic effects. Race riots in Detroit, Washington reported, had caused more than 300 engagements to be canceled, with a loss of $10,000 daily to the musicians' union.[16]

Washington urged theatrical audiences to activism, not just by attending recommended shows and shunning others but by bombarding the industry as well as political representatives with letter campaigns supporting works that helped, and protesting works that harmed, the cause: "I can't remind you too often to make your voices heard in Hollywood."[17] In the pages of the *People's Voice*, standards for theatrical criticism were based almost entirely on content, what *Voice* columnist Joe Bostic labeled "propaganda quotient."

> We look on the entertainment world as a prime propaganda medium. This because we feel that no other activity offers quite so many opportunities for the subtle planting of propaganda, to the rank and file of the masses. It is for this reason that all of our appraisals of things theatrical have been—and will continue to be—colored by the actual or potential P.Q. (propaganda quotient) contained therein.[18]

Some of the era's most celebrated entertainments, like *Cabin in the Sky*, *St. Louis Woman*, *Stormy Weather*, or *Carmen Jones*, which featured extraordinary artistic achievement by performers Ethel Waters, Lena Horne, Bill Robinson, and Dorothy Dandridge, received relatively low PQ, due to what city editor S.W. Garlington called "glorified segregation,"[19] the ghettoization and restriction of African-American talent to musical entertainment and stereotypical characters or situations. Powell himself railed against *Cabin in the Sky* as a "totally unprovoked insult"; Washington more generously labeled it a well-intentioned "blunder."[20] Works that rated high "PQ," including the films *In This Our Life*, *Casablanca*, *Sahara*, *Bataan*, and *Mission to Moscow*, and stage plays *Finian's Rainbow*, *Beggar's Holiday*, and *Street Scene*, were those that depicted African-American performers in supporting, but non stereotyped roles, as "part of the national life of America,"[21] in equal and varied relationships with white characters, or as individuals whose achievements lay outside the province of musical or comical entertainment or crime. Washington considered Canada Lee's casting as de Bosola in *The Duchess of Malfi* a minor triumph, despite the fact that he played the role in white makeup.[22] Washington also had high praise for plays or films that treated racial and/or working class themes seriously, including *The Ox-Bow Incident* and *Strange Fruit* (mob violence), *Decision* and *Jeb* (discrimination in employment), *Deep are the Roots* (interracial romance), and *On Whitman Avenue* (discrimination in housing). For Washington and her colleagues the artistic and political triumphs of the decade were Paul Robeson's performance in *Othello* (1943-44) and his contract stipulating that he would not play in segregated theatres. Washington urged other stars to follow his lead in fighting Jim Crow in theatres and proudly reported on those, like Lena Horne and Katharine Dunham, who did so. In 1946 she reported the picketing of the Lisner auditorium and the National Theatre to end racial segregation in Washington, D.C. theatres, and in 1947 she celebrated the Actors Equity resolution providing that no Equity member "shall be required to perform in a theatre that practices racial discrimination . . . on either side of the footlights."[23]

Washington censured Hollywood films like *St. Louis Woman* and *The Song of the South* for perpetuation of racist stereotypes, but she did not spare her own race in condemning negative theatrical presentations. She dismissed Earl Dancer's musical *Africana* as a "sorry excuse for entertainment"[24] and fired off a blistering attack of certain Apollo comedy acts as "razor wielding, name calling, liquor drinking, woman debasing, vulgar, stupid brand of so-called comedy which has no place in the new order of the new Negro." Washington warned the performers that "offensive" performances onstage and "rude disgusting behavior" offstage were retarding race progress.[25] Washington did not hesitate to goad even Robeson into appropriate action, leading a campaign to persuade him to accept the role of Denmark Vesey in Dorothy Heyward's *Set My People Free*. She also published an open letter to *Native Son* star Canada Lee, scolding him for failing to participate in a three-day conference held by the Writers Congress in Los Angeles on the treatment of racial subjects in film and radio.[26]

Despite her moratorium on degrading stereotypes, Washington's strong prolabor stance made her reluctant to disparage working class characters in general. She made clear that she did not object to servant roles per se, but only to "the stereotypical servant with his bowed head, ridiculous dialect, and idiotic, brainless stupidity. No one is or should be naive enough to think that we object to maid or butler roles when they are a part of normal integral situations and are convincing characters."[27] She defended a number of servant roles, including those in Lillian Hellman's *Little Foxes* and *Another Part of the Forest* and Edward Chodorov's *Decision*, as dignified and sympathetically drawn human beings with something to say. When Butterfly McQueen quit the Jack Benny show because she felt her maid's role was a negative reflection of her race, Washington protested in the pages of the *Voice*. McQueen's character, Washington insisted, was neither stereotypical nor racially specific: she was simply an American maid, and McQueen's comedic talent was a "highlight" of the program. In fact, Washington insisted that McQueen's artistic and commercial success "has done a service to the American Negro," and Washington urged readers to write Benny asking him to bring McQueen back.[28]

Formal critical comments were rare, although the *Voice* frequently quoted from reviews published in other sources, and Washington occasionally offered general, aesthetic evaluations. Rather than condemn Jimmy Baskett for accepting the despised role of Uncle Remus in *Song of the South*, she interrupted her denunciation of Disney's racist cartoon to pay tribute to Baskett's "fine, sensitive performance."[29] For the most part, however, the talent of African-American performers was not the primary issue, but how that talent was being used or abused.

Whether her criticism targeted the white or African-American community, Washington's critique of discriminatory practices was invariably constructive; her harshest diatribes generally concluded with practical suggestions to solve the problems. She promoted more acceptable treatment in films by suggesting that studios hire a technical advisor, perhaps thru the auspices of the NAACP or the Harlem Library, for all films dealing with race or featuring African-American characters. She proposed production of short educational films on African- American history and challenged the NAACP to organize a drive to fund it. She promoted the controversial work of the NAACP and the Hollywood Mobilization Emergency Committee to guarantee better roles and working conditions for minority actors (controversial to many minority actors who feared these efforts would result in total unemployment). She published lists of books suitable for theatrical adaptation and the names of individuals whose lives she deemed suitable for theatrical dramatization, including Crispus Attucks, Harriet Tubman, Frederick Douglass, Booker T. Washington, and George Washington Carver. She challenged African-American authors to write stories depicting authentic African-American experience. She advised nightclub comics to go to the Harlem library and read up on some of the "magnificent material there" and "to read the papers more carefully and adapt timely events to comedy."[30]

Despite her personal, unequivocal position regarding Tom and Mammy roles, Washington addressed her fellow actors with somewhat more sympathy than other *Voice* writers. Whereas Bostic had accused Lincoln ("Step-in-Fetchit") Peary of "traitorism," and Dodson had accused Hattie McDaniel of not giving "a tinker's damn for any of us,"[31] Washington advised McDaniel to have more confidence in her ability as an actress: "wise up Hattie, no one is riding you for the mammy roles you must play, but I for one am riding you for your defense of the overall picture these roles create in the minds of the movie-going public." She reiterated that she was not out to put actors out of work but to get better roles for them. Washington then issued a rhetorical challenge to Hollywood to film the Mary McCleod Bethune story with McDaniel in the lead.[32]

From the outset Washington and her *Voice* colleagues had recognized the powerful role a Negro Theatre might play in meeting the economic, cultural and political needs of their community, championing the work of little theatre organizations such as the Ira Aldridge Guild, the Rose McClendon Players, and, especially, the American Negro Theatre, founded in 1940 by Frederick O'Neill, Abram Hill and members of the Rose McClendon Players.[33] During Washington's tenure, she tried to move community support beyond "lip service to the cause" by promoting a fundraising drive for the American Negro Theatre in fall 1944.[34]

Offstage performance by celebrities as well as ordinary citizens was also subject to "PQ" criteria. As Washington assented, "we are a minority group with the finger always pointed at us, we must adhere to 'the best foot forward' at all times."[35] She admonished young people for wearing zoot suits, for vile language on street corners, and for rude or boisterous behavior in the audiences of theatrical performances.[36] She recommended clean and wholesome material onstage and moderation and sobriety offstage. She especially warned "weedheads" on "weed row" (52nd Street) to stop using marijuana, which she characterized as "one of the most insidious and deadly narcotics in existence."[37] Washington seemed especially concerned that using marijuana led to familiarity between the races, which could be deadly indeed on southern tours. Although her warnings against interracial romance seemed based on fear of violent repercussions rather than her personal disapproval, Washington and her *Voice* colleagues did attempt to prescribe "New Negro" sexual morality. Bostic preached a heterosexist and homophobic party line, complaining that a Pigmeat Markham routine "parades the obscenity of homosexualism"[38] and admonishing the police department for allowing a public dance for lesbians at the Lido: "To permit kids (few if any were twenty-five) to publicly flaunt their carnal excesses . . . is to let the moral level of our community sink to a sewer level low."[39]

If less overtly homophobic, Washington nevertheless advocated marital monogamy from a heterosexist perspective: "if we in the profession are going to utilize our medium for molding opinion in the right direction, we must set an example in our personal lives, the starting place for decency and proper human relations, is in the homes."[40] Washington, whose own marriage to Duke Ellington trombonist Lawrence Brown was disintegrating, devoted several columns to sexual irresponsibility among musicians, who were, according to Washington, particularly incompetent at handling their private lives.[41] In January 1947 Washington expressed indignation at an appalling rise in separations and divorces among professional entertainers and suggested they ask God for a keener appreciation "of our marital vows, our children, and our homes." [42]

If personally conservative, however, Washington was steadily gaining a reputation as politically radical—in fact, as a Communist or Communist sympathizer. The prolabor, pro-union *Voice* had, from its inception, been associated with Communism. Powell himself had referred to the paper as the "Lenox Avenue edition of the *Daily Worker*,"[43] and the FBI read it "with great care."'[44] The *Voice* was one of thirteen African-American publications under government investigation during this time. Given that one investigator criticized the Oklahoma City *Black Dispatch* for using "well-known Communistic phrases" such as "civil liberties," and "inalienable rights,"[45] it is not surprising that the FBI labeled the even more radical *Voice* "a transmission belt for the Communist Party." Washington had actively campaigned for

Ben Davis, Communist candidate for city council, and was strongly sympathetic to dramatic works that depicted the Soviet Union favorably. She insisted that every citizen should be compelled to see *Mission to Moscow*, and she identified *Heroic Stalingrad*: *The City that Stopped Hitler* as the best war movie of 1943.

In May 1944, Washington devoted her column to her political affiliation. Although denying membership in the Communist party, her denial included strong approval of party policies.

> Whether or not I am a Communist does not interest me nearly as much as what makes people think that I belong. Is it because I have continually for the past year used these columns to fight for the rights of the Negro in the theater and tried to show that his destiny is tied with that of every Negro—in this land—to improve relations between white and Negro artists?
>
> Personally, I don't care what a man or woman's tag is if he believes in and works toward the fundamental rights of all men. Toward this end, the Communist seems to have worked a lot more diligently than the rest of us. . . . I shall work with anyone who wants the same thing, be he Communist or any other named group.[46]

In September 1945, Washington once more denied Communist party membership in print.[47] In December 1946, Adam Clayton Powell, Jr, then Congressman Powell, severed his ties with the paper, according to the *New York Times*, because of its politically dangerous association with the Communist Party.[48]

According to Marvel Cooke, Washington did join the Communist Party, recruited by Cooke.[49] If so, perhaps it was after her printed denials. From February through September 1947, unionism, labor activism, red baiting and the HUAC dominated her columns. She railed against the anti-union, anti-labor, anticommunist, and racist actions of individuals such as Walt Disney, Cecil B. DeMille, William Randolph Hearst, Hedda Hopper, Mississippi Congressmen Theodore Bilbo and John Rankin, and Actors Equity Association President Frank Fay. She denounced Lowell Thomas' documentary on South Africa for omitting any mention of Apartheid. She devoted a column to recruiting performers—especially "names"—into the Cultural Division of the National Negro Congress.[50] She applauded artists' resistance to red baiting and exhorted the "fence sitters" to "make up your minds what kind of America you want to live in."[51] She devoted columns to discussion of anti-labor legislation, especially the Taft-Hartley bill, pressuring readers to "bombard Congress with mail. Act now or forever hold your peace—and your empty purse."[52] After Taft-Hartley passed, she reported angrily on attempts by the League of New York Theatres to use it to fight Equity's anti-discrimination efforts. She devoted a column to protesting film censorship and another to celebrating Equity's ban on the segregated National Theatre in Washington, D.C. Her calls for political activism increased in frequency and urgency:

> "Don't sit at the bars and bemoan the fact that you can't get work because you are a Negro. . . . [D]o something about it."[53]

"Who said we can enjoy democracy without fighting for it?"[54]

"Artists must have the courage to fight!"[55]

Meanwhile, Washington and her colleagues were drawing increasing attention from the HUAC. Some thought that the government had planted spies in the newsroom.[56] Red baiting, economic and other problems finally caused the paper to stop publication in April 1948. Washington had written her last column six months earlier, in which she devoted one paragraph to praising William C. Smith's performance in a revival of *Showboat* and five paragraphs to a segment of NBC's "America's Town Meeting." The program had aired the previous week, posing the provocative question: "Is There Really a Communist Threat in Hollywood?" Thus Washington had one final opportunity to denounce red baiting in Hollywood and to celebrate the stars who were speaking out against it, a list that included Paul Robeson, Lena Horne, Bette Davis, Katharine Hepburn, Edward G. Robinson, John Garfield, and Frank Sinatra: ". . . these are the people who speak our language—the language of freedom and democracy for all peoples, regardless of color, race, or creed. I know which side I stand on and all the Rankins, Thomases, and Tenneys can't dupe me into giving up the fight for my rights as an American. How about you? "[57]

With this final rhetorical challenge, Washington ended her career as a theatrical columnist as she had begun it—exhorting her community to keep fighting for a new world order. According to Marvel Cooke, both she and Washington and a number of other *Voice* staffers were fired for causes both economic and political.[58] Washington returned to acting for a few years, appearing in five politically progressive and short-lived stage plays, and CBS-TV's *The Goldbergs*, in which she portrayed one of the atypical servant roles she had championed in her columns—a highly competent and caustic housekeeper.[59] Divorced from Brown in 1951, she married in 1952 Hugh Anthony Bell, a dentist from Connecticut. After her second marriage, Washington disappeared from public life, living quietly with her second husband until his death in 1984, and alone in Connecticut until her own death ten years later. Before her death, she was recognized by the African-American community for her artistic and social contributions by induction into the Black Filmmakers Hall of Fame in1975, a CIRCA Life Achievement Award in 1979, and an AUDELCO award in 1981.

Although evidence does not allow conclusions demonstrating direct, causal relationships between the radical rhetoric of *The People's Voice* and specific legal or cultural events, the theatrical columns of Fredi Washington promoted and encouraged the positive developments that occurred during the years of the paper's operation, including the negotiations between the NAACP and the Hollywood studios, the formation of various committees to combat racist representations, the anti-segregation stands taken by artists like Robeson, Dunham, and Horne, the boycotting of Jim Crow theatres, the gradual disappearance of the most overtly minstrel-show characterizations and the equally gradual emergence of more varied and realistic depictions.

Attempts by this radical civil rights publication to arbitrate the private and public acts of a racial community in order to create a new social identity for that community confirm contemporary arguments that identity *is* performance. That Washington and some of her colleagues combined anti-racist liberation rhetoric with compulsive heterosexist and homophobic rhetoric highlights the moral and political complexity, in fact the coercive potential, of such arbitrations.

The questions debated within the pages of *The People's Voice* regarding politically acceptable personal and artistic choices are still being debated. The "razor-wielding, woman-debasing" stereotypes Washington denounced have, arguably, been replaced by gun-wielding, woman-debasing "gangsta" types. Last year's double-Oscar win for African-American actors Denzel Washington and Halle Berry sparked controversy in some corners from those who felt that both roles they'd won for were negative stereotypes (in the words of one writer, a "gangster and a ho").[60] Washington's prescriptions for "New Negro" performance in art and life, while not always consistent or necessarily laudable, were borne of her own personal struggles, as a woman, an artist, and a member of a politically disenfranchised social group, to reconcile conflicting artistic, economic, and social goals. The personal and economic sacrifices she demanded were those she herself had made.

Washington's passionate anti-discrimination exhortations remain as evidence of a surreal moment in U.S. history, when the most democratic, humane, and just actions, deliberately designed to exemplify first class American citizenship, were labeled "Un-American"; when a culture of fear effected a preemptive strike just when the country was perhaps on the verge of radical social change. If, as Powell, Washington, and many others believed, U.S. participation in World War II provided an optimum moment to combat domestic fascism, the moment was lost to postwar anxiety over the perceived threat of Communism.

Moments like these from our past remind us that the U.S. never quite won that war against "domestic fascism." More than five decades after Fredi Washington described Senator John Rankin as Mississippi's "gift to white supremacy," the current Mississippi Senator Trent Lott made headlines by lamenting South Carolina Senator Strom Thurmond's unsuccessful bid for the presidency as the "Dixiecrat" candidate of 1948.[61] More than five decades after Washington denounced red baiting in Hollywood, the Screen Actors Guild decried a "disturbing trend" in current debates about the possibility of war with Iraq: "Some have recently suggested that well-known individuals who express 'unacceptable' views should be punished by losing their right to work."[62] Fredi Washington's efforts to achieve the rights of full citizenship for a particular, racially defined, social group led her into a related struggle for "freedom and democracy for all peoples, regardless of color, race, or creed." Her admonition to "make up your minds what kind of America you want to live in" is strikingly, and perennially, relevant.

NOTES

1. Activist minister, New York City Councilman, and later, Congressman from the newly created Harlem district, Adam Clayton Powell, Jr., was one of the era's most influential civil rights leaders. During his twenty-five years in Congress (1944-1967) Powell continued to fight segregation and racial discrimination, eventually achieving considerable influence as Chair of the Committee on Education and Labor. In the late 1960s, Powell's flamboyant lifestyle (he was married three times), frequent

absenteeism, and allegations of financial misconduct led to an investigation by the House Judiciary Committee. In 1967 Congress took the unprecedented step of excluding Powell from Congress, a move declared unconstitutional by the Supreme Court in 1969. Powell resumed his seat, but lost the next election. He died in 1972.
2. Editorial policy, *The People's Voice*, 14 February 1942, 34.
3. The concept of a 'New Negro' identity had been developed over the course of at least four decades. In 1900, Booker T. Washington detected "signs of the New Negro" in increasing economic and educational achievement. In 1925, Professor Alain Locke articulated a "New Negro" spirit manifested in "race pride" and a desire to contribute to and share equally in "American culture and institutions." The "New Negro" of 1942, championed by Powell, combined educational and economic achievement, race pride, and desire to share equally in the nation's cultural and social life with a more militant and uncompromising attitude. For the "New Negro" citizen of 1942, the time for compromise was past; the time for first class citizenship and racial equality was *now*. See Booker T. Washington, N. B. Wood, and Fannie Barrier Williams, *A New Negro for A New Century* (New York: Arno Press, 1969. Orig. pub. Chicago: American Publishing House, 1900); Alain Locke, ed. *The New Negro* (New York: Atheneum, 1968; orig. pub. 1925); Neil A. Wynn, *The Afro-American and the Second World War* (New York and London: Holmes & Meier, 1993, rev. ed.).
4. Wynn, 19-25, 97-100. See also Aimin Zhang, *The Origins of the African American Civil Rights Movement, 1865-1956* (New York & London: Routledge, 2002), 101-122. For unity of the wartime approach of the Black Press, see Lee Finkle, "Conservative Aims of Militant Rhetoric: Black Protest During WWII," *Journal of American History*, vol. 60, no. 3 (1973), 692-713.
5. *The Amsterdam News* was established in 1909; in 1944, the first year for which circulation statistics are available for *The People's Voice*, the *Amsterdam News'* circulation (48, 932). was roughly twice that of the *People's Voice* (24, 167) The circulation of the *Voice* peaked in 1946 at 29, 243. The *Voice*'s circulation was very close to that of its closest ideological ally, the *Daily Worker* (maintained a circulation of about 22,000 throughout the 1940s). Source: *N. W. Ayer & Son's Directory, Newspapers and Periodicals* (Philadelphia: N. W. Ayer, 1930-69). That the *Voice* offered the *News* "strong competition" is confirmed by Ronald E. Wolseley, *The Black Press USA* (Ames, IA: The Iowa State University Press, 1971), 51.
6. Richard Robbins, "Counter-Assertion in the New York Negro Press," *Phylon*, vol. 10, no. 2 (1949), 132.
7. Besides Dodson and Bostic, who were both sportswriters, *Voice* features writer Ken Jessamy, assistant managing director Marvel Cooke, and Washington's sister Isabel (then Mrs. Adam Clayton Powell, Jr.) also contributed theatrical columns during the paper's first year of operation or while Washington was on vacation.
8. As a light-complexioned African-American actor who refused to pass as white or to "black up" for roles, Washington found suitable roles scarce. Despite these limitations, she developed a remarkable career, making her stage debut in 1921 in the hugely successful *Shuffle Along*. Subsequent stage appearances include *Black Boy*

(1926), *Singin' the Blues* (1931), *Run Little Chillun* (1933), and *Mamba's Daughters* (1939); screen credits include the musical shorts *Black and Tan* (1929) and *Hi-de-Ho* (1933), and feature films *The Emperor Jones* (1934), *Drums in the Jungle* (1935), *Imitation of Life* (1934), and *One Mile From Heaven* (1937). For a detailed analysis of Washington's performing career, see Cheryl Black, "Looking White, Acting Black: Cast(e)ing Fredi Washington," forthcoming in *Theatre Survey*, May 2004.

9. Marvel Cooke, interview by Kathleen Currie for the Washington Press Club Foundation, 1 November 1989, **http://npc.press.org/wpforal/cook5.htm**, accessed 25 February 2003, 97-98. Before joining the *Voice*'s staff, Cooke had worked at the *Amsterdam News* and the *Crisis*; she later became the only woman and only African-American journalist for the New York *Daily Compass*.

10. "White-Looking Sepias Get Casting Brush-off," *The People's Voice*, 16 May 1942, 28.

11. Fredi Washington, "Headlines and Footlights," *The People's Voice*, 10 April 1943, 26.

12. Ibid.

13. Fredi Washington, "Fredi Says," *The People's Voice*, 10 June 1944, 22.

14. Fredi Washington, "Headlines and Footlights," *The People's Voice*, 19 February 1944, 22 and 29 April 1944, 22.

15. Fredi Washington, "Headlines and Footlights," *The People's Voice*, 7 August 1943, 26; and 14 August 1943, 24.

16. Fredi Washington, "How Detroit Riots Affected Show Folk," *The People's Voice*, 10 July 1943, 24. According to historian Neil A. Wynn, "the outbreaks of racial violence during World War II surpassed those of any previous period" and reached a peak in 1943. Wynn lists 242 instances of racial violence in 47 cities, including 70 "major disturbances" in Harlem. The riot in Detroit lasted 3 days and resulted in the deaths of 34 African-Americans. See Wynn, 68-70.

17. Fredi Washington, "Headlines and Footlights," *The Peopleís Voice*, 15 May 1943, 24.

18. Joe Bostic, "Headlines and Footlights," *The People's Voice*, 2 January 1943, 30.

19. S.W. Garlington, quoted by Ken Jessamy, "Headlines and Footlights," *The People's Voice*, 12 December 1942, 30.

20. Adam Clayton Powell, Jr., review of *Cabin in the Sky*, *The People's Voice*, 5 June 1943, 24. See also Washington's "Headlines and Footlights" column, *The People's Voice*, 1 January 1944, 26.

21. S.W. Garlington, 30.

22. Fredi Washington, "Fredi Says," *The Peopleís Voice*, 16 November 1946, 22. Washington reminded her readers that Clarence Muse had performed in whiteface at the Lafayette Theatre.

23. "Fredi Says," *The Peopleís Voice*, 9 November 1946, 22; 23 November 1946, 22; 1 February 1947, 22.

24. Fredi Washington, "Headlines and Footlights," *The People's Voice*, 19 June 1943, 24.

25. Fredi Washington, "Headlines and Footlights," *The People's Voice*, 31 July 1943, 24.

26. Fredi Washington, "An Open Letter," *The People's Voice*, 1 January 1944, 26.

27. Fredi Washington, "Headlines and Footlights," *The People's Voice*, 5 August 1944, 22.
28. Ibid. McQueen had made several earlier broadcasts as Rochester's girlfriend (Benny's butler, played by Eddie Anderson), but quit when Benny asked her to play a maid. McQueen later elaborated on her reasons for leaving the popular show: "I was going through a stage where I couldn't say "yes, ma'm." I don't know why. Maybe it was because we were so stereotyped . . . I just choked on that "yes, ma'm." See Transcript of Interview by Don Hillegas, 6 April 1972, in *Artist and Influence*, Vol. 16 (New York: Hatch-Billops Collection, 1996), 79. McQueen has also listed anti-African remarks by Benny as a contributing factor. Butterfly McQueen, "Miscellanea," TS, Butterfly McQueen clippings file, Schomburg.
29. Fredi Washington, "Fredi Says," *The People's Voice*, 30 November 1946, 22. She then directed readers to send letters of protest to Disney.
30. Fredi Washington, "Headlines and Footlights," *The People's Voice*, 31 July 1943, 24.
31. See Nell Dodson, "Hattie McDaniel Toms on Air," *The People's Voice*, 10 October 1942, 29, and Joe Bostic, "See Here, Mr. Lincoln (Stepinfetchit] Peary," *The People's Voice*, 9 June 1945, 22.
32. Fredi Washington, "Fredi Says," *The People's Voice*, 26 April 1947, 22.
33. The Rose McClendon Players were founded in 1937 by actor Dick Campbell and actress Muriel Rahn to honor actress Rose McClendon after her death in 1936. The Ira Aldridge Guild (not to be confused with the Ira Aldridge Players at Howard University) was organized in 1943 in an attempt to revive a stock company in Harlem along the lines of the famed Lafayette Players (1915-1932).The company included former Lafayette Players Abbie Mitchell, Susie Sutton, Lionel Monogas, Percy Verwayen, and Charles Moore.
34. Fredi Washington, "Headlines and Footlights," *The People's Voice*, 9 September 1944, 22. The American Negro Theatre (1940-49) was one of the most notable theatrical organizations of the era. Among its most successful productions were *On Strivers' Row* by Abram Hill and *Anna Lucasta* by Philip Yordon.
35. Fredi Washington, "Headlines and Footlights," *The People's Voice*, 10 June 1944, 22.
36. Ibid.
37. Fredi Washington, "Headlines and Footlights," *The People's Voice*, 16 October, 1943, 30; see also Fredi Washington, "Fredi Says," *The People's Voice*, 17 November 1945, 26.
38. Joe Bostic, "Headlines and Footlights," *The People's Voice*, 6 March 1943, 26.
39. Joe Bostic, "Headlines and Footlights," *The People's Voice*, 14 July 1945, 22.
40. Fredi Washington, "Fredi Says," *The People's Voice*, 11 January 1947, 22.
41. Fredi Washington, "Orchestra Wives at Home," *The People's Voice*, 5 January 1946, 22; "Fredi Says," *The People's Voice*, 11 January 1947, 22.
42. Fredi Washington, "Fredi Says," *The People's Voice*, 11 January 1947, 22. Brown and Washington separated in 1947 and divorced in 1951.
43. Charles V. Hamilton, *Adam Clayton Powell, Jr.: The Political Biography of an American Dilemma* (New York: Atheneum, 1991), 105.

44. Ibid., 177.
45. G. Banister to Director, Federal Bureau of Investigation, 23 November 1942, quoted in Patrick S. Washburn, *A Question of Sedition: The Federal Government's Investigation of the Black Press During World War II* (New York and London: Oxford University Press, 1986), 170.
46. Fredi Washington, "Headlines and Footlights," *The People's Voice*, 27 May 1944, 26.
47. Fredi Washington, "Fredi Says," *The People's Voice*, 29 September 1945, 26.
48. Hamilton, 185.
49. Cooke interview, 81, 93-94.
50. Fredi Washington, "Fredi Says," *The People's Voice*, 7 June 1947, 22.
51. Ibid.
52. Fredi Washington, "Fredi Says," *The People's Voice*, 10 May 1947, 22.
53. Fredi Washington, "Fredi Says," *The People's Voice*, 8 March 1947, 22.
54. Fredi Washington, "Fredi Says," *The People's Voice*, 17 May 1947, 22.
55. Fredi Washington, "Fredi Says," *The People's Voice*, 21 June 1947, 22.
56. Wil Haygood, *King of the Cats: The Life and Times of Adam Clayton Powell, Jr.* (Boston and New York: Houghton Mifflin Company, 1993), 147.
57. Fredi Washington, "Fredi Says," *The People's Voice*, 13 September 1947. The individuals referred to are Senator John Rankin, Representative R. Parnell Thomas, and Jack Tenney of the California HUAC
58. Cooke interview, 94.
59. The plays in which Washington performed included *Lysistrata* (October 1946), American National Theatre and Academy's *A Long Way From Home* (February 1948), Sarett and Herbert Rudley's *How Long til Summer* (December 1949), Sherwood Anderson's *The Triumph of the Egg* (1950) and Josephine Niggli's *Soldadera* (1950), She appeared on *The Goldbergs* in January 1949.
60. Donna Murch, "The Price of Popular Culture," *The Black Scholar*, vol 33, no. 1, p. 25. Implying that these "breakthroughs" were actually steps backward, Murch declares that Sidney Poitier would not have been "caught dead" in Washington's film *Training Day*, nor Dorothy Dandridge in Berry's (*Monster's Ball*). See also Nancy Kendrick, *Philadelphia Daily News*, 29 July 2003, accessed 14 August 2003, **www.philly.com/mid/dailynews/news/local/6409865.htm;** Erin Aubry Kaplan, "Hollywood Hype, Black Stereotype," *London Guardian*, 4 June 2002, p. 14, accessed through Lexis-Nexis, 21 July 2002; Liz Smith, "Angela's Bashes," *Newsday*, 27 June 2002, section A, p. 15; Leonard Pitts, Jr., "Denzel Washington has the Right to Play Bad," *Chattanooga Times Free Press*, 21 October 2001, F3.
61. Lott's remarks, widely reported, were made during the celebration of Senator Thurmond's 100th birthday in December 2002.
62. "Screen Actors Guild Releases Statement Regarding Free Speech," 3 March 2003, **www.sag.org/pr/pressreleases/pr-la030303.html,** accessed 4 March 2003.

Cheryl Black is Assistant Professor of Theatre and Director of Graduate Studies at the University of Missouri-Columbia. She is author of *The Women of Provincetown*

(University of Alabama Press, 2002), numerous journal articles, and co-author of a chapter in *Creating a Cultural Paradigm: The Personal and Political in American Drama* (Palgrave, 2002).

Theatre History Studies 24 (June 2004)

The Cherry Sisters in Early Vaudeville Peforming a Failed Femininity

PEACH R. PITTENGER

The Cherry Sisters earned their place in American popular entertainment by virtue of their complete and total lack of talent. They first presented their novelty act—which consisted of original songs, sentimental skits, and moralizing essay recitations—in Marion, Iowa, in 1893. After touring the Midwest for nearly four years, they came to the attention of impresario Oscar Hammerstein, who engaged them for a month-long run at his Olympia Theatre in New York in November 1896. Their appearance reportedly saved Hammerstein from an impending bankruptcy.[1] When the Cherry Sisters returned to the Midwest, they enjoyed a short-lived boost in salary as a result of their New York résumé. After a decade of performing, the Cherry Sisters retired in 1903, the same year that the youngest sister, Jessie, died. Addie and Effie Cherry returned to the stage in 1905 and continued to perform intermittently with a series of nostalgic appearances through 1938.

These are the basic facts of the Cherry Sisters' career. However, their history—as a struggling, itinerant female variety act at the turn of the century—is buried beneath a theatrical legend of innocent incompetents who muddled along as the "world's worst actresses," succeeding in spite of themselves. The Cherry Sisters entry in the *Cambridge Guide to American Theatre,* which reflects the humorous aspects of the legend, concludes with a commonly held belief of Cherry Sisters' great financial success: "The peculiar act ('so bad it was great') made them a fortune."[2]

The Cherry Sisters' career has been relegated to little more than an amusing footnote in American popular entertainment, due to the novelty aspects of their act and their limited success. However, the Cherry Sisters phenomenon was firmly grounded in the theatrical and social conditions of the 1890s, and it is within that historical context that their career gains significance and transcends mere theatrical trivia. In an era noted for popular female performers whose primary assets were youth and beauty rather than talent, the Cherry Sisters—middle-aged, morally righteous, and plain spinsters—performed a satire of theatrical femininity, especially the sexualized female spectacle found in 1890s burlesque. The decade was marked by rapid economic and social changes, including financial depressions and the emergence of the New Woman, which challenged prevailing beliefs about male privilege and superiority. These cultural conditions helped create a niche for the Cherry Sisters, who served as a theatrical scapegoat for all that had gone wrong in contemporary society, as seen from a male point of view. Young men's frustration, confusion, and anger, and the resulting misogyny that could not be openly expressed in proper society, found release under the guise of audience rowdyism. Hostile male audiences and critics consistently focused on the women's failed femininity—their appearance and spinster status—characterizing them as grotesque freaks. As a result of one particularly brutal newspaper review, Addie Cherry sued for libel and took the case to the Iowa Supreme Court. The landmark decision in 1901, in favor of the newspaper, established the broad standard for a critic's right to fair comment that stands today. The lawsuit and decision are not only important within the context of American theatre history; they are also indicative of the extreme hostility and harsh reality that the Cherry Sisters faced throughout their career, both of which have been erased by the humorous legend.

The Cherry Sisters mythos that survives today includes both inaccurate and apocryphal stories, all of which can be traced to a single source. In December 1944—just four months after the death of the last sister—*Coronet* magazine published Avery Hale's lighthearted article "So Bad They Were Good," which included nearly all of the elements of the Cherry Sisters legend.[3] Hale's article has been reprinted and quoted liberally, with the result that his account has survived as the accepted history of the Cherry Sisters. For instance, Anthony Slide relied almost exclusively on Hale's popular biography in his three vaudeville reference books. He printed the article in its entirety in *Selected Vaudeville Criticism* and used it as his single source for *The Vaudevillians: A Dictionary of Vaudeville Performers.* In his *Encyclopedia of Vaudeville,* Slide cited Hale's article for general information and Michael Gartner's 1982 article, "Fair Comment," which summarizes the libel lawsuit.[4]

In Hale's account, the artless Cherry Sisters blithely worked their way toward a small fortune. Supposedly they earned as much as $1,000 a week and lived "almost thirty years principally on money they had earned around the turn of the century."[5] Hale also proclaimed that the Cherry Sisters performed behind a net to protect themselves from the barrage of rotten fruits and vegetables routinely thrown by audiences. Yet despite the assault by audiences, the Cherry Sisters remained oblivious to their lack of talent. They naively believed, Hales reports, that the tossed vegetables were either unrestrained tributes to their talent or acts of jealousy by less talented people. Like most legends, this one serves to mask a much more complex reality. In fact, the records indicate that the Cherry Sisters likely created and perpetuated their comic image of naïveté, often struggled to earn survival wages, and almost certainly never performed behind a net. Additionally, the audience response to their amateur theatrics was more than traditional rowdyism and sometimes developed into virulent attacks and riots. Instead of the idyllic, romanticized life portrayed in Hale's article, the Cherry Sisters' career was a long, dangerous, and hardscrabble chase after an elusive dream of financial security.

The Cherry Sisters made their first public appearance at Daniel's Opera House in their hometown of Marion on January 20, 1893, supposedly for the purpose of raising money for a trip to the Chicago World's Fair later that year. The show was a hodgepodge variety act, with Jessie singing "Why Did They Dig Ma's Grave So Deep?" and Ella, in blackface and male drag, performing an original song titled "Old Sam Patch."[6] According to local newspapers, the women earned about $100 for the single performance. These figures are in line with Effie Cherry's report of gross box office receipts of "close to Two Hundred Dollars," if we assume that the theatre took a substantial cut of the proceeds.[7] In 1893, $100 would have been an astounding windfall for the Cherry Sisters, who were unskilled farm women. In one performance, the group earned nearly 10% of a teacher's annual salary, which was estimated as

$1,146 in 1896. A more germane comparison comes from an 1892 article in *Household*, a farmwoman's magazine that encouraged young women to earn money by poultry raising, beekeeping, dairy work, or sewing, all of which paid between $5.00 and $7.50 per week. In fact, Effie Cherry noted that they had already tried poultry raising and dairy work.[8] Obviously, show business paid much better and the women must have been financially motivated from the beginning.

The Cherry Sisters were the five surviving daughters in a family of eight children. They were Ella, born 1854; Elizabeth (Lizzie) born 1857; Addie, born 1859; Effie, born 1867; and Jessie, born 1871. The parents owned a small, isolated twenty-acre farm outside of Marion, Iowa. The mother died in 1876 and the father died in 1888, leaving the farm to the unmarried sisters. Effie wrote that the "five girls were left orphans to battle [their] way through life alone" after their father's death, even though they ranged in age from 17 to 34 at the time.[9] As unmarried, unskilled rural women in the late nineteenth century, their options were limited and performing offered an irresistible opportunity for financial security.

Consequently, immediately after their hometown success, the Cherry Sisters booked themselves into Greene's Opera House in nearby Cedar Rapids, where they were subjected to scathing critical and audience responses. A reporter for the *Cedar Rapids Gazette* wrote, "They couldn't sing, speak or act. . . . Possibly the most ridiculous thing of the entire performance was an essay—think of it—an essay—read by one of the poor girls." Claiming that the audience was filled with "the best people of the city," the reporter nevertheless noted, "[N]othing could drive [the Cherry Sisters] away and no combination of yells, whistles, barks and howls could subdue them. . . . Cigars, cigarettes, rubbers, everything was thrown at them, yet they stood there, awkwardly bowing their acknowledgments and singing on."[10]

So, from the beginning the Cherry Sisters encountered extremely negative responses to their show. The fact that they carefully clipped and pasted this review, along with myriad other critical articles, into a scrapbook confirms that they could not have remained oblivious to the negative criticism.

Throughout their career, the Cherry Sisters publicly maintained a persona of innocents abroad in the alien world of theatre. However, at the same time, they exhibited a savvy talent for self-promotion through adversarial relationships with newspaper reporters, which often included attention-grabbing squabbles and lawsuits. The first of these "publicity lawsuits" occurred as a result of the coverage for their Cedar Rapids appearance. The Cherry Sisters filed a libel suit against the *Gazette* and newsman Fred P. Davis, but were then "persuaded" by their lawyer and the *Gazette* to settle for a mock trial of Mr. Davis during an encore performance at Greene's Opera House on March 14, 1893, thus insuring that they would earn one more tidy sum for themselves. Effie claimed that they agreed to the mock trial on the advice of their attorney: "[S]ince we were mere schoolgirls and knew nothing whatever about court business . . . we concluded to do as the lawyer suggested and try the case at the opera house."[11] The "mere schoolgirls" were 22 to 39 years old and had been self-supporting for five years. Newspaper coverage for the show suggests that all parties—the *Gazette* and the theatre, as well as the Cherry Sisters—were financially motivated. The *Gazette* was instrumental in orchestrating the publicity for the mock trial, with an eye to the Cherry Sisters' financial gain. Even Effie admitted that the editor told them, "I am going to do the right thing by you girls . . . [and] by handling the matter this way it will increase your receipts at the box office." The newspaper ran several articles prior to March 14th, including one with a large headline that read, "A Second Exhibition of the Cherry Freaks."[12] The plan worked and the Cherry Sisters faced a sold-out crowd for the second performance and mock trial.

With this performance, the Cherry Sisters learned that public humiliation could pay handsomely. The very appearance of the women on stage was enough to send the audience into a frenzy. The *Gazette* reported that "not a dozen words uttered by the sisters was heard" and the *Marion Sentinel* confirmed that "It might have been a pantomime for all that the listener could discover." Their show was little more than a warm-up act for the mock trial that followed, in which the all-male jury of local attorneys found Davis guilty of libel and a judge, costumed in a Shriner's outfit, sentenced him to management of the Cherry farm and marriage to one of the sisters, beginning with the eldest and moving down the line to the first one who would consent to entering the "holy bonds of matrimony."[13] The Cherry Sisters may have endured ridicule of their appearance, rural background, and spinsterhood, but they netted at least $150.00 in the process.[14] At this early point in their career, the Cherry Sisters had performed three times—suffering humiliation, ridicule, and rowdy assaults twice—and had netted several hundred dollars in the process. They had discovered a gold mine.

The Cherry Sisters capitalized on their growing notoriety and embarked on a tour of Iowa that spring. Between March 1893 and October 1896, they toured Iowa and then the Midwest on an intermittent basis, appearing whenever they could obtain bookings. Addie, Effie, and Jessie Cherry performed, while Lizzie and Ella continued to work the farm. (Lizzie stayed involved in the act, often serving as business manager and performing with her sisters on an irregular "as needed" basis.) During these years, the Cherry Sisters' reputation as the worst act in show business grew, spreading throughout the Midwest. Contemporary accounts indicate that audiences, predominately male, were drawn by the opportunity to mock and revile the women and to participate in rowdy mob scenes. At least initially, the popular novelty act continued to draw a substantial crowd and income. Effie Cherry reported that they received "only $150" for their performance in Dubuque in May 1893, even though the box office take was "Over seven hundred and fifty dollars, of which seventy-five per cent came to us by our contract."[15] While Effie's aggrieved account of the box office gross may be somewhat exaggerated, her figure of $150 seems plausible based on their solidly booked tour that spring. However, the Dubuque money was hard earned. The audience quickly turned into a violent mob and the Cherry Sisters experienced the first premeditated, full-scale riot of their career.

While prior audience responses could be explained away by theatrical tradition—i.e., booing, hissing, and throwing rotten fruit at a bad performer—the Dubuque audience's brutality could not.[16] According to the *Dubuque Herald* (as reprinted in a *Gazette* article headlined "He Hurled a Wash Boiler"), the audience consisted of "seven or eight hundred people, only a few of whom were women." The riot was expected and premeditated. A Bellevue newspaper offered the opinion, "The Newspapers in advance told of what latitude was to be allowed, the theatre manager sanctioned it, and the police laughed at it." This is supported by a report that the theatre manager took the precaution of replacing the stage curtain with an old one that was "a misfit for the proscenium, leaving open spaces on either side." Additionally, the audience came equipped with seltzer syphons, fire extinguishers, and a large wash boiler. The Cherry Sisters were violently assaulted and repeatedly driven from the stage. The usual fruits, vegetables, eggs, and tin cans soon gave way to seltzer spray, forceful discharges from fire extinguishers aimed at their faces, and large missiles, including the wash tub that was thrown from the balcony and aimed directly at the women. When one of the "eldest sisters," presumably Effie, was driven from the stage, she returned with "a shotgun and a defiant look" that created a momentary pause in the rowdy behavior. However, the performance was terminated shortly thereafter (without gunfire) and the crowd followed the Cherry Sisters into the street, where the men pelted them with rocks, sticks, and eggs until they reached the safety of their hotel.[17]

The Dubuque audience's behavior not only transgressed the acceptable boundaries of audience behavior, but also moved beyond the realm of theatre when the men took the riot into the streets. The mob assault indicates how dangerous the Cherry Sisters' enterprise had become. In fact, the city censured the theatre manager and city marshal for dereliction of duty in their failure to protect the women.[18] After a three-month retreat to Marion for regrouping, the Cherry Sisters ventured out on tour again in the fall of 1893, with renewed commitment and vigor. It is indisputable that the Cherry Sisters reentered show business with open eyes. Although they continued to publicly profess a belief in the public's adulation, Dubuque forced them to face reality. Privately, they had to know that adulation does not result in riots that threaten the performers' safety, driving them from the theatre and through the streets of the city. In fact, the Cherry Sisters continued to experience violent physical assaults on a periodic basis, even in their hometown of Marion in 1895. According to the *Marion Pilot* that riot broke out immediately after the opening religious tableau, stopped the show, and continued uncontrolled for about an hour. The Cherry Sisters were assaulted with meat—tenderloin and liver—and their manager sustained a serious injury when an audience member broke a chair over his head.[19] Yet the Cherry Sisters apparently took the Marion riot in their stride and continued their tour.

During the next ten years, the Cherry Sisters toured throughout the Midwest variety circuit, where the combination of their greenhorn performance of a failed femininity and predominately male audiences continued to prove volatile. According to Effie, they began to write their own songs and sketches, which, in retrospect, suggest a conscious decision to emphasize their amateurish status. A 1895 program provides a typical sampling of a Cherry Sisters' performance. Jessie sang "Bicycle Ride to the Fair," and "Fair Columbia," which she reportedly performed while draped in an American flag. She also recited her temperance essay, "Corn Juice." Both Addie and Effie appeared in male drag, delivering moralizing essays titled "The Modern Young Man" and "The Traveling Man." The program often featured grand tableaus, including Jessie's signature "Clinging to the Cross." Contemporary reports of that tableau describe Jessie suspended on or clinging to a giant crucifix; in Odebolt, Iowa, red lights and a musical rendition of "Rock of Ages" accompanied the pose.[20] The program content—earnest patriotism, temperance, and melodramatic religiosity—provided fodder for audience ridicule. Addie and Effie's drag performances of moral essay recitation, both of which criticized young men specifically, appear to be direct challenges, even male baiting, to the young male audience.

The Cherry Sisters' performance of "The Hypnotizing of Trilby" further illustrates that the women consciously created a self-deprecating act. George du Maurier's 1894 novel permeated the popular culture, both in America and abroad, and parodies of the book and subsequent play were wildly popular. The Cherry Sisters performed the scene in which young Trilby, completely oblivious to her lack of musical talent, first sings "Ben Bolt" for Svengali. By choosing that particular scene, which featured Trilby's initial ineptitude rather than her later accomplishments, the Cherry Sisters performed a double parody—of *Trilby,* as well as their own act. The "Ben Bolt" scene closely reflected their own situation, giving them further inspiration and support for their stage career. They not only appropriated the material, but also adopted Trilby's artless persona as their own theatrical persona. The element of theatrical ineptitude was essential to the Cherry Sisters' relationship with their male audience, who could then attribute their own raucous, hostile, and assaultive behavior to socially acceptable theatrical rowdyism.

The second essential element of the Cherry Sisters' appeal was their performance of a failed femininity. In late nineteenth century theatre, both legitimate and popular, a female performer's beauty and youth was often more important than her talent. In popular entertainment, this was most evident in burlesque, which put the issue of female sexuality on center stage. According to Robert C. Allen, burlesque was responsible for creating a new, highly sexual theatrical image of female beauty. In the mid-nineteenth century, troupes such as Lydia Thompson and the British Blondes were largely responsible for a radical shift in societal ideas of female beauty, moving from the Victorian ideal of a "slender, asexual steel-engraving lady to the large-breasted, big-hipped ideal." Women in burlesque performed as sexualized female spectacle, complete with an impertinent, naughty, and winking-to-the-audience manner. Allen characterizes the relationship between performer and audience as a "system of display and gaze" that was driven by male pleasure.[21] Male audiences, situated in a position of power and privilege, assumed the right to look, judge, objectify, and accept or reject the female performer. By the 1890s, burlesque's influence throughout popular entertainment was evident. The sexualized, voluptuous body type had become a stage ideal of female beauty and men expected female performers to be beautiful, sexy, and compliant in the gendered "display and gaze" dynamic.

The Cherry Sisters were the antithesis of the late nineteenth century theatrical ideal of femininity in both appearance and decorum. They were not young, beautiful, or graceful; they were neither voluptuous nor sexy; they were far from charming or endearingly flirtatious; and, above all, they were not compliant. The Cherry Sisters played up their Iowa farming background, performing in homemade dresses—highnecked, longsleeved, and utilitarian—and seldom wore any makeup, thus cultivating a no-nonsense, asexual stage persona. As a result, they challenged the male audience's complacent belief that female performers' primary purpose was to provide sexual pleasure by submitting to their gaze. Instead of competing with theatrical images of beauty, the Cherry Sisters satirized the very standards that excluded them from a traditional career. They burlesqued burlesque.

Their signature song, "Eulogy on the Cherry Sisters," illustrates the Cherry Sisters' burlesque of theatrical femininity. They typically opened their act with the "Eulogy," a parody of the popular song "Ta-Ra-Ra-Boom-De-Ay," sung to the accompaniment of Jessie's bass drum (See fig. 1). British music hall star Lottie Collins had popularized the original song in 1891, building her American career on the suggestive lyrics, delivered with "deceptive demureness" and a 'kick dance' version of the cancan. The song was a "smash hit," and audiences, especially male ones, were certainly well acquainted with its titillating elements. The song celebrated the New Woman who remained a "good girl" at the same time that she flaunted her sexuality in a flirtatious manner:

> Never forward, never bold,
> Not too hot, and not too cold,
> But the very thing, I'm told,
> That in your arms you'd like to hold![22]

In contrast, the Cherry Sisters' nonsensical parody avoided flirtatious or sexual references, instead "introducing" themselves to the audience:

> Cherries Red and Cherries Ripe
> The Cherries they are out of sight
> Cherries Ripe and Cherries Red
> Cherry Sisters are still ahead.[23]

In contrast to the flirtatious Lottie Collins' delivery style, the Cherry Sisters opened their act standing stiff and awkwardly, covered in modest calico from head to toe, and singing the parodic lyrics with straight faces and seemingly deadly seriousness.[24] A comparison of carte de viste photographs of Lottie Collins and Jessie Cherry, in which their facial features and hairstyles are remarkably similar, helps illustrate the parodic aspect of the Cherry Sisters' performance of a failed femininity. Collins' photograph includes a knowing half-smile directed to the camera, long and curly hair falling to her waist, a corseted hourglass figure that is emphasized by draped material around her hips and shoulders, and shapely arms shown off by closely fitted gloves (See fig. 2). In contrast, Jessie's straightforward pose and serious demeanor convey an image of a non sexualized school girl rather than a flirtatious, sexy woman (See fig. 3). Although her dress is similar in style to Collins' dress, her figure is uncorseted and fails to replicate Collins' hourglass silhouette; Jessie's bulky, long sleeved dress conceals rather than reveals her body. By performing the "Eulogy" as their first number, dressed in unstylish and modest dresses, the Cherry Sisters firmly established the theatrical persona that served as the basis of their entire career in the first moment of performance. While maintaining an air of earnest innocence, the women offered themselves up for ridicule as parodies of the sexy and flirtatious femininity that was highly popular in contemporary entertainment.

The Cherry Sisters' act, incorporating both an amatuerish persona and a failed theatrical femininity, appealed to a predominately male audience, most of whom were young, confused, and angry about the cultural developments of the 1890s. According to Gail Bederman, men's traditional bases of power were threatened on numerous fronts. First, a series of depressions created financial uncertainty, loss of confidence, and a compromised ability to fulfill the traditional male role of breadwinner. Secondly,

Figure 1. Addie, Jessie, and Effie Cherry with their famous bass drum. Photo courtesy of Orville and Jane Rennie Collection, State Historical Society of Iowa—Iowa City.

changing job markets severely limited prospects for advancement, with the result that young middle-class men faced the possibility that access to male power and status would be closed to them forever. Finally, the male sense of superiority and privilege was further undermined as the New Woman entered public life through college education, social reform work, and professional careers normally reserved for men. Traditional ideas about masculinity were being challenged on several fronts, with the New Woman's success being particularly threatening. Biederman argues that women's advances "undermined the assumption that education, professional status, and political power required a male body" and that "men reacted passionately by ridiculing these New Women."[25] While the Cherry Sisters were not typical New Women, their refusal to participate in the compliant "display and gaze" arrangement between female performer and male audience directly challenged the young men's threatened sense of privilege, authority, and power. The combination of cultural upheaval of the decade and the Cherry Sisters' confrontational performance of amateurism and failed femininity created the niche for their novelty act. The Cherry Sisters served as a cultural scapegoat, allowing respectable young men to vent their frustration, anger, and misogyny within a contained and socially acceptable theatrical environment. Although it is unlikely that the Cherry Sisters masterminded the phenomenon, they took advantage of it once they realized the financial potential of their act, actively pursuing a long term career in popular entertainment.

However, despite the Cherry Sisters' perseverance, they failed to become rich on the Midwestern variety circuit. While they continued to attract curious and rowdy male audiences, their initial financial windfall soon dwindled to a much lower and sporadic income, and they spent the remainder of their career chasing after the possible wealth promised by their earliest performances. Winifred Van Etten reports that the Cherry Sisters hired a number of managers during their first year, including A. J. Wheeler who contracted, as early as May 1894, to pay the three women a flat $200 per month. Throughout the decade, they lived the lives of itinerant variety performers, precariously from day-to-day, and were sometimes stranded on the road without work. In December 1894, Addie wrote home to Lizzie for money: "If you will send $5.00 we will send you all we can spair [sic] next week. . . . Now Lizzie if you don't send us 5.00 I am not so sure as we will send you any money next week but will keep it so we will not get broke again. But $5.00 is not much to ask of you. We do not want $15.00."[26] The Cherry Sisters soldiered on in their pursuit of the elusive fortune promised by their early success, attributing their financial problems to unscrupulous theatre managers and unfair newspaper editors.

The Cherry Sisters' relationship with newspapermen was complex and mutually manipulative. The male critics shared the misogynistic attitudes of the male audience and their articles often reviled the women—their performance and their failed femininity—in extreme terms. However, it appears that the Cherry Sisters purposely encouraged, even goaded, the newspapermen into an antagonistic relationship in order to gain publicity and keep their name in the public arena. When confronting the press, the Cherry Sisters portrayed themselves as innocent victims in a baffling, hostile world. Their libel suit against the *Cedar Rapids Gazette* and mock trial created the model for the Cherry Sisters' long term relationship with the press. The Cherry Sisters' most

Figure 2. British music hall star Lottie Collins, who popularized "Ta-Ra-Ra-Boom-De-Ay." Photo courtesy of Library of Congress, Prints and Photographs Division LC-USZ62-101298.

Figure 3. Jessie Cherry, who bears a striking resemblance to Lottie Collins in appearance and dress, although Jessie Cherry fails to convey the same sense of flirtatious femininity. Photo courtesy of Orville and Jane Rennie Collection, State Historical Society of Iowa—Iowa City.

effective boost came from a *Dubuque Times* article in March of 1896, which reported on the installation of a net to protect the women during performance. The story captured the imagination of the public and became the most enduring aspect of the Cherry Sisters' legend. The article read:

> [The Cherry Sisters] have at last succeeded in effecting a way to protect themselves from everything except pistol bullets. They carry with them a wire screen, such as is put up in front of base ball grand stands. . . . This is put up immediately back of the footlights and is securely held in place with guy ropes. Mr. S. G. Arnold of [Dubuque], who was in Osage Saturday evening, says that . . . the show went along without any further trouble, the girls looking like people giving a performance in a cage.[27]

While the installation of a net could be true, it is more likely a part of a pattern of unsubstantiated mythos surrounding the Cherry Sisters. Despite the detailed description, the newspaper report is suspect. The *Dubuque Times* article, which appears to be the only Iowa newspaper account of the Osage net, relies upon one man's unsupported eyewitness account in a small town located about 150 miles from Dubuque.

In fact, allusions to a net were present from the beginning of the Cherry Sisters' career. During their first Cedar Rapids appearances in 1893, the *Gazette* reported that the theatre manager suggested a second performance with a protective screen and then followed with its own suggestion that the onstage jury be protected by a net during the mock trial.[28] Apparently, the *Gazette* not only played a role in promoting the Cherry Sisters' early career, but was also responsible for planting the seed for further speculation about the need for a net as well. Despite its suspect origins, the net story is the most enduring aspect of the Cherry Sisters' legend. While Hale only noted that "there came the day when they were obliged to perform behind fish netting and wire screens," other accounts often claimed—without any evidence—that the first net appeared during the Cherry Sisters' New York run in 1896. For instance, in 1928 the *Des Moines Register* reported that a net was installed as a result of a rowdy opening night audience in New York and was used thereafter throughout the Cherry Sisters' career. In 1982, Gartner also assumed a New York origin, suggesting that Oscar Hammerstein himself may have masterminded the idea. By 1994, even Slide had accepted the New York origin as fact.[29]

If the Cherry Sisters had performed behind a net, we would expect to find mention of it in more than one newspaper review. Although the New York newspapers covered the Cherry Sisters' 1896 New York appearance extensively, no paper ever mentioned a net and details in articles argue against its presence. The *New York Herald* reported that a man was ejected for throwing things onto the stage. The *New York Dramatic Mirror* coverage suggested a remarkably mild audience reception and reported that the Cherry Sisters were pleased to receive flowers instead of shoes and eggs. *The New York Times* critic, who was appalled by the apparent poverty and ignorance of the Cherry Sisters, as well as by the entire spectacle of their performance, also failed to mention a net; if one had been present, it would likely have added to his horror and garnered mention in his review. Finally, immediately following their New York appearance, the Cherry Sisters played Chicago, where the management placed a sign on the stage that prohibited the audience from throwing anything except flowers. The presence of a sign, and the reporter's account of it, strongly suggests that a net was not in place for the Chicago performances; it would have been highly unlikely that the reporter made note of a sign but not the net.[30]

Eyewitness and anecdotal accounts of shows with the net in place do exist, but in each case the credibility of the report is open to question. In the Junior League of Cedar Rapids Oral History project, Eleanor Cook Thomas claimed that when she saw the Cherry Sisters perform, "they had netting up." However, Thomas also claimed that she saw Jessie Cherry's "Clinging to the Cross" tableau, which was impossible; Thomas was born in 1909, six years after Jessie died. In the early 1960s, Orville Rennie ran an ad in the *Cedar Rapids Gazette* searching for eyewitnesses. His single response came from a man who claimed to have seen the Cherry Sisters perform behind a screen in Boston, but with no corroborating information regarding date or place. This claim is compromised by the fact that Effie wrote in her autobiography—three decades earlier—that they regretfully never played Boston.[31] Regardless of the veracity of the net story, Arnold's widely circulated March 1896 article brought the Cherry Sisters to the attention of people outside of the Midwest and probably played a role in their big break—New York—later that same year.

The Cherry Sisters' legendary role in Hammerstein's financial recovery appears to be true. Hammerstein's lavish Olympia Theatre opened in October 1896, and was an immediate financial failure, leaving Hammerstein overextended and in bankruptcy court when he engaged the Cherry Sisters for a limited run in November. Just twelve days after the Cherry Sisters opened, *The New York Times* reported that Hammerstein's creditors had agreed to temporarily suspend bankruptcy proceedings against Hammerstein, subject to full payment of his debts totalling $84,000.[32] It appears that the Cherry Sisters, playing to sold-out houses from November 16th to December 11th, helped stabilize Hammerstein's immediate financial situation.

The New York engagement was supposedly a financial turning point for the Cherry Sisters as well, catapulting them into the upper echelons of high-paid entertainers. In his 1910 memoir, producer Robert Grau reported that the "incompetents" were so popular that they were paid $1000 a week. Grau's unconfirmed figure eventually hardened into a "fact" cited by both Hale and Slide.[33] The surviving evidence indicates that the Cherry Sisters never received $1000 a week. In a 1962 interview, Rennie pegged their New York salary at only $100 a week plus expenses.[34] According to Van Etten, upon returning to the Midwest, the Cherry Sisters reportedly commanded $400 weekly for their appearance at the Imperial Music House in Chicago. That figure matches Effie's claim that their post-New York tour included Chicago, St. Louis, and Cincinnati, and that the largest salary they received on the trip was $400. Effie also claimed that six months after the New York engagement, the Cherry Sisters earned $600 for two 4th of July shows at Hubinger's Park in Keokuk, Iowa.[35] These post-New York engagement appear to be the largest salaries that the Cherry Sisters commanded.

Upon their return to the Midwest, the Cherry Sisters continued to face extreme hostility from both male audiences and reporters. Critics became increasingly virulent, incorporating violent language and imagery in their assessment of the women. Their criticism changed from discussion of the Cherry Sisters amateurism and failed femininity to hostile condemnations of the women as grotesques. For example, the *Oskaloosa Daily Times* reported that Jessie "swooned away like a cow when knocked on the head with an ax. . . . She would make a lovely corpse." Other reviews of the post-New York era were equally hostile and cruel, dehumanizing the women by routinely comparing them to heifers, mules, and automatons.[36]

One particularly virulent review, published in the *Odebolt Chronicle* and reprinted in the *Des Moines Leader* in 1898, reflected the prevailing journalistic treatment of the Cherry Sisters by the late 1890s, and resulted in the landmark libel lawsuit. The article in question, written by William Hamilton, characterized the Cherry Sisters as grotesque in extreme terms:

> Effie is an old jade of 50 summers, Jessie is a frisky filly of 40, and Addie, the flower of the family, a capering monstrosity of 35. Their long, skinny arms, equipped with talons at the extremities, swung mechanically. . . . The mouths of their rancid features opened like caverns, and sounds like the wailing of damned souls issued therefrom. . . . Effie is spavined, Addie is knock-kneed and string halt, and Jessie, the only one who showed her stockings, has legs without calves, as classic in their outlines as the curves of a broom handle.[37]

Hamilton dehumanized the women, comparing them to infirm and diseased horses, taloned creatures, and rancid, damned souls and, ironically, failed to address their performance. At the trial, Hamilton defended his article as a satiric piece and Addie Cherry, at the request of the judge, performed a sampling of the variety act.[38] The court ruled that there was no evidence of intentional malice, which is the basis for libel, concluding:

> One who goes upon the stage to exhibit himself to the public, or who gives any kind of a performance to which the public is invited, may be freely criticised [sic]. He may be held up to ridicule, and entire freedom of expression is guaranteed dramatic critics, provided they are not actuated by malice or evil purpose in what they write.[39]

Although this ruling stands as the broad standard for performance criticism today, it is predicated upon Hamilton's misogynistic attack on the Cherry Sisters' personal appearance rather than their dramatic performance. For the Cherry Sisters, operating within a nineteenth-century male dominated judicial system, "fair comment" was synonymous with "fair game." Even the Iowa Supreme Court acknowledged that the ruling was based on an exception made in the case of the Cherry Sisters: "Ordinarily publication of such an article as the one in question would of itself be an indicium [sic] of malice, but, as applied to the facts of this case, we do not think it should be so held."[40]

The newspaper reviews, as well as the details of the failed lawsuit, can be viewed as evidence of the hostile, misogynistic environment that the Cherry Sisters routinely encountered. Between 1897 and 1902, they began to hire off-duty policemen for protection during their performances, which indicates that the women were compelled to continue performing under dangerous conditions.[41] Although the Cherry Sisters managed to continue performing, their career increasingly became a litany of despair and poverty, a sharp contrast to the fortune heralded in the Cherry Sisters' mythos.

By the turn of the century, the Cherry Sisters had to travel farther from home in search of venues and earned less money for their efforts. After a disappointing Western tour in 1900, the Cherry Sisters returned to the more familiar territory of the Midwest, but circumstances failed to improve. Jessie's 1901 diary reads as a record of troubles inherent to the life of itinerant actors:

Jan 1, 1901	Fulton, Ill. took in $16.
Jan 6.	Morrison, Ill. took in $22.
March 18	Rockford Iowa. took in no $ blizzard didn't play.
March 21	Addie had the lawyer at Ogden send for Effie's jewelry. She paid him $5.
March 29	Addie gave the lawyer 50¢ to send for Effie's jewelry at Dayton. Our lawyer from Ogden came to room to get 50¢ more which was mean.
April 6	We played at Seamore Iowa. took in 11.20 the house was rude and very small. We cut the concert at the intermission
June 11	We played Colimes Iowa took in no $
June 12	We left Colimes for Lisbon Iowa. Left our board bill unpaid.
August 6	Effie took her revolver out on the stage with her. Took in $57.
October 31	Okland IA. . . . The opera manager had to advance us the tickets to get us there. . . . We couldn't get any musician and it was best that we couldn't. Our share after the entertainment was $3. The Anita opera man attached our baggage. We had just $1 left after expenses were settled.[42]

In many ways, Jessie's journal entries serve as a microcosm of the Cherry Sisters' career, encompassing the constant pursuit of money in an unfriendly world of bad weather, rude and dangerous audiences, unpaid bills, lawyers, and financial disappointments. They held on to their precarious touring career until 1902, when they settled in Hot Springs, Arkansas, to run a resort restaurant, but that endeavor also failed. Jessie Cherry died of typhoid the following year and Addie and Effie returned to Marion, where they stayed for two years before venturing onto the stage again.

Between 1905 and 1938, the two surviving Cherry Sisters performed when and where they could, as a means of supplementing their income. Addie and Effie primarily supported themselves by operating a bakery in Cedar Rapids from the late 1910s until 1932.[43] Newspaper records indicate that they limited their performing career to short tours, special appearances, and a series of nostalgic comebacks in Iowa and Chicago until 1932. After the bakery closed, they made a concerted effort to return to the stage fulltime, going out on the road for Midwestern tours once again.

Their series of comeback performances, beginning in 1905, were devoid of virulent audience responses. The gendered cultural upheavals of the 1890s had leveled out and the Cherry Sisters' niche as theatrical scapegoat was no longer relevant.

Instead, the shows were nostalgic in nature, playing to both male and female audiences who focused on the amateurism of the act, and there was a decidedly pathetic aspect to them. Publicity photos of Addie and Effie that appear to have been taken decades apart show the women wearing the same dresses and accessories; while the clothing may have been retained as costume staples, they give the appearance of "genteel" poverty, whether intended or not (See figs. 4 and 5). Recounting a 1918 performance, Van Etten reported that Lizzie assisted by playing the part of the young lady in "The Gypsy's Warning," a skit that became more ludicrous as the women aged:

> Addie, stouter now by a good many pounds, in [a] garment that stagehands at the Majestic described as patent-leather pants, still played the Spanish Cavalier, the vile seducer. Lizzie, now some sixty years of age, a perfect pelt of hair hanging in hanks down her back, her gaunt face made gaunter by quantities of eye makeup, played the maiden and languished on the shoulder of fat Addie, who was much too short to be languished ongracefully.[44] (See fig. 6)

As the women aged, the audience progressively viewed them as parodies of their younger selves, with the result that they evoked sympathy and pity rather than hilarity.

The nostalgic performances provided a sporadic income during the 1910s. Based on signed contracts dating from 1909 to 1911, the Cherry Sisters earned $100 to $125 per week, with a few contracts paying as much as $150, when they could find work. As late as 1918, they were paid $125 for a three-day engagement at the Majestic Theatre in Des Moines.[45] By the 1930s, however, the well had finally run dry. The Cherry Sisters could not sustain a viable career at a time when it was desperately needed. In 1935, they returned to New York to appear at the Gay Nineties nightclub; Addie was 76 and Effie was 68. The sisters appeared so elderly and pitiable that the audience was mortified. Van Etten, quoting an unnamed source, reported that Tallulah Bankhead and Gracie Allen were in the audience and both women wept.[46]

Financial records and personal correspondence from the 1930s indicate that all of the Cherry sisters were living in poverty, with Lizzie and Ella fighting to survive on the farm. Addie and Effie received $200 for the 1935 Gay Nineties appearance and, hoping that once again a New York engagement would provide a short-term boost, used the money to bankroll a Midwestern tour that failed dismally. Stranded on the road, Effie regretfully wrote to Lizzie, "I wish we had come right home from New York with our $200."[47] While Addie and Effie struggled on the road, Ella and Lizzie lived in extreme conditions on the farm. The farmhouse collapsed in 1934, and Ella and Lizzie retreated to the basement:

> [T]hey set up a stove which fed by inserting one end of a log into the firebox, pushing it gradually further in as it was consumed. The method was accompanied by . . . smoke . . . and made their eyes sore but they no longer had sufficient strength to cut wood. Beds were heaps of rags on the basement floor. . . . By February no one could endure the situation any longer. [Authorities] came and carried Ella out. . . . In March she died.[48]

Figure 4. Effie and Addie Cherry in the early years of their nostalgic comeback career. Photo courtesy of Orville and Jane Rennie Collection, State Historical Society of Iowa—Iowa City.

Figure 5. Effie and Addie Cherry in the later years of their career, still wearing the same dresses and accessories. Photo courtesy of Orville and Jane Rennie Collection, State Historical Society of Iowa—Iowa City.

Figure 6. Addie, Lizzie, and Effie Cherry in their signature skit, "The Gypsy's Warning," in the later years of their career. Photo courtesy of Orville and Jane Rennie Collection, State Historical Society of Iowa—Iowa City.

After her own hospitalization, Lizzie returned to the family farm and attempted to live there alone. Correspondence between Addie and Effie, and Lizzie during the Cherry Sisters' 1936 tour was filled with health and financial concerns. In January, Lizzie wrote, "[M]y hands are numb, my feet are numb, I can hardly light the fire;" on February 4th, the county sheriff once again removed her from the premises and placed her in the Linn County Home.[49] Meanwhile, Addie and Effie were stranded on the road. On February 24, 1936, they wrote to Lizzie: "We are going to stay another week where we are which will make 3 weeks, for it was such bad weather here that we could not get any other place as the theatres were all empty as they said the St. Louis people will not get out when the weather is bad."[50]

A month later, Addie and Effie still hadn't made enough money to return home. On March 28, Effie wrote, "I know that you will be dispointed [sic] that we did not come home from Peoria Ill, but we did not have money enough. I thought he would keep us another week."[51] The letters of that winter paint a picture of desperation for Lizzie, confined to the county home against her will, and for Addie and Effie, stranded on the road without steady engagements or income. The archived correspondence ends with the March 28th letter, which suggests that the sisters managed to return home before Lizzie's death on May 13th. Addie and Effie retired to Cedar Rapids, applying for their old age pensions in 1938 and sharing a room in a boarding house. They made their last public appearance at the Strand Theatre in Cedar Rapids in 1938, when Addie was 79 and Effie was 71 years old. Van Etten wrote, "Addie, old and heavy, had to be helped onto the stage."[52] Addie died in 1942 and Effie followed in 1944. Effie died in poverty and debt; Rennie bought the Cherry Sisters' collection from her landlady in exchange for back rent.[53]

Effie's *The New York Times* obituary was an affectionate celebration of the Cherry Sisters' mythos. It made no mention of the harsh reality of their career—the very real hostility of the audiences, the physical attacks and riots, or the deeply entrenched misogyny that acted as the psychological core of the decade-long sustained novelty act. It also failed to mention the paper's own 1896 review, in which the critic wrote that the women were untalented, poverty-stricken Western versions of "poor whites."[54] Instead, the obituary resurrected all the elements of the Cherry Sisters' legend: the first show that paid for a trip to the Chicago World's Fair, the women's perpetual naïveté, a bizarre but idyllic career built on good-natured rowdyism, the $1,000 a week salary, the net installed by Hammerstein, and a comfortable retirement.[55] In all likelihood it was the source for Hale's popular article later that year.

NOTES

[1] Bernard Kelly, "Those Fabulous Cherry Sisters," *The Denver Post Empire Magazine*, 18 November 1962: 8.

[2] *Cambridge Guide to American Theatre*, ed. Don B. Wilmeth and Tice L. Miller (New York: Cambridge University Press, 1993): 106.

[3] Hale, "So Bad They Were Good," *Coronet* (Dec. 1944):92-96.
[4] See Anthony Slide's *Selected Vaudeville Criticism*, (Metuchen: Scarecrow Press, 1988): 45-50, *Vaudevillians: A Dictionary of Vaudeville Performers*, (Westport: Arlington House, 1981): 25, and *The Encyclopedia of Vaudeville*, (Westport: Greenwood Press, 1994): 94. Also see Michael Gartner, "Fair Comment," *American Heritage* (Oct./Nov. 1982): 28-31.
[5] Hale, 94-5.
[6] Effie Cherry, unpublished autobiography, 12, Rennie 2:14. My major sources of primary materials come from the Orville and Jane Rennie Collection, Ms. 178, Historical Society of Iowa, Iowa City, IA. It includes Effie Cherry's unpublished autobiography (circa 1930), playbills, programs, publicity photos, songbooks, personal correspondence, diary fragments, scrapbooks, contemporary newspaper articles, and Winifred Van Etten's unpublished 1940s biography, "The Queens of Corn." All notes for sources from the collection include the box and folder of the material (i. e. 2:14).
[7] See *Marion Sentinel*, 26 January 1893 and *Marion Pilot*, 26 January 1893, Rennie 1:12. Newspaper articles from the Cherry Sisters' scrapbook are identified by newspaper and/or publication date as available, followed by location in the Rennie collection. Also see Effie Cherry, 12. All income figures represent group income, not income per member.
[8] See Mary J. Oates, "Organized Volunteerism: The Catholic Sisters in Massachusetts, 1870-1940," *Women and Power in American History*, ed. Katheryn Kish Sklar and Thomas Durbin (Englewood Cliffs: Prentice Hall, 1991): 123; "Girls Be Practical," *The Household* 25 (1892), reprinted in ed. and comp. Norton Juster, *A Woman's Place: Yesterday's Women in Rural America* (Golden CO: Fulcrum, 1996): 271; and Effie Cherry, 7-9.
[9] F. John Herbert, "The Cherry Family," Rennie 1:1; Effie Cherry, 8.
[10] *Cedar Rapids Gazette*, 18 February 1983, Rennie 1:12.
[11] Effie Cherry, 19; Rennie 2:14.
[12] Ibid., 20; *Cedar Rapids Gazette*, 15 March 1893, Rennie 1:12.
[13] *Cedar Rapids Gazette*, 15 March 1893 and *Marion Sentinel*, 16 March 1893, Rennie 1:12.
[14] *Marion Sentinel* reported gross receipts of $690.00, with 25%, or $172.50, going to the Cherry Sisters. *The Des Moines Register* confirmed a sold out house of 1200 and reported a 75¢ admission price, resulting in gross receipts of $900.00; if the Cherry Sisters received 25% of these figures, they would have earned as much as $225.00. Effie Cherry corroborates that gross receipts were nearly $1,000.00, so it appears that the Cherry Sisters probably earned at least $150.00 for the show. See *Sentinel*, 16 March 1893, and *Des Moines Register*, 15 March 1893, Rennie 1:12 and Effie Cherry, 21; Rennie 2:14.
[15] Effie Cherry, 24; Rennie 2:14.
[16] The Cherry Sisters performed during a period when rowdyism had fallen out of favor. American audiences became more well-mannered during the 1830s and 1840s, with the rowdy elements relegated to some "lower-class" houses and variety theatres by the 1860s and 1870s; hissing had nearly disappeared by the 1860s. Nevertheless,

rowdyism was a well-known theatrical tradition in the memory of variety audiences of the 1890s. See Richard Butsch, *The Making of American Audiences: From Stage to Television, 1750-1990,* (Cambridge: Cambridge University Press, 2000): 5 and Robert C. Allen, *Horrible Prettiness: Burlesque and American Culture,* (Chapel Hill: University of North Carolina Press, 1991): 70.

[17] *Dubuque Herald,* May 1893, Rennie 1:12; unnamed Bellevue Iowa newspaper quoted in Effie Cherry, 24, Rennie 2:14. The *Herald* report that one of the Cherry Sisters threatened the audience with a shotgun seems apocryphal at first glance. However Jessie's diary entry of August 5, 1901 (quoted in Van Etten, n. p., Rennie 3:7) includes a note that "Effie took her revolver out on stage with her." Consequently, there are at least two documented instances in which a sister, presumably Effie, pulled some kind of gun on the audience.

[18] *Cedar Rapids Gazette,* 23 May 1893, Rennie 1:12.

[19] *Marion Pilot,* 17 November 1895, Rennie 1:12.

[20] Marion Opera House Program, November 1895, Rennie 1:10. Also see Lord Richard Acton and Patricia Nassif Acton, *To Go Free: A Treasury of Iowa's Legal Heritage,* (Ames: Iowa State University Press, 1995): 207.

[21] Robert C. Allen, *Horrible Prettiness,* (Chapel Hill: University of North Carolina Press, 1991), 78, 138, and 283.

[22] William Brooks, "Ta-Ra-Ra-Boom-De-Ay" Liner Notes, *The Hand That Holds the Bread* Compact Disc (New York: New World Records, 1978): 34-35.

[23] Van Etten, "Notes," Rennie 3:7.

[24] "Cherry Sisters Certainly Unique," *New York Herald,* 17 November 1896:12.

[25] Gail Bederman, *Manliness and Civilization,* (Chicago: University of Chicago Press, 1995): 12-14.

[26] Van Etten, 71 and 73, Rennie 4:1. While Van Etten's manuscript lacks citations, it is especially important because a portion of the collection was lost in a flood in 1956 and her manuscript is the only surviving documentation of some lost primary materials. I tend to accept Van Etten's account as accurate for several reasons. She was an English professor at Cornell College in Mt. Vernon, Iowa from 1937 to 1968. Her manuscript is well researched, with some notes included in the Rennie collection. I have been able to verify portions of her manuscript. For instance, the Rennie collection includes only two pages of detailed financial information from Jessie's 1901 diary. Van Etten's manuscript includes this information— without error— as well as additional figures from missing pages covering the remainder of the year. Van Etten also quotes from personal correspondence between the sisters and I have been able to verify her accuracy in the surviving letters, which makes me trust her account of the lost letters also.

[27] *Dubuque Times,* reprinted in *Cedar Rapids Republican,* 13 March 1896, Rennie 1:11.

[28] *Cedar Rapids Gazette* 13 March, 1893 and 14 March 1893, Rennie 1:12.

[29] See Hale, 95; "The Cherry Sisters' Nice, Clean Act is on the Stage Again," *Des Moines Register,* 2 September 1928: 3; Gartner, 29; and Slide, *Encyclopedia,* 94.

[30] See "Cherry Sisters Ask Fair Play," *New York Herald,* 18 November 1896: 12; "Hammerstein's Olympia," *New York Dramatic Mirror,* 5 December 1896: 17; "Four Freaks from Iowa," *The New York Times,* 17 November 1896: 5; and "Vaudeville

Correspondence," *New York Dramatic Mirror*, 26 December 1896: 20.

[31] See Eleanor Cook Thomas, interview by Laura Derr, transcribed by Renae Blasdell, Junior League of Cedar Rapids Oral History Project, 14 June 1985, Cedar Rapids Public Library; Bernard Kelly, "Those Fabulous Cherry Sisters," *The Denver Post Empire Magazine*, 18 November 1962: 9; and Effie Cherry, 30; Rennie 2:14.

[32] Hammerstein's Creditors," *The New York Times*, 28 November 1896: 7.

[33] See Robert Grau, *The Businessman in the Amusement World* (New York: Broadway Publishing, 1910): 245; Hale, 94; and Slide, *Vaudevillians*, 25.

[34] Kelly,18. Although Rennie did not cite his source, it is possible that he had access to information that is no longer in the collection— i.e. lost in the flood.

[35] See Van Etten, 119, Rennie 4: 1 and Effie Cherry, 29-30; Rennie 2:14.

[36] See *Oskaloosa Daily Times*, 29 September 1896, Rennie 1:11; *Cedar Rapids Gazette*, 15 March 1893, Rennie 1:12; and *Quincy (IL) Herald*, undated, Rennie 1:12. The *Gazette* described the Cherry Sisters as "a band of enrobed skeletons that were worked like automations" and the *Herald* claimed Lizzie had "the gyratorical abandon of a yearling heifer."

[37] William Hamilton, *Odebolt Chronicle*, reprinted in *Des Moines Leader*, 23 February 1898, quoted in "Cherry v. Des Moines Leader et al," *The Northwestern Reporter: All the Decisions of the Supreme Courts of Minnesota, Wisconsin, Iowa, Michigan, Nebraska, North Dakota, South Dakota, June 1-August 3, 1901*, vol. 86 (St Paul: West Publishing, 1901): 323.

[38] Although the original lawsuit was filed by all three performing Cherry Sisters, only Addie Cherry continued the suit as far as the State Supreme Court.

[39] *Northwestern Reporter*, 325.

[40] Ibid., 323-4.

[41] Van Etten, n. p., Rennie 4:1. Van Etten had access to records that covered the content of the Cherry Sisters' later performances, as well as contracts and financial records. I assume that this portion of the collection was lost in the 1956 flood. Consequently, I have relied extensively upon Van Etten's manuscript for this portion of the Cherry Sisters' history, supplementing her account with newspaper articles and surviving personal correspondence.

[42] Ibid., n. p.

[43] Ibid., 236.

[44] Ibid., 223.

[45] Ibid., 214 and 222.

[46] Ibid., 269.

[47] Ibid., 272.

[48] Ibid., 262.

[49] Ibid., 270-1.

[50] Addie and Effie Cherry to Lizzie Cherry, St. Louis, 24 February 1936, Rennie 1:2.

[51] Addie Cherry to Lizzie Cherry, Indianapolis, 28 March 1936, Rennie 1:2.

[52] Van Etten, 322 and 276, Rennie 4:1.

[53] Kelly, 9.

[54] See "Four Freaks from Iowa," note 28.

[55] "Effie Cherry Dies; Last of Sister Act," *The New York Times*, 6 August 1944: 37.

Peach R. Pittenger is a Ph.D. candidate in the Department of Theatre at Ohio State University.

Theatre History Studies 24 (June 2004)

The New Theater of Chicago: Democracy 1; Aristocracy 0

KATHY L. PRIVATT

In his book, *Democracy in America*, Alexis de Tocqueville contrasts "the taste for ideal beauty" present in an aristocracy with democracy's application of imagination to "devise what may be useful, and to represent what is real."[1] His assessment is echoed in *The Craftsman* in 1905. Calling for a "civic Renaissance for Chicago," the author advocates "uniting the useful and the beautiful" to influence "good order and the health of society."[2] However, the era referred to as the Chicago Renaissance exhibited both the aristocratic intent of presenting the "ideal" and the democratic aim of more "useful" applications. The New Theater is a snapshot of the aristocratic-democratic or ideal-pragmatic struggle embodied by the Chicago Renaissance at the turn of the century, of which the theater was a part. Formed by a cohesive, elite group, the New Theater's mission was riddled with conflict between business and artistic goals from the outset. Its failure within a single season was a predictable outcome for an essentially aristocratic endeavor.

The Chicago Renaissance, usually dated from the 1880's, encompassed the founding of many of the cultural institutions that still define that city. The New Theater project in 1906 was an attempt to include the theater in this movement combining "idealistic notions of culture" and a desire to apply culture to social goals.[3] The Renaissance sprang from industrialists- and businessmen-turned-philanthropists attempting to raise the status of Chicago to meet or exceed that of New York. The Chicago fire in 1871 wiped the architectural slate clean, and the World's Fair provided the venue for competition.

Organizing as late as they did in the Renaissance, the New Theater's supporters were a cohesive group of Chicago elite. Many in the group were born into the new industrial money that was shaping Chicago society. Although only a second generation rather than the extended lineage necessary for Alexis de Tocqueville's usual view of aristocracy, the insular nature of their interactions closely matches his description of the American aristocrats. In his first volume, he discusses the "remains" of the aristocracy in the United States and predicts that members of that group would withdraw from political involvement, and concentrate their efforts on private life, forming "a particular society that has separate tastes and enjoyments."[4] Sharing backgrounds, geographical location, social clubs, and philanthropic interests, the New Theater Trustees formed a new, local aristocracy. The moneyed patrons represented a cross-section of industry, banking and real estate, commingled with a few lawyers, professors and newsmen (See Table 1).[5] Many of these gentlemen, inheriting money from the entrepreneurship of their fathers, banded together to support cultural institutions. The Field family tree represents the interconnections formed by business relationships and the art world:

Stanley Field, Marshall Field's nephew, established a career as a financier, then became his uncle's vice-president. Playwright Preston Gibson married the niece of Marshall Field, connecting that family to the commercial theater world. Many of Gibson's plays opened at the Belasco Theater. Both Stanley Field and Gibson were on the New Theater Board, and Mrs. Marshall Field was a subscriber.[6]

Table 1
New Theater Board of Trustees - Professions

Aldis, Arthur - Real Estate in Lake Forest
Baker, Alfred L. - Banker/Broker then Lawyer
Bartlett, Frederic Clay - Artist
Bentley, Cyrus - Lawyer
Bissel, Arthur - Piano Company
Booth, W. Vernon - Fishing/Packing/Shipping
Carpenter, Frederick Ives - University Professor (English)/Author
Carpenter, G. A. - Judge
Chatfield-Taylor, H.C. - Author (inherited manufacturing money)
Dick, A. B. - Lumber Manufacturing - Mimeograph
Fargo, Livingston - American Express Company
Farnham, Harry J. - Real Estate and Renting Agent
Field, Stanley - Financier - Marshall's nephew & VP
Frost, A. C. - Banker and Railway Official
Gade, F. Herman - Lawyer and Mayor of Lake Forest
Gibson, Preston - Playwright/Tribune Writer
Herrick, Robert - English Faculty/Writer
Howland, G. C. - University Professor/Tribune editorials
Hulburd, Charles H. - President of Elgin Watch Co.
Hutchinson, Charles L. - Banker
Jones, David B. - unknown
Lathrop, Byron - unknown
MacVeagh, Franklin - Merchant/Grocer
Martin, Horace H. - Lawyer
Norton, Charles Dyer - Banker/Life Insurance
Porter, George F. - Director of Daily News - Land Co.
Ryerson, Martin A. - Capitalist/Lumber
Sprague II, A. A. - Merchant/Grocer
Vincent, George Edgar - University Professor
Wacker, Charles Henry - Executive of beer company/RR
Walling, Willoughby - Dr./Consul to Edinburgh/Secretary of Trust & Savings Bank
Wooley, Clarence E. - unknown

A board of trustees formed a "corporation not for pecuniary profit" and assembled a group of subscribers.[7] Approximately 71 percent of the original trustees were members of the University Club or the Onwentsia Club (See Table 2).[8] Onwentsia, an

"Indian word signifying a meeting place for sporting braves and their squaws,"[9] developed as a country club, while the University Club included the "promotion of literature and art" in its stated goals.[10] Both very exclusive social clubs, the University Club was Chicago-based, while the Onwentsia Club was founded in the Lake Forest suburb. Eleven of the 32 trustees had ties to Lake Forest. Arthur Aldis, president of the group, operated a real estate business which developed the Lake Forest suburb. He and nine other trustees lived there. Charles Wacker and Arthur Bissel graduated from Lake Forest Academy. Bissel went on to Lake Forest University. Albert Blake Dick and Charles Dyer Norton were trustees, and Alfred Baker was president of the board of Lake Forest College/University. Shared professional, social and geographical affiliations provided the opportunity for formation of a cohesive and elite group. When paired with major philanthropic efforts of the era, the involvement of this group indicates an idealistic approach to community improvement.

The Chicago Renaissance, fueled by the World's Fair, produced the Art Institute, the Field Museum (following the World's Fair), the Chicago Orchestra, and several libraries. Readily available records indicate the Trustee's involvement in these various projects (See Table 2). Stanley Field used money left by his uncle and his own funds to establish the Field Museum. He also was a primary benefactor of the Art Institute. Frederic C. Bartlett, an artist with inherited money, painted a mural and donated the first collection of modern art to the Art Institute for which he served as Trustee. The University of Chicago also emerged from this Renaissance, claiming eight New Theater Trustees as faculty and academic trustees. George Howland, Frederick Ives Carpenter, George Vincent, and Robert Herrick were all faculty members. Willoughby Walling was a Library Board Trustee, Franklin MacVeagh was a trustee, Charles Hutchinson was a trustee and treasurer, and Martin A. Ryerson was a trustee, VP and later President for the University. The evidence of a cohesive community is laid out like a spider web. Not everyone is involved in every project, but the interconnections and shared "mission" are unmistakable. The New Theater supporters functioned as a unit with what de Tocqueville defines as aristocratic intent.

Like their other philanthropic projects, the New Theater was founded and endowed with idealistic (aristocratic) artistic goals.[11] The clearest statement of these objectives was made in retrospect by Victor Mapes, but it is consistent with less complete purpose-statements published previously:

> 1. The elimination of the "star" system. There was to be no "star" in the cast and no "featured" players. The company was to be formed of as capable actors as could be procured, who were all to be on a basis of equality and ready to accept any part that might be assigned them.
> 2. There were to be no "long runs." Whatever the success of any play the number of its performances was to be strictly limited, so that new productions might follow one another at stated intervals.
> 3. As to the selection of plays the guiding principle was summed up succinctly in the words "plays worth while." No one cult or school was to dominate. The general effort would be to offer as wide a variety as possible of plays, new or old, that should interest intelligent people, without making them feel that they were wasting their time.
> 4. No pretensions were to be made in the way of elaborate scenery, costumes or

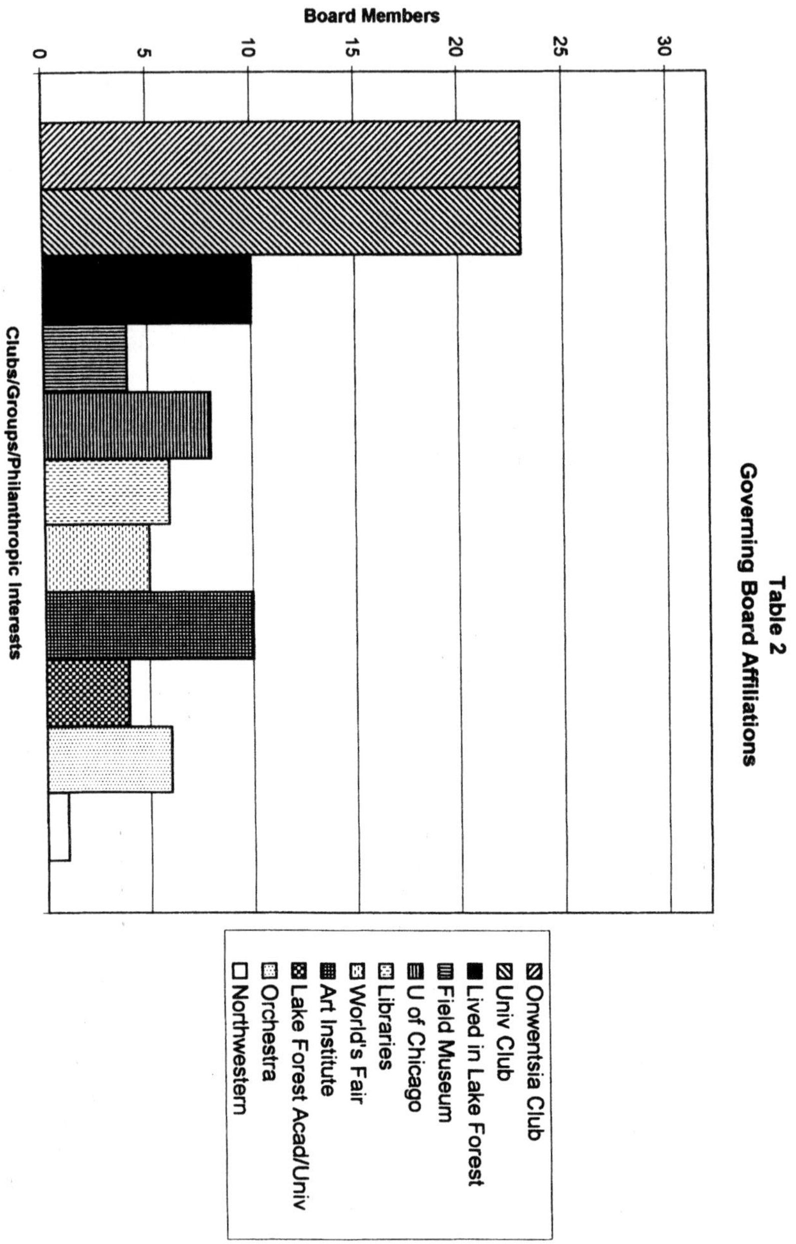
Table 2
Governing Board Affiliations
Board Members
0
5
10
15
20
25
30
Clubs/Groups/Philanthropic Interests
Onwentsia Club
Univ Club
Lived in Lake Forest
Field Museum
U of Chicago
Libraries
World's Fair
Art Institute
Lake Forest Acad/Univ
Orchestra
Northwestern

Table 2.

accessories, the aim being merely to give each play an adequate, if modest, presentation as nearly correct as possible.[12]

Contradictions abounded immediately. Samuel P. Gerson was chosen as business manager, and Victor Mapes was selected as artistic director. Despite goals that contradicted the whole commercial theater process of play selection and promotion, the trustees employed men firmly rooted in the commercial theater. Gerson came to the New Theater from Chicago's Garrick Theater and the Shubert Organization.[13] The Garrick was under the supervision of J. J. Shubert, General Manager, the most spectacle-driven and most financially successful of the Shubert brothers.[14] In the year preceding Gerson's hire by the New Theater, The Garrick billed itself as The Parlor Home of Amusement and produced musical comedies such as *The Woggle=Bug* [sic] by L. Frank Baum, *Sweet Kitty Bellairs* by David Belasco, and *Mexicana: A Comic Opera in Three Acts* by Clara Driscoll and Robert B. Smith.[15] The business practices in Gerson's immediate past were in direct conflict with the aims of the New Theater. Mapes came to Chicago via a stint as stage manager for Charles Frohman and stage director of Daly's Theater.[16] Using Mapes' own statements about the New Theater, Rich and Seligman argue convincingly that his selection of the acting company revealed "less enthusiasm for the principles of the New Theatre than might have been expected"[17] since he talked of only being able to hire actors willing to "sacrifice their aspirations and professional prestige."[18] Additionally, Rich and Seligman concluded that most of the actors were inexperienced, and two of the three with professional standing had connections to a Frohman company. Mapes additional appeal was not artistic background, but an "ancient family" of New York, putting him on equal footing with his elite employers.

Contradictory impulses seem to have driven season selection as well. Despite his position as Artistic Director, Mapes received suggestions from "prominent" subscribers.[19] He accepted and classified the various suggestions, and in his retrospective look at the New Theater endeavor, used passive voice to communicate that "the first five bills were decided upon."[20]

The opening night bill, October 8, 1906, included *Sainara* by Ernest d'Hervilly, *Engaged* by W. S. Gilbert, and *Marse Covington* by George Ade. In response to that event, reviews in both *The Chicago Daily Tribune* and *The Chicago Record-Herald* had praise for the theatre and its decoration: "a house which suggests exclusiveness and elegant refinement and as such is a desirable addition to the city's places of amusement,"[21] which speaks in support of the trustee's goal of raising the cultural status of Chicago, and "the atmosphere of a millionaire's residence,"[22] which reflects the wealthy, aristocratic tastes of the founders. Both papers recognized the "society" presence at the opening. Hubbard complimented that audience as one "which in its fashionableness, its dressiness, and its behavior recalled opening night audiences at the grand opera." *The Chicago Record-Herald* article described successful efforts by "Trustee Bissell" to engage the audience in drawing room behavior at intermission, with "little groups paying visits and at their ease." The same article further cemented the aristocratic image of the trustees by describing the insular, invitation-only "little house-warming celebration" they held in the French tearoom after the performance. The writer for *The Chicago Record-Herald* was complimentary of the plays selected and

Figure 1. Opening Night Audience: After the performance of *Sainara* "the curtain parted again and the audience had its picture taken by flashlight."[23] Photograph from Library of Congress, Prints and Photographs Division [LC-USZ62-125357 DLC].

assigned the acting deficiencies to first-night jitters. Hubbard, writing for *The Chicago Daily Tribune* was not so kind, and blamed Mapes' cuts in *Engaged* for its failure, since some of the audience left at intermission and more at the conclusion of this piece.

The bill changed on October 22 to Jose Echegaray's *The Great Galeoto* and Robert Marshall's *Shades of Night.* As noted by Rich and Seligman in their account of the New Theatre season, reviewers praised the literature chosen, and expressed reservations about the acting company.[24] More importantly, the reviews included pleas to support the theatre, with *The Chicago Record-Herald* castigating the audience attitude: "If a considerable number of the somewhat extraordinary assemblage which was present at the play last night gave evidence of knowing little and caring less what the simple ethics of Jose Echegaray's masterpiece are all about that is not the fault of the New Theater. Perhaps it was born to correct just that fault."[25] Apparently, the reviewer still saw the New Theater as an institution that could educate the masses, rather than the separate entertainment Alexis de Tocqueville predicted, appealing to aristocratic interests only. Not surprisingly, as the theater experienced financial trouble, the solutions offered by its staff were commercial answers with predictable results. Beginning to feel the financial constraints, Mapes took, or was allowed, leeway in promoting the third offering, *The Spoilers,* which was scheduled to be opened by Charles Frohman in New York later that season.[26] While in rehearsal, an article appeared in *The Chicago Daily Tribune* reporting a conflict over the use of a "hammer lock" in a fight scene. Associated with commercial melodrama, Mapes "rose up in his art protecting majesty and swore by the shades of Echegary and night that never, never, never on the stage of The New Theater should a 'hammer lock' be starred."[27] The play was replaced, then reinstated and sold-out for a two-week run. After opening, the whole affair was revealed as a publicity stunt like those used in the commercial theater.[28] The script itself was not outside the producing realm of the commercial theater, and was sold to its Chicago audience, not through the merits of the producing group, but through a commercial trick.

November found the theater with only that one profit-producing effort - *The Spoilers.*[29] Still, reviewers supported the theatre, and audiences still stayed away. W. L. Hubbard's review of the next offering, *The Son-In-Law* by Emile Augier and Jules Sandeau, preceded by *The Goal* by Henry Arthur Jones, took a new tack to attract an audience. Suggesting that subscribers could be "confidant" of worthy evening, Hubbard suggested that the "general public" could "invest" in a "pleasantly amusing evening."[30] Although not a stellar review, he was unconsciously promoting the trustees goal that the New Theater provide plays "that should interest intelligent people."[31]

In December, following additional financial difficulty, Chrystal Herne was hired as a star. Although her debut was in Gerhart Hauptmann's *Elga,* never before seen in English, her presence was in direct violation of the New Theater's mission to combat the star system. However, since she was an established Chicago actress, Mapes and the trustees hoped she would draw some much needed audiences. Her employment was followed by that of her mother as stage director, which precipitated Mapes resignation. Neither hire prevented the financial demise of the theater.[32]

From December forward, press reports took a negative turn. Reviews for *Elga,* despite Chrystal Herne's efforts, were as dismal as the audience turnout. *The Chicago Daily Tribune* review began "Wherefore?" and suggested that the New Theater had never established its reason for being.[33] *Sweet Lavender* by Arthur W. Pinero was offered for the holiday season, and Hubbard drew a distinction between potential audiences that reflected the gap between the trustees and their fellow citizens. Suggesting that someone who has no play-going experience might be pleased by the performance, and subscribers trying to support the New Theater might try to justify its presentation, Hubbard was unwilling to grant the production a "moderately adequate" epithet[34] James O'Donnell Bennett, writing for *The Chicago Record-Herald* was less directly negative toward the two pieces offered in early January: *Dora* by Victorien Sardou and *Masquerade* by Ludwig Fulda. He disparaged the actors' ability in each performance, but softened the criticism by consuming most of the review with a description of the story.[35]

Ironically, the new year brought more favorable reviews for productions of James A. Herne's *Margaret Fleming* and *The Whole World* by S. Marshall Ilsley. *The Chicago Daily Tribune* gives particular credit to Mrs. Herne's work as a replacement for Victor Mapes.[36] In his essay "America's First Art Theatre," James L. Highlander argues that *Margaret Fleming* was, of the season, the most appropriate work for an "art theater" because it matched the "new drama" pursued by the "Continental forerunners" of the New Theater.[37] At the time, however, the audience attendance did not increase and *The Whole World* did not complete a two-week run. Prior to either opening, Board of Trustees President Arthur T. Aldis had announced the closing of the New Theater.[38]

In October 1906, W. L. Hubbard, writing for *The Chicago Daily Tribune*, wrote "Opening of New Theater Gives Promise of Much." In January 1907, he wrote "Failure of New Theater Surprise to Few Persons."[39] The artistic aims of the New Theater were impure in intent from the beginning. Conceived by an aristocratic elite with their taste for the "ideal," the trustees were functioning in a community (democracy) that equated artistic institutions with social improvement. What resulted was an artistically-commercially mixed attempt to improve the standing of the community by adding an "art theater' to its cultural institutions. The failure was assured from the point of conception. The New Theater was born from an aristocratic group dictating what the theater should offer. Hubbard suggested that, all due respect for the founders aside, "it is a great question if there be any demand for such a playhouse here in Chicago." He goes on to suggest that the elite nature of the founders was well known and unappreciated: "The promoters of the undertaking seemed to have devoted so much attention and energy to the collecting of a fashionable audience that they overlooked the necessity of assembling a company of competent players." Further support of this dictation and preference for elite audiences is presented in an anonymous piece soon after the opening of the New Theater. In response to small audiences, the executive committee announced discount tickets for the University of Chicago, Northwestern University, and Lake Forest Academy so that students "may have an opportunity to take advantage of the educational features of the endowed playhouse."[40] Noting the didactic assumption and the close connection between the trustees and two of the scholastic institutions, the philanthropic nature of this offer is questionable. The icing on the aristocratic cake is Aldis' 1917 confession that billboards announcing the opening of the theater listed, not the names of the plays and players, but the elite trustees.[41] For Alexis de Tocqueville, the conclusion of this project would confirm the power of the masses to exercise their will.

The one enduring aspect of this failed attempt is also the most pragmatic. The New Theater was the first endowed art theater in America, beginning an arduous and ongoing main streaming of endowments into our American theater heritage. Technically, Red Wing, Minnesota boasts the first endowed theater, procured through a deed of gift from a deceased citizen in 1905. Theodore B. Sheldon left money and land to construct a theater. Although his stated intent was providing a theater as an "educational factor in the community for the better development of the artistic feeling both in those who may tread its boards and in those to whom it is a gift," his instructions established a road house that lured commercial acts visiting Minneapolis, a thoroughly practical arrangement.[42] Thus, Chicago's attempt is the first endowed "Art" Theater.[43]

Theaters operated with pure artistic objectives frequently do not draw enough audiences to support themselves in a democracy's market economy; if a group desires a theater that is not driven by the box office, an endowment is the most practical means of support. In the early nineteen hundreds, even that practical arrangement encountered resistance from a segment of the population skeptical of the product of that "generosity." In 1908, an anonymous author for *Current Literature* summarized the flaw in this path: "it is only talented mediocrity whose path can be smoothed by municipalities and millionaires."[44] Obviously, not all potential benefactors agreed with that author's assessment.

The failure of the New Theater did not signal the end of attempts to establish a theater free from the subjugation of the box office. However, a subtle shift occurred in the professional backgrounds of those with artistic control. The Chicago's Women's Club had planned a theater opening in 1906, just like the New Theater, but postponed until 1907. The group named Donald Robertson, with an established career as actor and director of more challenging, literary pieces, as the director of the Players' Theater. Like many of his later endeavors, this first project still involved the commercial theater world (the Shuberts provided the entire company and management for one endeavor), but Robertson always retained artistic control. He also allied himself more closely with other artists than those who served on the New Theater Board. In 1911, his company, the Drama Players, was supported by the Chicago Theater Society, an organization founded by the Cliff Dwellers with Hamlin Garland as secretary. Always endowment based, though never entirely successful, Robertson's projects reflect the continual refinement of his funding to provide buildings, maintenance monies, and audiences, into the 1920's.[45]

Theatrical history is more cognizant of another Chicago-based art theater, credited as part of the Little Theater Movement in the United States. In 1912, an art theater was opened by theater artists for a subscription audience: Maurice Browne's Chicago Little Theater. After their second season, Browne received an anonymous gift (endowment) that insured the continuation of that project and its well-documented influence on later projects. While no causal links remain between the New Theater and others that tried to follow its stated idealistic aims, the evolution still unfolds. From the New Theater's failure, more successful paths emerged, finding the pragmatic approach to ideal beauty predicted by Alexis de Tocqueville.

NOTES

1. Alexis de Tocqueville, *Democracy in America*, trans. Henry Reeve, vol. 2, 4th edition. New York: Langley, 1843) 75-76.
2. L. M. McCauley, "Municipal Art in Chicago: A Civic Renaissance Planned for the Western Metropolis," *The Craftsman* 9 (December 1905): 340, 321.
3. Helen Lefkowitz Horowitz, *Culture & the City: Cultural Philanthropy in Chicago from the 1880's to 1917* (Lexington, KY: Univ. Press of Kentucky, 1976) x.
4. Alexis de Tocqueville, *Democracy in America*, trans. Harvey C. Mansfield and Delba Winthrop (Chicago: Univ. of Chicago Press, 2000) 170-2.
5. Frederic Bartlett is the exception. Secure with inherited money, Bartlett is the only pure artist by profession. Information for both Table 1 and Table 2 came from several sources— John W. Leonard, ed. *The Book of Chicagoans: A Biographical Dictionary of Leading Living Men of the City of Chicago* (Chicago: A.N. Marquis, 1905); *Chicago Blue Book of Selected Names of Chicago and Suburban Towns for the Year Ending 1906* (Chicago: Chicago Directory, 1905); *University Club of Chicago Year Book for 1906-1907* (Chicago: Club House); *The Biographical Dictionary and Portrait Gallery of Representative Men of Chicago, Minnesota Cities and the World's Columbian Exposition* (Chicago: American Biographical Publishing, 1892); James Grant Wilson and John Fiske, eds., Charles Dick and James Edward Homans, eds., 1914 rev., *Cyclopedia of American Biography* (New York: Press Association Compilers, 1915-1931); Onwentsia Club Yearbooks for 1895, 1945, 1946, Lake Forest-Lake Bluff Historical Society, Marquis Who's Who, *Who Was Who in America*, vol. 1 (Chicago: Marquis Who's Who, 1963).
6. A partial list of subscribers is offered in L. France Pierce's article "Chicago to Have Two Subsidized Playhouses," *The Theatre Magazine* 6 (July 1906): 195.
7. Wallace Rice, "'The New Theater' of Chicago," *The World Today* 11 (August 1906): 846.
8. Information for Table 2 came from sources listed in note 5.
9. Multiple published and unpublished sources of information provided by Elizabeth Hedsund, Collections Manager of the Lake Forest-Lake Bluff Historical Society all use this phrase without citing an original source.
10. Quoted in Franz Schulze, *A Heritage: University Club of Chicago 1887-1987* (Chicago: University Club of Chicago, 1987) 29.
11. The endowment was collected using the Chicago Orchestra as a model. Rice, "'The New Theater' of Chicago," 845.
12. Victor Mapes, "An Art Theatre in Operation," *The Theatre Magazine* 7 (August 1907): 202.
13. J. Dennis Rich and Kevin L. Seligman,"The N ew Theatre of Chicago, 1906-1907," *Educational Theatre Journal* 26 (1974) 56 and L. France Pierce, "Chicago to Have Two Subsidized Playhouses" 195.
14. See *The Boys From Syracuse: The Shubertís Theatrical Empire* by Foster Hirsch for an in-depth examination of producing patterns and aesthetics.
15. *Garrick Theater Bound Programs*, vol. 2, Chicago Historical Society.
16. Wallace Rice, "'The New Theater' of Chicago," 845.

17. J. Dennis Rich and Kevin L. Seligman, "The New Theatre of Chicago, 1906-1907," 56-7.
18. Victor Mapes, "An Art Theatre in Operation," 202.
19. Ibid, 203.
20. Ibid, 205.
21. W. L. Hubbard, "The New Theater," *Chicago Daily Tribune*, October 9, 1906, 8.
22. "Brilliant Opening of Chicago's New Playhouse," *Chicago Record-Herald*, October 9, 1906, 8.
23. W. L. Hubbard, "The New Theater," 8.
24. J. Dennis Rich and Kevin L. Seligman, "The New Theatre of Chicago, 1906-1907," 61.
25. James O'Donnell Bennett, "Music and the Drama," *Chicago Record-Herald*, October 25, 1906, 8.
26. Victor Mapes retrospective, "An Art Theatre in Operation" claims that *The Spoilers* was chosen during the initial selection of plays (p. 205). Conversely, Rich and Seligman in "The New Theatre of Chicago, 1906-1907," claim that "confronted with the possibility of failure," Mapes acquired *The Spoilers* as a potential box office success (p. 61). Either way, it was a commercial melodrama.
27. "News of the Theaters," *Chicago Daily Tribune*, October 31, 1906, 8.
28. J. Dennis Rich and Kevin L. Seligman, "The New Theatre of Chicago, 1906-1907," 61.
29. Victor Mapes, An Art Theatre in Operation," 202-09.
30. W. L. Hubbard, "News of the Theaters," *Chicago Daily Tribune*, November 21, 1906, 8.
31. Victor Mapes, "An Art Theatre in Operation," 202.
32. Two articles present detailed accounts of the complete season, rise and fall, of the New Theater: Rich and Seligman listed in a previous note and James L. Highlander, "America's First Art Theatre: The New Theatre of Chicago," *Educational Theatre Journal* 11 (1959): 285-90.
33. "News of the Theaters" *Chicago Daily Tribune*, December 6, 1906, 10.
34. W. L. Hubbard, "News of the Theaters," *Chicago Daily Tribune*, December 20, 1906, 10.
35. James O'Donnell Bennett, "Music and the Drama," *Chicago Record-Herald*, January 3, 1907, 6 and January 16, 1907, 8.
36. W. L. Hubbard, "News of the Theaters," *Chicago Daily Tribune*, January 30, 1907, 8 and February 6, 1907, 8.
37. James L. Highlander, "America's First Art Theatre: The New Theatre of Chicago," 290.
38. "Frost Nips New Theatre," *Chicago Daily Tribune*, January 19, 1907, 3.
39. W. L. Hubbard, "Opening of New Theater Gives Promise of Much," *Chicago Tribune*, October 14, 1906, sec. X1 and "Failure of New Theater Surprise to Few Persons," *Chicago Tribune*, January 20, 1907, sec. X1.
40. "Plays & Players," *Chicago Tribune*, October 21, 1906, sec. X5.
41. Arthur T. Aldis, "Adventuring In the Drama," *The Drama* 7 (February 1917): 129-135.

42. L. France Pierce, "The First Municipal Theater in America," *The World To-day* 8 (June 1905): 664.
43. James L. Highlander, in "American's First Art Theatre: The New Theatre of Chicago," frames his history of events as a step in the evolution of the art theater in the United States. J. Dennis Rich and Kevin L. Seligman, in "The New Theatre of Chicago, 1906-1907," frame the inception of the New Theater as another failed attempt to have a national theater. I find the evidence more compelling for Highlander's thesis.
44. "The Chimera of a National Theater," *Current Literature* 44 (June 1908): 665.
45. I re-constructed Robertson's activities from the following sources, using multiple reports to confirm a timeline: Kenneth Sawyer Goodman, "The Chicago Theatre Society," *The Nation* 98, no. 254 (March 19, 1914): 308-9; "The Chicago Theatre Society," *The Dial* 51, no. 603 (August 1, 1911): 63-5; "Another Stage Experiment," *The Nation* 93 (July 13, 1911): 41; Hamlin Garland, "'Starring the Play,'" *The Nation* 93, no. 2403 (July 20, 1911): 54; L. France Pierce, "Chicago to Have Two Subsidized Playhouses," 194; "What Chicago's 'Drama Players' Did," *The Literary Digest* 44 (May 18, 1912): 1039-40; "The Upward Trend of the Theater in America," *Current Literature* 47 (December 1909): 673-5; Martyn Johnson, "The Chicago Theatre Society; A Step Toward the Future Theatre," *The Drama* 12 (November 1913): 194-99; David H. Wallace, "Donald Robertson, the Idealist," *The New York Dramatic Mirror* 70, no. 1817 (October 15, 1913): 1; Thomas Wood Stevens, "Robertson: A Record," *The Play-book* 1, no. 2 (May 1913): 3-9; Matthew White, Jr., "Chicago's Bid for Better Drama," *Munsey's Magazine* 46 (January 1912): 585-90; "The Chicago Civic Theatre," *The Drama* 13 (March 1923) 214 and 228; Hamlin Garland, "A New Idea in Theater Management," *Metropolitan Magazine* 35 (February 1912): 21-3; *New York Times*, "Drama Players for Lyric," November 2, 1911, http://www.proquest.com; *New York Times*, No Title, April 10, 1910: XX1, http://www.proquest.com; *New York Times*, "Donald Robertson Here for 'Beethoven,'" March 22, 1910, http://www.proquest.com; *New York Times*, "'Beethoven' at New Theatre," March 15, 1910, http://www.proquest.com; *New York Times*, "A Chat With Donald Robertson," April 17, 1910, http://www.proquest.com; *New York Times*, "Society at Home and Abroad," November 12, 1911, http://www.proquest.com; *New York Times*, "Chicago Opera Hurt by Ticket Scalping," November 22, 1911, http://www.proquest.com; *New York Times*, "'Joyous' Drama in Chicago," June 30, 1911, http://www.proquest.com; *New York Times*, "Ibsen Play Given by Drama Players," November 2, 1911, http://www.proquest.com; *New York Times*, "New Organization to Give Best Plays," September 18, 1911, http://www.proquest.com.

Kathy L. Privatt received her Ph.D. from the University of Nebraska-Lincoln in 1999, specializing in 20th century American theatre. Currently an Assistant Professor of Theatre Arts at Lawrence University in Wisconsin, she has presented at ATHE and in the history and pedagogy symposiums of MATC.

Theatre History Studies 24 (June 2004)

Christopher Smart's *Old Woman's Oratory* and the Patent Theatres: Legitimacy, Transgression, and "Rational Mirth"

NOEL CHEVALIER

First, a children's riddle-one that is neither exactly a riddle, nor entirely intended for children:

Like W------TON, in different dress,
  I either sex can ape,
And like her, all mankind confess,
  Have comeliness and shape:
Had she the innocence of me,
  And I her air and arts,
She would a perfect goddess be,
  And I should gain more parts.[1]

Buried within the pages of the first children's periodical, *The Lilliputian Magazine; or, The Young Gentleman and Lady's Golden Library* (1752), this riddle's solution unrealistically demands of its young readers an awareness both of the Drury Lane theatre company of the late 1740s and of the tradition of theatrical cross-dressing. The riddle, primarily a puff for *The Midwife* (1750-53), the adult-oriented miscellany written and edited by *The Lilliputian*'s editor, Christopher Smart, combines multiple layers of signification in an unusual piece of entertainment for this most unusual children's publication.

This poem is presented as the fourth of a series of "New Riddles, By Members of the Society" [i.e., subscribers to the magazine], and is attributed to "Master Hunter." Karina Williamson has noted that "Master Hunter" is Smart's nephew, also named Christopher.[2] The first three riddles in the series, all attributed to young girls, are answered in a poem, "The Last Ænigmas Answer'd," in the following issue. However, this fourth riddle is left unsolved. The solution, however, can be deduced from its first line. The elided name is fairly obviously Peg Woffington, a member of David Garrick's acting company at Drury Lane Theatre, who was celebrated for her skill in breeches parts, and who therefore specifies "different dress" as gender difference.[3] However, "I either sex can ape" can refer equally to a woman imitating a man (as with Woffington) or to a man imitating a woman, as is the case with the subject of the riddle. Adult readers in 1752 who knew anything about Smart could easily guess the subject of the riddle to be Mrs. Mary Midnight, the editor of *The Midwife* and mistress of ceremonies at *The Old Woman's Oratory*, the miscellany vaudeville show Smart conducted in the Little Haymarket Theatre from 1750 until his confinement for madness in 1756.[4] Knowing the solution also reveals the bawdy pun implied in the reference to "gain[ing] more parts." If the subject of the riddle were as good an actor as Woffington, she would, the poem declares, gain more roles; were she equally as good at crossing gender lines, should could "gain more parts" in the sense of assuming the phallus which exists within the breeches donned by the woman who assumes male roles.

The use of the cross-dressing Peg Woffington in the *Lilliputian* riddle is significant, since Woffington's assumption of male dress, a subversive act outside of its theatrical context, is politically neutralized and legitimized by her enacting this assumption within the licensed space of Drury Lane theatre. By extension, then, Woffington's act of (non)-transgression sanctions Smart's grotesque, freewheeling assortment of animal acts and musical virtuosi on saltboxes and spoons, all presided over by the transvestite figure of Smart/Mary Midnight. Smart's appropriation of Woffington's legitimacy is similar to his appropriation of legitimate literary figures in *The Midwife* itself, which combined serious essays, such as reprints of Johnson's Rambler numbers, with farcical *Gentleman's Magazine*-style reports on such matters as petrified turds.

The curious figure of Mrs. Midnight, and the magazine and vaudeville show she presided over, have received relatively little critical attention. Smart's biographer, Arthur Sherbo, sees Smart primarily as a great classical scholar who chose to fritter away his talent on ephemera until his mental breakdown and religious conversion. In fact, he seems almost embarrassed by the gusto with which Smart assumed the role of Mary Midnight,[5] even though Smart clearly regarded *The Old Woman's Oratory* as of equal or even greater importance than *The Midwife* itself. More recent critics, such as Robert Erickson in *Mother Midnight* (1986), have focused on the character of the wise old woman, such as Mrs. Midnight sometimes pretends to be, as a challenger of social norms. However, Ross King has noted that Smart's old woman "serves more conservative purposes,"[6] in effect to satirize female education and wisdom, and to underline the essential disorder that occurs when women rule. Fraser Easton, too, has remarked on how Smart reworks the transvestite figure of Mrs. Midnight in *Jubilate Agno*,[7] so that her transgressive nature is reined in by Smart's Christian purpose in the poem. Yet no one has yet specifically noted how Smart uses Mrs. Midnight both as a magazine editor and as a stage figure to engage the patent playhouses — specifically, to critique the patent theatre's failure to address the questions of theatrical freedom and cultural monopoly that were raised by the ultimate legitimization of theatrical culture in the Licensing Act of 1737. Smart's Mrs. Midnight is both a figure of disorder and misrule, but she is also a figure of reason, an arbiter from the margins of theatrical culture, who interposes to restore order in the theatre wars that frequently erupted between the two patent houses.

Mrs. Midnight, then, reminds us of the place of marginal and the illegitimate within a culture ruled by centrality and legitimacy. The need for legitimized theatre ostensibly grew out of a need to control potential political subversion in the playhouses, and to maintain social order. This locative aspect of legitimacy, however, was supplemented and reinforced in literary theory by a generic aspect: certain types of stage entertainment were deemed inappropriate for patent theatre houses, and therefore relegated to the unlicenced, illegitimate, bastard venues. In short, comedy, tragedy and opera became the exclusive property of the legitimate playhouses; other forms of entertainment were fit only for illegitimate venues. As far as the post-Licensing Act stage was concerned, legitimacy and authority had tangible representatives only within the walls of Drury Lane, Covent Garden and the Royal Opera House.

Under the Licensing Act, the patent theatres became *de facto* guardians of a high culture that became increasingly the property of a middle-class patronage who had the disposable time and money to spend on stage plays. In this way, legitimate plays could be treated as cultural commodities that reached their fullest expression only within the walls of the playhouse itself.[8] In reality, of course, the patent houses indulged in illegitimate genres all the time, though not without considerable grumbling about the need to mount pantomimes and musical variety shows mainly in order to keep the legitimate venues open. Richard Bevis, in *The Laughing Tradition*, notes that, "Then, as now Shakespeare was hard pressed to out draw a variety show"[9] Burlesque, farce, and even puppet-theatre offered audiences more diverting shows than straight comedy and tragedy. Bevis observes that the development of variety entertainment was "the most significant development on the eighteenth-century stage,"[10] because it revealed that the audiences that existed for these shows were not simply the uncultured who frequented fairground sideshow, but were the same audiences who attended the licensed playhouses. In the mind of apologists for the licensed stage, all this boiled down to a simple maxim: poverty of public taste generated the popularity of illegitimate entertainment. This maxim was often combined with a nostalgia-tinged corollary that asserted that, in more enlightened ages, comedy and tragedy used to be enough to satisfy the public.

Mrs. Midnight therefore appears transgressive primarily because she appears against a theatrical paradigm that constructs legitimacy primarily in terms of rigid classification, both of genre and of gender. In fact, legitimate theatre actually helped to create what Jane Moody terms "an illegitimate theatrical culture,"[11] by defining itself in terms of its antithesis. Legitimate theatre is respectable, serious, important, and lasting; illegitimate theatre is irresponsible, superfluous, superficial, and ephemeral. Smart interposes between this binary and attempts to undermine the monopoly of legitimacy held by the patent playhouses, while at the same time utilizing elements of illegitimacy for essentially legitimate ends.

In order to understand fully how Smart situated his vaudeville show within theatrical culture, it is important to trace Mrs. Midnight's origins in Smart's humor magazine, *The Midwife*. Originally created for *The Midwife* as its eidolon-editor, whose role was to gather together as many contradictory texts as she could find, ordered only by her always-tangible presence within the magazine itself. In doing so, Mrs. Midnight blurs the distinctions between literary and theatrical legitimacy and illegitimacy, between serious commentary and nonsense, between the respectable and the prurient. As Lance Bertelsen says of *The Midwife*, "In its ontological promiscuity . . . [it] suggests a world where conceptual boundaries are obscure and transitory, and where mad humor reigns."[12] The frontispiece to the collected edition of *The Midwife* (1753) cleverly embodies the transgressive nature of the magazine, and its origins in Grub Street. It is an astonishing image of two men in drag-ostensibly, Christopher Smart and John Newbery, the author/editor and publisher respectively-at work composing the magazine.[13] (See fig. 1) Neither of them attempts to appear as anything but transvestite men, although their postures suggest a naturalness that leads the viewer away from reading them as freakish. The Grub-Street nature of the whole production is signified by the close-stool next to the pen-holding figure on the left-presumably Smart-labelled, "The Jakes of Genius," a clear indication of at least one source of the magazine's inspiration. Smart, as Mrs. Midnight, normalizes what should be an unsettling, or even just plain funny, image.

By December 1751, however, Mrs. Midnight's textual self was supplemented with a performative self: Mrs. Midnight was incarnated on stage as another kind of "editor," the mistress of ceremonies of the outrageous variety show, titled *The Old Woman's Oratory*. The show played at both the Castle Tavern and the Haymarket Theatre during its first season, December 1751-May 1752; at its height, the show ran exclusively at the Haymarket for 68 performances between December 1752 and March 1753.[14] While the show was running, Smart continued issuing numbers of *The Midwife*, although he quickly began to use the magazine as a promotional vehicle for the show, while using the show itself as a source of material for *The Midwife*. Even after *The Midwife* ceased publication in 1753, the show continued under various names. *The Old Woman's Oratory* was, by far, its most frequent title, but by 1752 it had also acquired the name *Mrs. Midnight's Grand Concert*. During the summer of 1754 the show was known as *The British Roratory*, while occasional titles such as *Caudle* and *Sack-posset*— clearly derived from Samuel Foote's vaudeville shows, *Tea* and *Chocolate* — associated the show with warming, restorative (but, unlike Foote's, alcoholic) drinks.

Stage-show and magazine therefore coexist to act as a context for each other. Recognizing this dual nature of the Mrs. Midnight character is also important to understanding the show's relationship to legitimate theatrical culture. While it was common for legitimate plays to be published as reading texts-in fact, in the case of censored or suppressed plays, publication was the only medium in which these plays could appear-illegitimate shows, vaudevilles, and variety shows were rarely recast as printed texts. Samuel Foote's progress from vaudeville director to patent-house playwright may serve as an example. Foote's satirical revue, *Diversions of the Morning* was initially staged at the Haymarket since 1747.[15] Although Foote and Smart never collaborated formally, they do pay tribute to each other: both use the name "Pentweazle," with Foote preferring the spelling "Pentweazel" (Foote's Lady Pentweazel, interestingly enough, was also a transvestite role). Smart used the name "Fardinando Foot" as one his many pseudonyms, while Foote introduced a character named "Smart" in his prologue to *The Minor*. The two authors also share a similar approach to satire. Matthew Kinservik has shown that Foote's satire quickly moves away from the tradition of direct attack on recognizable individuals-the mode of satire that led Fielding to be dubbed "the English Aristophanes"-to a less subversive brand of mimicry that satisfied the terms of the Licensing Act and made satire "tolerable" to the new theatrical world order. As Kinservik notes, "Foote's satire and the Licensing Act were able to coexist to the mutual satisfaction of both satirist and censors."[16]

Figure 1. Ostensibly, Christopher Smart and John Newbery composing *The Midwife*. Courtesy of the Thomas Fisher Rare Book Library.

Foote, however, quickly moved away from pure vaudeville to scripted, narrative farces that combined elements of the early variety shows reworked into legitimized forms for the patent houses. Although related to the Haymarket show, *An Auction of Pictures, Taste* was staged at Drury Lane on January 11, 1752, as an afterpiece to Edward Young's tragedy *The Revenge.* Despite this rocky start[17], Foote followed up with the well-received *Englishman in Paris* at Covent Garden in March 1753, and a new version of *Diversions*, called *Mr. Foote Gives Tea* or simply *Tea at Drury Lane* in November, this time with a Fieldingesque satirical rehearsal in Act II. At this same time, Smart continued his *Old Woman's Oratory* at the Haymarket, with no thought of adapting the shows for the patent houses. My point here is that Foote's printed works begin only with plays staged at the patent playhouses, while Smart steadfastly remained on the fringes of theatrical legitimacy.

Although Smart and his creation stand on the fringes of the theatre world, even the opening number of *The Midwife* establishes Mrs. Midnight as a figure directly involved even in that world's internecine quarrels. The verse selections in this number (I.i.36-40), if read as a sequence, form a commentary on a brief theatre war between Drury Lane and Covent Garden which took place in late September and early October 1750. Smart reprints both David Garrick's "New Occasional Prologue," spoken 8 September 1750, and Spranger Barry's prologue reworking of the same theme delivered exactly one month later at Covent Garden. He then uses these two Prologues as the occasion for a third, in which "either Mr. *Garrick* or Mr. *Barry*, or both" (39) appear as apologists for the theatre war, each blaming the other for the wrong. Mrs. Midnight, in her first "stage appearance," interposes between the two:

> Great is the Noise, and clamorous is the Clash
> When two such *weighty Wights* together dash!
> Wit's Mirth oft takes its Rise from *Folly*'s Ire,
> As *Flint* strikes *Steel*, and Quarrels into *Fire.*
> I, even I, old Woman, as I am,
> Have just Pretence your Poetry to damn;
> To fix the Standard between wrong and right,
> And call you both a couple of---Good Night.
> (ll. 13-20)

The two warring parties leave the stage, after which Mrs. Midnight comments on her role as mediator in a curious metaphor:

> While *Garrick* smart, and blustring Barry jar,
> Like rough and smooth, or Oil and Vinegar,
> I, like an hard-boil'd Egg come in between,
> And mix their Matters, as I intervene;
> I form (*for Rhyme's sake* add, with JUST INTENTION)
> Betwixt the fighting Fluids a Convention;
> Which being thus conjoin'd, please ev'ry Palate,
> And make a pretty Figure in a Sallad. (21-28)

Mrs. Midnight refers to herself as a "convention," in the sense of an agent that brings together various parties for a common purpose, an emulsifier between disparate elements like oil and vinegar.[18]

The term "convention" suggests that Mrs. Midnight regards her magazine as a neutral ground where the conflict may be successfully resolved. The magazine, therefore, usurps the authority and autonomy each manager would maintain in his own space. Smart, as Smart, holds no power among these two theatrical demagogues, but as Mrs. Midnight he/she can appropriate the conflict, embodied in the two Occasional Prologues actually spoken at both theatres, and can play out the process in her own context and on her own terms. In this poem, then, the legitimacy of the patent theatres, and the power the both Garrick and Barry derive from their legitimized status, is both revealed to be problematic and divisive; at the same time, the solution can be found only within the pages of Smart/Mrs. Midnight's illegitimate publication.

Having neutralized the authority of Garrick and Barry in her Prologue, Mrs. Midnight offers her own comment of Garrick and Barry's theatre war. At the beginning of the sequence Smart reprints his own ballad "The Distressed Damsel," which in this context can be read as an ironic allusion to *Romeo and Juliet* itself, since it is the song of a young girl who, at the age of fifteen, bemoans the fact that she is still a virgin. The distressed virgin of the ballad echoes the character portrayed in the theatre; the distressed actress representing Juliet is likewise condemned repeatedly to lamenting her virginity and participating in the tragedy that arises because of it. Rounding out the whole sequence is a witty quatrain, signed "I H-----t," that had also appeared in the *Daily Advertiser*, "On the Run of *Romeo and Juliet*":

Well--what's to Night? says angry Ned,
    As up from Bed he rouses:
Romeo again--and shakes his Head,
    *Ah! Pox on both your Houses! (40)

The lines refer to the fact that since 28 September the two theatres had run rival productions of *Romeo and Juliet*, each house offering added features to the play not found in the other's production. The speaker of the poem, representing the opinion of many theatre patrons, expresses his exasperation with both theatres for continuing the run of these productions to the extent that play-going has become boring for regular playgoers.

In addition to commenting on the banality of the competition that is inevitable with only two patent theatres, Smart also used his miscellany to challenge conventional notions of the hierarchy of dramatic genres, in the guise of providing puffs for shows at Drury Lane. For example, early numbers of *The Midwife* include a number of references to Henry Woodward's afterpiece, *Queen Mab*, which opened on December 26, 1750 and ran until the end of the season. *The Midwife* I.iv (published early in 1751) opens with "A Dissertation on Dumb Rhetoric," which is essentially an account of the pantomime designed partly as a puff for the company, partly as a genre study of pantomime itself. He concentrates on the "Machinery" — both the mimed action and the stagecraft — which "will always please more with its Novelty, than offend with its Absurdity" (146). He also notes that "*The Talismans*, the *Genii*, and many other Things out of Nature, afford astonishing Delight to young Readers, and I own I like them to this Day" (146). The pleasure of novelty and the delight in the fantastic are reason enough not to condemn pantomimes as "unmeaning Things," as Smart argues.

For all his attacks on the cultural snobbery of the patent houses, however, Smart is well aware that he is using his magazine and his transgressive Mrs. Midnight persona to promote as well as to satirize. Smart picks on Garrick and Drury Lane in part because he was a member of Garrick's social circle.[19] The satires of Garrick are good-natured jests, not serious challenges to Garrick's authority. Smart sometimes puffed Garrick's plays in *The Midwife*, and even included a "Letter to Mr. Garrick"[20] that encourages him to revive more of Fletcher's plays, and to leave off plays such as Edward Ravenscroft's *The London Cuckolds*, which had been performed at both Drury Lane and Covent Garden on October 29, 1750.[21]

The prologue from *The Midwife*'s inaugural number quoted above demonstrates how the Mrs. Midnight figure, although at this stage still confined to the pages of the magazine, had already been conceived as participating on stage. The stage show, therefore, was less an opportunistic, moneymaking venture for Smart, as Sherbo suggests, as it was a fulfilment of ideas present even in the magazine's opening number. Like *The Midwife*, the *Old Woman's Oratory* recognized its mission promote diverting spectacle, using its illegitimate status seemingly to challenge the authority of the patent theatres, and apparently to suggest that illegitimate entertainment offers opportunities to erase boundaries, such as those that govern gender roles, that legitimate drama now has to reinforce. Smart's use of ephemeral, unsophisticated, and unusual entertainments was popular, and predictably censured by the established theatres for its lack of seriousness. He used the orations featured in the show as opportunities to speak on a variety of subjects, often in defense of the principles of the Oratory itself and to attack the established playhouses for indulging in similar entertainments, while both bemoaning the need to do so and monopolizing main piece genres. Yet the Orations do not carry the carnivaleqsue sense of inverting the established order; if anything, they are more a plea for acceptance of hitherto rejected forms of entertainment. In Mrs. Midnight's world, nothing is legitimate or illegitimate; her attack on the patent theatres is primarily against the value-judgements themselves, not the authority that sanctions them.

Ironically, however, despite Smart's apparent promotion of "dumb Rhetorick" as a legitimate means of communication, our only lasting traces of the substance of *The Old Woman's Oratory* come not from the musical numbers or the animal acts, but from the orations and poems that were first spoken in the show, then printed. Even detached from the context of the show, these pieces are fascinating in their own right. For example, Mrs. Midnight's Inaugural Oration, delivered at the Haymarket on December 27, 1751,[22] outlines the principles upon which the show was based. She declares that she intends

> To raise a Fund of rational Mirth, and to support and variegate it with perpetual Novelty. . . . To despise every thing that is really despisable, and admire every thing that is truly admirable. . . . *To be a Citizen with Politeness and a Courtier with Integrity*, or (that I may comprehend all these Predicaments in one Word) to be *Mary Midnight, Author of the Old Woman's*

Magazine.[23]

The term "rational Mirth" is striking-rationality is the antithesis of the carnivalesque, while "Mirth" suggests something pleasant, yet safe. Like Sgt. Pepper's band, Mrs. Midnight's show is "guaranteed to raise a smile," but do little more. Despite its comically overblown style, this inaugural oration reads like a manifesto of one who represents order rather than chaos, who reveals her transgressive persona to be yet another costume.

This idea is reinforced in the "Prologue to Mrs. Mary Midnight's Oratory,"[24] also delivered on December 27, in which Mrs. Midnight declares her principles in verse:

To brand the Murderer of Common Sense,
With all his accessary Audience;
To give up Infamy to Ridicule,
And in impartial Colours paint the Fool;
....
This is our Task-And if we shou'd succeed,
'Twill be a true *Herculean* Feat indeed.
(ll. 1-4; 11-12).

Again, the emphasis on promoting common sense, instead of misrule, suggests that Mrs. Midnight is less a carnivalesque construction and is looking to use the madness of her Oratory in the service of establishing reason.

Part of Mrs. Midnight's point, of course, is that the social world outside of the Oratory is so disordered that only a carnival can set it right:

But lest the manly Miss, or Female Beau,
Shou'd think our Satire Nonsense, Stuff and Low;
Shou'd 'gainst poor Salt-Box arm their Critic Rage,
And hiss the harmless Jew-Strump off the Stage.
We between whiles ('tis hop'd without Offence)
Shall introduce that honest Exile SENSE.
Whom, tho' he's *English*, Beaus must needs prefer,
He'll seem to them-so like a Foreigner.
(ll. 14-20)

Mrs. Midnight here ironically attacks the fashionable world for its inversion of gender roles (the "manly Miss" and the "female Beau"), suggesting that her show, not those of the patent theatres, can alone restore order. Instead of being transgressive, then, Mrs. Midnight repeatedly speaks from a position of order, sense, and reason.

Finally, Mrs. Midnight justified her character in a speech delivered January 14, 1752: "A Defence of her Own Existence."[25] Why does Mrs. Midnight need to defend herself at all? Ostensibly, to answer remarks made by John Henley himself — the "*Stentorian* Orator . . . in the University of *Clare-Market*" — who "has barbarously endeavour'd to annihilate, or rather to metamorphose" Mrs. Midnight's existence (49). Her fear of metamorphosis is a fear that Henley's attempt to identify her as "a Printer

. . . a Bookseller . . . and a Fellow of a College" (49) — that is, as either Newbery or Smart[26] — will rip off the transgressive mask that enacts the representation of the author/editor by identifying her as more conventional than she appears. She declares that she will not "suffer Logick to destroy my being," and insists that she is not, as Henley claims, a man dressed as a woman, but is "*ipso facto*, and *bona fide*, an old Woman" (50).

Mrs. Midnight's need to defend her existence can be read as an affirmation of an authority that appears not to have been taken for granted. Henley's attack on the "truth" of Mrs. Midnight's identity is more than an attempt to provoke the actor in the costume to reveal himself. It is an attempt to declare Mrs. Midnight's authority on the stage invalid by arguing that, since there is no representation of who she is, there can be no truth in what she says. Henley's desire to discover the author behind the name, to interpret the text by appealing to the authorial intention behind it, ignores the whole process of representation upon which both the Oratory and the miscellanies are based.

Mrs. Midnight's response to Henley, apart from offering a few easy cuffs at a figure who was largely a joke anyway, does suggest a certain uneasiness with the persona Smart has constructed for himself. At the same time, Smart is willing, in the context of the show itself, to play with the idea of revealing his dual nature. A "Prologue" featured in the Oratory show reveals Mrs. Midnight as sexually ambivalent. From hints given in the prologue, the situation appears to be that Mrs. Midnight has appeared on stage not as the *bona fide* old woman, but as Christopher Smart, revealed as a "Fellow of a College" in petticoats:

> Well, Ladies, what d'ye think of me To-night?
> Say, Don't you think I make a shocking Sight?
> By various Arts we various Creatures ape,
> And metamorphose into twenty Shapes;
> Sometimes in Breeches, then in Petticoats again,
> And all your Loves and Favours to obtain;
> Then let not our Endeavours prove in vain?
> Don't think because I Petticoats put on
> I cannot act the Part a Lover can,
> And shew myself sometimes a brisk young Man?
> To serve a Turn I can my Coats lay by,
> And with the best that's here my Manhood try.
> Then pray what needs this mighty Pother then,
> Without my Cloaths, I'm like another Man.
> Nay, never let a Blush your Thoughts disguise,
> You all love Men, — I see it in your Eyes.
> But lest some dull censorious Fool shou'd say,
> *God's Curse*; such Transformations spoil the Play.
> Let 'em fret on, I care not for their Noise;
> I heed them not, so I have your Applause.
> But hold! There's one Thing I've forgot to say;
> Besides, there is my Compliments to pay; —
> First to the *Ladies* I my Thanks return,

And this kind Favour I'll for ever own;
And if you ever should in Wedlock join,
Then may your Husbands to your Will combine.
Now for the *Men* — Faith, I don't know what to say,
Unless I chuse the good old-fashion'd Way,
And thank you for the Favour done To-day.
However, one I'll chuse, do what you can,
And he that claps me most shall be the Man.[27]

Although she declares that she, like any actor, can "metamorphose into twenty Shapes," Mrs. Midnight is careful to point out that the transformation is temporary, as the circumstances of the role demand. Mrs. Midnight teases the audience further, by suggesting that the figure on stage may not be the Midwife revealed in her true nature, but merely an old woman donning breeches for the occasion. The ambiguity is furthered by her declaration that "without my Cloaths, I'm like another Man" (14), an echo of the "more parts" of the *Lilliputian Magazine* riddle, this time gained not by assuming a breeches role, but by eliminating dress altogether, to reveal that "natural" signifier of masculinity that clothes mask. Mrs. Midnight ends her prologue ambiguously, with a bawdy pun that again echoes the *Lilliputian* riddle. On the surface, this prologue is a conventional call for applause; however, the line "[h]e that claps me most shall be the Man" also suggests ambiguity of sexuality as well as of gender. After having assured the ladies that, because he wears petticoats, he "cannot act the Part as Lover can," he now suggests that he is available to the men as well, adding the ironic suggestion that whoever is successful in infecting him with syphilis ("he that claps me most") shall both "his Manhood try" and reveal his homosexuality. This prologue, therefore, out of all the pieces to survive from *The Old Woman's Oratory*, most clearly reveals how the Mrs. Midnight character plays with signifiers of gender and sexuality, but at the same time seeks to point out how those signifiers do have definite signifieds outside of the space of the theatre. Mrs. Midnight does not want "Logick to destroy [her] being" when the logic means dismantling the persona; yet she is all for raising "rational Mirth" within the context of the show itself.

The Old Woman's Oratory continued running until the early 1760s, and was successful enough to spawn *Mrs. Midnight's Orations* (1763), a collection of reprints from *The Midwife* and hitherto unpublished pieces.[28] The collection provides a number of important texts that, apart from *The Midwife*, offer the only record of texts performed at the Oratory.[29] The texts, however, stand at the fringes of the Smart canon in part because the collection itself bears little evidence of any connection with him. It is an odd volume in many ways. The title page lists no publisher; instead, it declares that it was "printed for the Editor." However, the editorship is left anonymous, even though this anonymous editor still saw fit to include a dedication to Lady Carolyn Seymour (3-6). Moreover, the volume seems to have been sold by subscription, but the list of subscribers is omitted. Such an omission would seem to eliminate one of the attractions of selling a volume by subscription, but the editor assures the reader that this was done "at the Desire of many of the Encouragers of this Work" (2). Even the dedication to Lady Carolyn Seymour seems formulaic, and indicates no trace of her having approved the dedication.

The Orations continue the attack on legitimate playhouses that Smart had begun in *The Midwife*. In *The Orations*, the attack centers predominantly on Garrick, who had actually been impressed by Smart's portrayal of Mary Midnight, and had presented a benefit night for him at Drury Lane. A "Prologue" to the Oratory ("When MARY MIDNIGHT first her Rostrum rear'd),[30] redefines Mrs. Midnight's relationship with the company of Drury Lane on the basis of her success with the show. Garrick, presented as the leader of "A Herd of Heroes arm'd with *Tragic Rage*" (5), addressing his company before an assault on Mrs. Midnight herself:

Shall I! the Admiration of the Stage,
Submit to Female Impotence and Age,
Be brav'd thus by a Beldam and her Doxies,
And play my LEAR to empty Pit and Boxes! (9-12)

Other members of the company offer their opinions both of Mrs. Midnight and her show. That assigned to Henry Woodward, author of *Queen Mab*, is particularly interesting, as it addresses the charge of nonsense of which Mrs. Midnight seems particularly proud:

Then in comes HARRY with his jemmy Switch,
Egad, Egad, I think she is a Witch,
That with her sort of Charm, charms People's Pence,
And cheats 'em with her Sort of Sort of Sense.
(32-35)

Here again, Smart's celebration of "unmeaning Things" comes under attack, but the established theatre's fear of the old woman's show derives not from its lack of sense, but from its popularity.

The Drury Lane actors play fictionalized versions of themselves in a mock-epic scene that parodies pre-battle conference scenes such as those featured in *The Iliad* or *Paradise Lost*. Instead of resolving their differences and joining to fight their common enemy, however, the actors begin a vicious fight among themselves:

With that a Battle furiously began,
The Little Hero [i.e. Garrick?] prov'd a mighty Man.
His well-try'd Steel he dealt with sudden Force,
And ev'ry Chief translated to a Cor'se:
Heaps lay on Heaps, the slaughter'd and the slain,
They drank, fought, dy'd, — then rose, fought, dy'd again. (42-47)

As befits a battle among actors, all the deaths described are mere stage-deaths, with each corpse rising and dying several times to simulate a battle between two large armies using only a handful of actors. Mrs. Midnight addresses the audience directly in the closing lines, to ask for protection for "ev'ry thing she's writ" (56). Her "Rostrum," because of its popularity, emerges as a victorious challenger to the established theatre of Garrick. Even the flattering remarks made about Garrick in *The Midwife* are now restructured in this prologue. Garrick is presented as a stodgy leader of a group of actors imitating epic figures; a buffoon in neoclassical dress. Garrick cannot bear the idea of a rival theatre featuring performers billed as "virtuosi" on comic instruments like the spoons or the saltbox, or "specialty" acts like Mons. Timbertoe, the wooden-legged dancer.

Apollo is featured in another occasional prologue attack on Garrick's theatre ("Mrs. Midnight enters with a WHISTLE, or CAT-CALL," 34-36). Here Mrs. Midnight brings a cat-call on stage and presents it as a device to introduce an allegorical tale: she relates how such a cat-call once dropped into the midst of Apollo and the Muses, who are informed by Momus that "'twas what the *Bucks* of this wise Age/Had form'd to fright the Muses from the Stage" (19-20). Erato indignantly points out that "what for Years they've written and have said/Has been without our Influence or Aid" (22-23). However, it is Apollo who is most indignant, and who issues a strong warning to the established theatres:

> "Go, Let your *Rich*'s and your *Garrick*'s know
> "That I'll take Vengeance, if they serve me so.
> "Shall I become a Laugh for Cits and Spouses?
> "Not I indeed! *A Pox of both your Houses* —
> ....
> "I'll pop on 'em from the *Zodiac* reeking,
> "And set them all a squalling and a squeaking."
> (41-45, 54-55).

Apollo's disdain for "Cits and Spouses" suggests that Garrick's theatre, even in its legitimacy, has been catering too much to middle-class taste — specifically, to the taste of those who expect the theatre to provide safe, respectable drama, with nothing new or daring or illegitimate.

The ambiguity of the Mrs. Midnight character reflects Smart's own ambiguous relationship with literary and theatrical legitimacy. Although lauded as a classical scholar, and clearly marked by Newbery as a rising poetic star, Smart seemingly wasted his talent on silly ephemera like *The Old Woman's Oratory*. Although he poked fun at Garrick numerous times, he retained enough of Garrick's friendship for him to offer Smart a benefit during his confinement. Finally, Smart himself, after his religious conversion, reconsidered his role as poetic transgressor and his involvement with the stage. Smart's apparent repudiation of the stage in *Jubilate Agno* (B.345) declares that "For all STAGE-Playing is Hypocrisy and the Devil is the master of their revels." Smart, however, is not Jeremy Collier; his attacks on the stage are not a commentary on immorality and profaneness. Smart's predominant theme in *Jubilate Agno* is praise and rejoicing; stage-playing, as conceived by the patent houses, emphasizes strictness of form, and concedes too much to secular authority for its legitimacy. The patent houses disallow the kind of exuberant, extemporaneous creativity that characterized Mrs. Midnight's shows, and that characterizes *Jubilate Agno* itself. This line quoted above occurs within the context of a discussion of the use of applause to be directed solely to the glory of God (B.343-45); the whole sequence reflects Smart's redefinition of himself in terms of his religious conversion and his confinement for madness. Smart does not merely repudiate aspects of his earlier life in *Jubilate Agno*; rather he rethinks them, and attempts a revision that will transform, though not abandon, all that he had previously stood for. Smart's concern in the poem is not merely to assert his authority through a different costume, but to transfer that authority to the supreme being, and to justify his resistance to conventions and his love of wordplay as acts of poetic praise.

NOTES

1. Christopher Smart, *The Lilliputian Magazine* (London, 1751), 47.
2. Karina Williamson, *The Poetical Works of Christopher Smart, Volume IV: Miscellaneous Poems, English and Latin* (Oxford: Clarendon Press, 1987) 4:395-96. Williamson notes that Betty Rizzo has attributed the poem to Smart, in part because the "Master Hunter" listed as the author was five years old in 1751. Christopher Hunter later edited *Poetical Works of the Late Christopher Smart* (Reading, 1791).
3. The reference may be further obscured by the fact that, in 1751, Woffington was living in Dublin. Her days of greatest fame were behind her, and it is unlikely that any child reader of *The Lilliputian Magazine* would know of her.
4. The show, however, kept running while Smart was confined, although it is not known who continued it.
5. Sherbo, *Christopher Smart, Scholar of the University* (East Lansing: Michigan State University, 1967), 75.
6. Ross King, "Insolent Women and Crest-Fallen Men: Christopher Smart, *The Midwife*, and Literary Transvestism." *The Glasgow Review* 2, 1993. http://www.arts.gla.ac.uk/SESLL/STELLA/COMET/glasgrev/issue2/king.htm#Title
7. See Fraser Easton, "Christopher Smart's Cross-Dressing: Mimicry, Depropriation, and Jubilate Agno." *Genre: Forms of Discourse and Culture*, 31:3-4 (1998 Fall-Winter), 193-243.
8. However, the idea of a fixed text as an additional commodity — the play published for reading purposes — also widened the gap between legitimate and illegitimate theatre; shows such as *The Old Woman's Oratory* were generally not printed and sold as reading texts.
9. Richard Bevis, *The Laughing Tradition* (Athens: University of Georgia Press, 1980), 65.
10. *Laughing Tradition*, 65.
11. Jane Moody, *Illegitimate Theatre in London 1770-1840.* (Cambridge: Cambridge University Press, 2000), 10.
12. Lance Bertelsen, "Journalism, Carnival, and Jubilate Agno" *ELH*, Vol. 59, No. 2. (Summer, 1992), 367. *The Oratory* he delightfully calls "street theatre [moved] indoors" (369).
13. This image is reproduced in Mahony and Rizzo, *Christopher Smart: An Annotated Bibliography* (New York: Garland Press, 1984), xxiv.
14. During this season, the show also featured an "Animal Pantomime."
15. Kinservik also notes that Foote's variety show was one of several staged in London at the time: Goodman's Fields, Sadler's Wells, and the New Theatre, Lemon St, among others, all saw concerts or revues staged.
16. Matthew Kinservik. *Discplining Satire: The Censorship of Satiric Comedy on the*

Eighteenth-Century London Stage. (Lewisburg: Bucknell University Press, 2002), 135.
17. *The London Stage* records an extensive note from Richard Cross that recounts how Taste was almost damned at its premiere, and how Foote himself played the part of the unscrupulous art dealer, Puff, after removing Richard Yates from the role.
18. Smart's use of this term in a culinary sense is not found in the OED, and may be a unique usage.
19. James Boswell records a number of anecdotes of Smart, mostly as told by Johnson. Frances Burney, too, recalls meeting Smart a few years before his death: in his youth he had been close friends with Charles Burney.
20. *Midwife* I.ii.87-88
21. Smart is obviously carrying on the same criticism of the patent theatres that he began in the previous issue. If both Drury Lane and Covent Garden are presenting the same play on the same night, then what option does the poor playgoer have? Fortunately, *The London Cuckolds* was played at both houses only on October 29.
22. *Midwife*, III.ii.37-42. The show at which the Inauguration Speech was delivered was actually the second night of the *Oratory*, the first night having been at the Castle Tavern on December 3.
23. *Midwife*, III.ii.39
24. *Midwife*, III.ii.57-58. See also Williamson, *Poetical Works Volume IV*, 388-89. Williamson includes this with the "uncertain" poems, mostly because it is unsigned. However, there is no compelling reason to believe it is not Smart's.
25. *Midwife*, III.ii.49-50
26. Smart was proud of identifying himself as "Scholar of the University" and as "Fellow of Pembroke-College Cambridge."
27. *Mrs. Midnight's Orations, and other Select Pieces* (London, 1763), 58-59.
28. The reprinted pieces are not necessarily those delivered at the Oratory, such as the fables, "The Bag-Wig and the Tobacco-Pipe" and "The Tea-Pot and the Scrubbing-Brush." Both of these poems had appeared in *The Midwife*; "The Bag-Wig" had even been reprinted in Smart 1752 *Poems on Several Occasions*. Their inclusion in the Orations was therefore presumably to increase the connection of this volume with Smart, and to provide purchasers with familiar titles.
29. The volume was privately printed and sold for Smart's benefit, probably, as Karina Williamson suggests, by John Newbery and Richard Rolt, Smart's co-editor on The Universal Visiter. See Williamson, *Poetical Works Vol. 4*, 400. It is difficult to speculate about Smart's intentions in either the texts or the volume as a whole, since it is possible that he may not have written the poems, edited the volume, or even known of its existence (he was still in confinement when it was issued). Scholarly opinion covers a wide range of possibilities: Sherbo believes the Smart wrote and edited the entire collection, while Williamson rejects the pieces for inclusion in Volume IV of *The Poetical Works*, mostly on the basis that there are no "reliable criteria" — by which I assume she means external evidence — for sorting out the canonical from the non-canonical pieces. It seems likeliest that the volume combines pieces Smart wrote for the show after *The Midwife* had ceased publication with pieces written by other hands after Smart was confined. Given that the collection has close ties to Smart, the pieces are a substantial body of "doubtful" attributions, and Williamson does readers a disservice by not including them.

30. *Mrs. Midnight's Orations,* 13-15.

Noel Chevalier is Assistant Professor of English at Luther College, University of Regina. He has edited David Garrick and George Colman's *The Clandestine Marriage* and other eighteenth century plays for Broadview Press. He has also published articles on Christopher Smart's *Jubilate Agno* and Frances Burney's *A Busy Day*, and is currently undertaking a study of representations of mercantilism in eighteenth century comedy.

Theatre History Studies 24 (June 2004)

Performance Practices of [Living] Open -Air Museums (And a New Look at "Skansen" in American Living Museum Discourse)

SCOTT MAGELSSEN

The silky white ribbon grew ever narrower as it slipped off the wooden spoon and drizzled into the bowl below. (See fig. 1) Despite the two-foot drop, the liquid maintained the integrity of its unbroken column all the way down. This is *long milk*, I am told by a hostess in the garb of a nineteenth-century Swedish farmworker. The food, she says—a sort of cross between yogurt and spoiled milk—gets its name from this physical property that she demonstrates several times a day for visitors to Skansen, the acclaimed open-air museum of Swedish life and culture in Stockholm. The nineteenth-century residents of this now-restored farmhouse would have made a daily meal of long milk, along with dried fish, cheese, and a hard-tack made with thirty-percent birch bark (in order to help spread the food stores out over the long winter months). Examples of these items are spread out on the table in front of her. "Do you ever eat this food?" I ask. "Yes, sometimes," she smiles, "It's not too bad."

This interchange, representative of thousands of similar ones that take place each summer at Skansen, happened in July of 2002 on my visit to the international tourist destination. I was there after four years of researching the ways in which American "living museums" negotiate the course between traditional display and the relatively recent performance practices of first-person costumed interpretation (role-playing), as a way of constructing historical narratives for visitors. Skansen has been posited in museum discourse as the world's first open air museum and, consequently, the inspiration for those that followed in Europe and abroad. One contrast between American museums and this Swedish model, though, is immediately clear. While the costumed hostess in Skansen remained in third-person, that is, telling me about the lives of nineteenth-century Swedish farmers, but not pretending to be one herself, American museums considered by scholars to be the most advanced in living history practices employ *first-person* interpreters. (See fig. 2)—Which means that if you go to the 1627 Pilgrim Village at Plimoth Plantation, say, you will encounter English Separatists who will tell you not only how they prepared their food, but who is coming over to eat it, and how much they miss their kitchens back in England.

Is the reason Skansen lacks first-person interpretation because it has fallen behind in museum evolution? Has Skansen plateaued at an early stage of development while its successors continue to add more advanced first-person, living interpretation to their

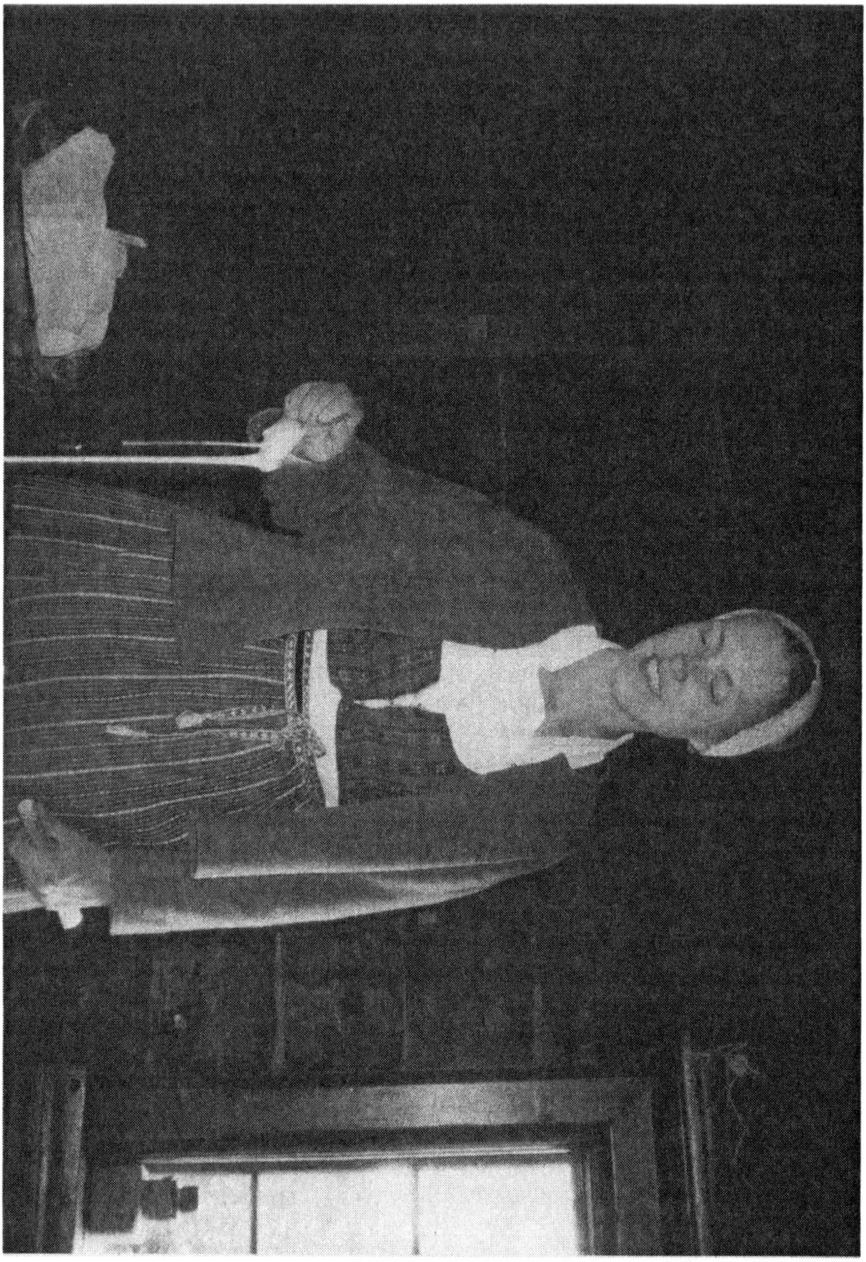

Figure 1. A costumed hostess demonstrates long milk at Skansen. June 2002. All illustrations courtesy of the author.

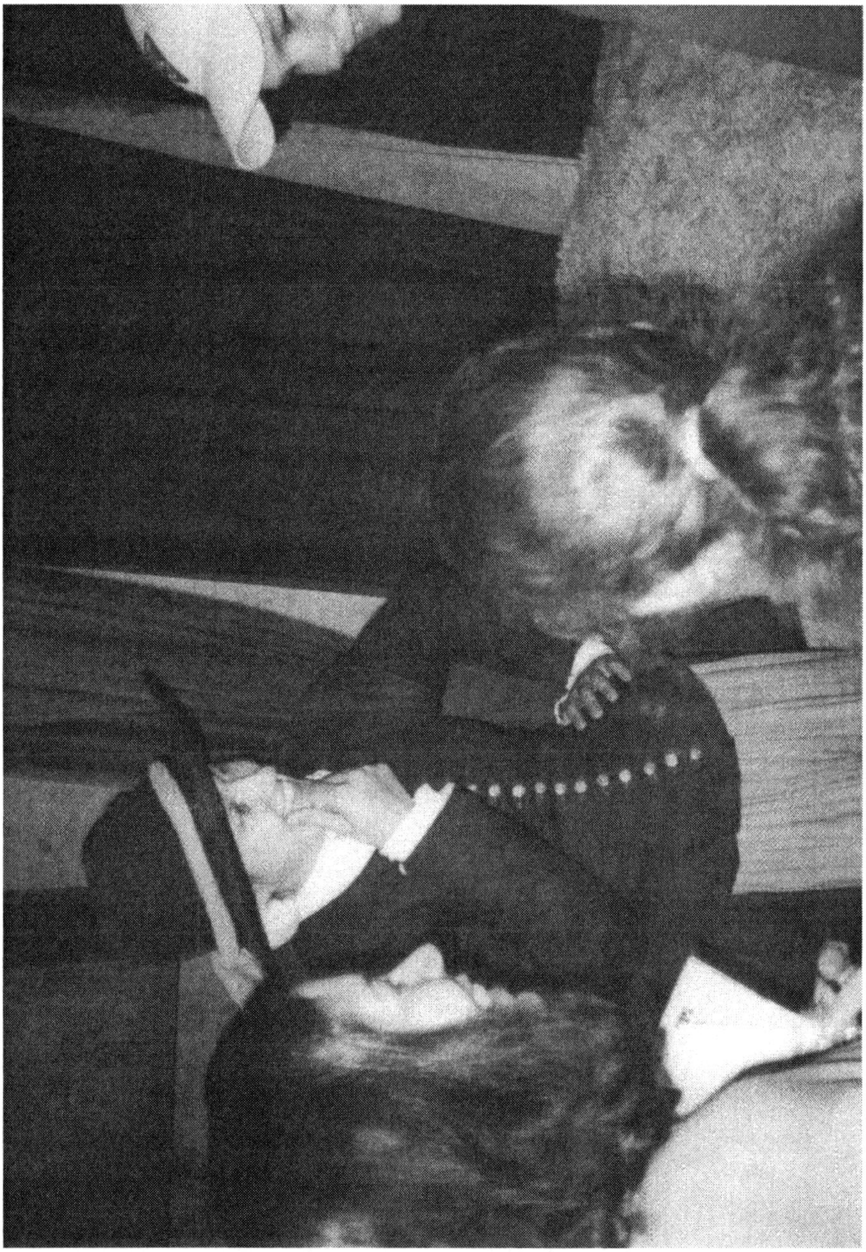

Figure 2. A first-person interpreter interacts with visitors at Plimoth Plantation. June, 2000.

programming? This seems to be the argument put forth by scholars like Jay Anderson.[1] I suggest that the problem is not that Skansen is somehow behind in the business of history museum performance, but that the way it has been positioned in discourse by people like Anderson sets it up as disappointment, precisely because it does not meet the standards he establishes. (See fig. 3) If living museums, in their fullest incarnation, are supposed to create three-dimensional historical *milieu* that visitors can enter in order to encounter the past as if they have just stepped from a "time machine," a museum like Skansen that does not feature character interpreters seems unfinished—underdeveloped. It becomes quickly apparent to the visitor, however, that Skansen is *not* trying to be a *living museum*. Nor does it claim to be in its literature or signage. It is also clear that Skansen is not a leftover from the early stages of open-air museum evolution, languishing in a state of arrested development, but that it has continued to change and shift, all the while retaining its popularity as a tourist destination throughout its existence. I do not propose that we reexamine Skansen's influence or role in the living history "movement." But, it would be very fruitful to remove it from its current discursive position (in North America) as a primitive "kernel of potential," and reexamine it as a performative operation in the present. This paper traces how Skansen's performance practices differ markedly from North American museums and thus, in a way, transcend tricky issues, not the least of which is the onus on American institutions of having to create "truth" for the visitor.

Skansen is, historically, more of an ethnographic park than a living history museum. (See fig. 4) Opened to the public in 1881 by Artur Hazelius, visitors to this *freilichtmuseen* could participate with costumed staff in revivals of popular customs and celebrate national holidays. With its motto, "Know yourself by knowing the past," Anderson writes, Skansen was an institution where Swedish people would affirm a sense of national consciousness through experiencing a "pocket edition" of all of the folklore and beauty of Sweden.[2] Hazelius founded it on the island of Djurgården, in the middle of the Stockholm archipelago, as a type of salvage mission in the face of what he perceived as threatening changes to Swedish folk traditions with the advent of industrialization. The site is charged with Hazelius' labor. Once a royal retreat where young princes played at soldiers, the island has been transformed into a heterotopic catalogue of agricultural farm life; its space reassigned politically from one associated with the monarchy and aristocracy to one that celebrates the life of Sweden's folk. (See fig. 5)

Hazelius is credited in the museum field not only for "founding" the open air museum movement, but also for changing the course of traditional museum development. Edward P. Alexander writes that, in the mid-nineteenth century, the exhibition function of western (primarily European) museums was dominant—pushing collection, conservation, and research into the background—and that displays were assembled to appeal to the "aesthete, scholar or collector."[3] The displays, as well as the imposing, "temple like" appearance of the museums themselves, intimidated and alienated the would-be general audience. Hazelius shifted the modes of perception and visitor-reception by restructuring exhibits for a "walk-through" experience of different stages of history, rather than falling back on the traditional arrangement of artifacts by "technical classification in chronological or stylistic order." Furthermore, Hazelius democratized the museum collection by moving his vernacular architecture and

Figure 3. Plimoth Plantation. June 2000.

Figure 4. Skansen, atop the Island of Djurgården in Stockholm, Sweden. June 2002

Figure 5. Costumed hosts greet visitors outside a restored nineteenth-century structure at Skansen. June, 2002.

artifacts into more approachable garden settings, employing "costumed craftsmen, musicians, dancers, and interpreters to bring the whole village to life."[4] The combination of the more informal, outdoor setting and the more visitor-friendly diorama-style exhibits, writes Alexander, allowed the layperson to experience history in a manner previously denied him or her. "No longer was the common man overawed by palace or temple; now the museum and the picnic could be combined and the whole family might share in enjoyment of the national heritage."[5]

Barbara Kirshenblatt-Gimblett traces the impetus for Skansen back to Hazelius' fascination with presenting "folk-life pictures": wax *tableaux* inspired by genre paintings of his time.[6] These three-dimensional scenes featured mannequins in folk dress among the furniture and artifacts Hazelius had collected in Sweden and other Scandinavian countries. He brought six of these folk-life pictures to the Philadelphia Centennial Exposition and the Paris *Exposition Universelle* (1876 and 1878, respectively). One tableau, entitled "The Infant's Death," or "The Little Girl's Last Bed" portrayed a family stricken with the passing of their youngest child. The mother wept over a cradle, while the father consoled an older sister of the deceased, the Bible on his lap turned, perhaps, to a comforting passage of scripture. A tiny coffin in the corner awaited its new occupant. The scene was based on an 1858 painting by Amalia Lindegren, and appeared at both the Philadelphia and Paris World Fairs.[7] James D. McCabe's *The Illustrated History of the Centennial Exhibition* describes a scene across the room, in which a Laplander in a reindeer-drawn sledge delivers orders to his wife before his departure: "Both figures are dressed in skins, and the sledge is a genuine article from 'the frozen north'. . . . The figures in all the groups are life-size, and are clad in the national dress of the classes they represent. The faces preserve the characteristics of each class."[8] *Frank Leslie's Illustrated Newspaper* described audience responses to the Philadelphia *tableaux* in 1876:

> All day long, and every day, the visitor to the western end of the Main Building will notice knots of much interested spectators gathered about certain groups of strangely costumed and strange-featured human figures—they are not human, upon a second and more critical glance, but only plaster—in the Swedish section. . . . The Swedish authorities have done the next best thing to bringing their peasantry here and exhibiting them in their everyday life, by sending groups of plaster figures dressed in the costumes of the different provinces, painted as to their faces and hands with a verisimilitude and accuracy that is really wonderful. The artist who made the figures is Professor Töderman, of the Royal Academy of Fine Arts in Stockholm, a sculptor of great reputation. Most of the subjects of the groups are taken from valuable paintings in the royal collection of the National Museum. Everybody recognizes the striking likeness of these figures to "the human form divine."[9]

Parisian newspapers had similarly positive reactions to the *tableaux* in Paris' Exposition Universelle two years later: "Never have wax or wooden figures or theatre decorations achieved such artistic effects of truth and life. All mothers cry beside the little one's last bed."[10] In inventing these scenes, writes Kirshenblatt-Gimblett,

Hazelius drew upon the tableau model that had been a staple in natural history museums and conflated it with the period rooms and travel panoramas he had encountered in his many visits to expositions and museums.[11]

Kirshenblatt-Gimblett, along with Anderson and Alexander, calls Skansen the prototype for the open-air and living museums to follow.[12] But, while the connection she draws between the *tableaux* of Hazelius' earlier career and Skansen may be correct, the exhibits peopled by living hosts in the open-air museum resembled their predecessors only in the costume, setting, and artifacts. The living hosts did not act out the parts formerly assigned to the wax mannequins, so the dramatic narrative found in *tableaux* like "The Little Girl's Last Bed" did not carry over into the Skansen model. Nor, it would seem, did darker themes like infant mortality.

One can see, upon visiting Skansen, that this museum began as one particular man's vision of what was worth preserving. The first buildings at Skansen, collected by Hazelius during the 1880s, were farms, churches, belfries, windmills, and the houses and workshops of Sweden's middling folk. The first building opened to the public was the Mora cottage, acquired in Dalarna in 1885. Next, Hazelius gained possession of Djurgården land on which stood the historic Bredablick tower. The early 1890s were devoted to adding folk buildings, animal pens, paths, and gardens.[13] As Annika Johansson, assistant director of interpretive programming told me, in Hazelius' efforts to save the "Old Sweden" the first buildings he chose to preserve were the farming houses, "so the houses of poor people aren't that much represented."[14] (See fig. 6) But, in the following decades, as Hazelius' enterprise was continued, aspects of town life, factories, and indigenous Sami culture were added.

Skansen bills itself as a "Sweden in miniature" echoing Anderson's description of it as a "pocket edition" of the country. The configuration of the exhibits on Skansen's grounds does indeed suggest a spatial metonym of Sweden's geography. A souvenir guidebook published for visitors to Skansen explains how this has been accomplished:

> Since the beginning of the twentieth century the principle that has been followed in the early buildings and farms has been to place those from the north of Sweden in the northernmost part of Skansen and the southern farms in the southernmost parts. So, for example, the Sami camp is to be found in the northern part of Skansen while the farm from Skåne is in the extreme south.[15]

Much of the Swedish flora and fauna on display are likewise arranged corresponding to their geographic origin. The reindeer are displayed in the northern area of the museum, with the Sami who raised (and continue to raise) them. The north is predominantly forested with birch, while beech trees stand among the southern farms and buildings.

Skansen is also very much a museum *of* Artur Hazelius. Unlike Colonial Williamsburg, which, as a staged environment, hides the evidence of J.D. Rockefeller JR's hand in restoring the eighteenth century Virginia capital (Rockefeller's name does not appear anywhere in the historic area), Skansen foregrounds its prime mover and *raison d'être*. (See fig. 7) The secondary entrance to the park, *Hazeliusporten*, features

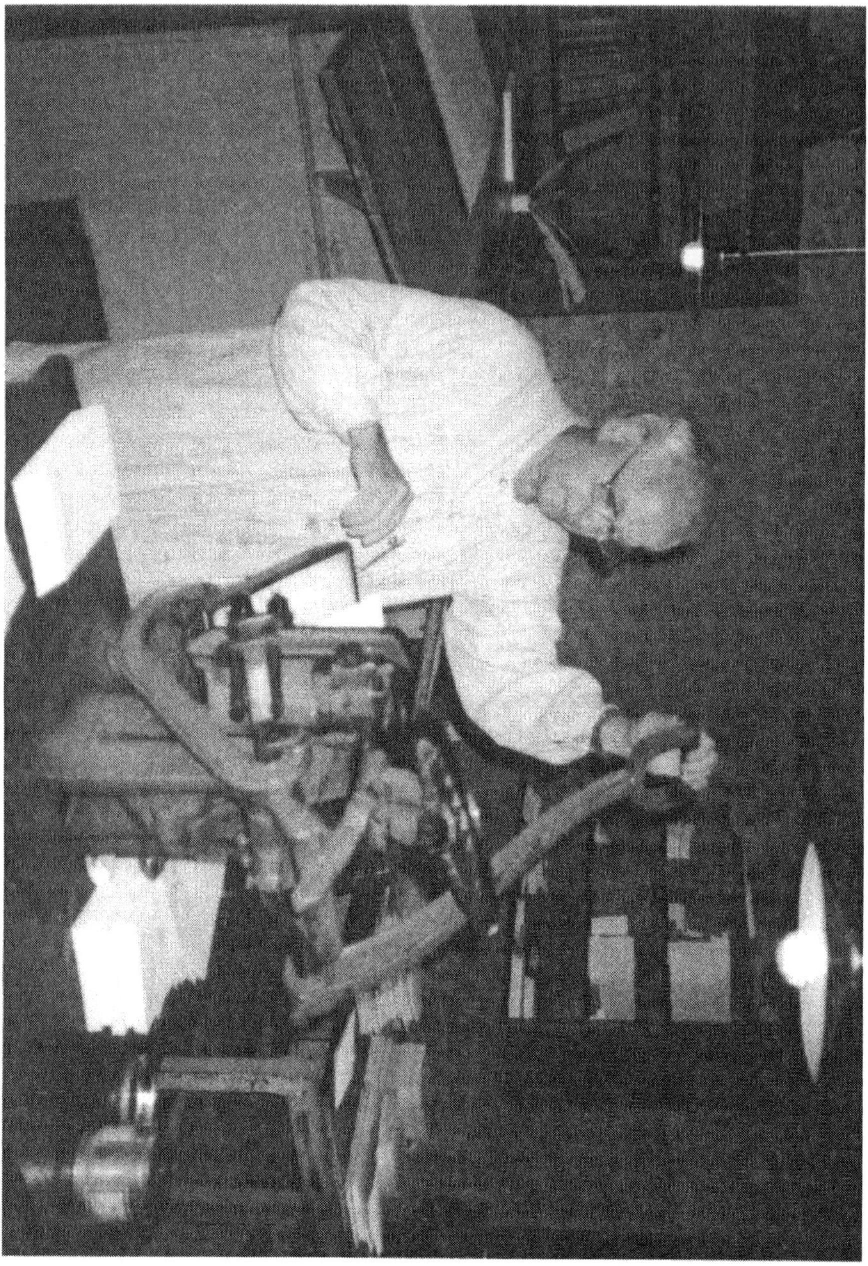

Figure 6. A costumed host demonstrates a nineteenth-century printing press at Skansen. June 2002.

Figure 7. The bust of Artur Hazelius outside Skansen's Hazelius Gate. June, 2002.

a shrine to Skansen's founder with his stern bust confronting those who wish to take the funicular railway to the center of the historic area rather than pass through the decidedly disney-esque main entrance. The bust trope is echoed on the Skansen visitor map and guidebooks. The first restored building one reaches after walking up the hill from Hazelius gate (not taking the funicular) is *Hazeliushuset*, the house in which Artur was born and raised, acquired and relocated to the museum in 1926. To complete the description of Skansen as the museum *of* Hazelius, it is probably worthy of note that his remains have been buried on the grounds. Not so much an exhibit, the grave is marked with a modest wooden sign: "Passerby. Stop for a moment by the grave of ARTUR HAZELIUS and reflect with reverence and gratitude on his memorable life."[16]

In this manner, the American museum to which Skansen bears the most resemblance is Greenfield Village, built by Henry Ford in his hometown of Deerborn, Michigan. In terms of recreating an authentic historical environment by way of performance and display, Greenfield Village is probably the least authentic of the American outdoor museums: buildings and exhibits were selected for inclusion largely based on Ford's whim or because of a (at times tenuous) connection with his personal history. Some buildings are restored originals like the Wright Brother's home and bicycle shop, Ford's own boyhood home, and the Postville, Illinois courthouse where Abe Lincoln once practiced law. Some are reconstructions, like Thomas Edison's Menlo Park laboratory and factory complex, or George Washington Carver's slave cabin. Still others are complete fabulations, like the Swiss chalet and clockmakers shop that Ford commissioned, simply because he too liked to tinker with watches and clocks in his spare time and wanted to commemorate this in his village. The Henry Ford Museum & Greenfield Village literature readily admits its founder's unorthodox acquisition practices:

> Uninfluenced by historic preservation or museum philosophies, Ford was not interested in professional standards or scholarship. Preservationists questioned the desirability of removing historic buildings from their original surroundings. Some of the buildings moved to or built in Greenfield Village did not approach the authenticity and accuracy of the Menlo Park project.[17]

While the brochures and signage are careful to point out which buildings are originals, the authoritative nature of the Village's institutional status as museum does allow for some slippage in visitor reception. . . . Not to mention visitor confusion with other museum sites like Plimoth and Colonial Williamsburg, that do try to assemble historic buildings or facsimiles with some degree of accuracy. Thus, being a simulacrum of a historical environment, many visitors have been "convinced that Ford, Edison, and the Wright Brothers actually lived next to one another in Michigan."[18] Such seemingly freewheeling policies on collection and display prompted harsh criticism from Michael Wallace in 1981. Citing Ford's bias against including banks, lawyer's offices, and homes of the wealthy in favor a collection of buildings associated with "blacksmiths, machinists, and frontier farmers," Wallace argues that Ford created, in effect, a "precapitalist Eden immune to modern ills":

> Ford's village was a *static* utopia. There was no conflict, no trouble within its

> grounds. Ford had banished war and politics. He had also—by excising banks, lawyers, and upper classes—precluded discussions of foreclosures, depressions, and unemployment. That, in turn, obviated the need to refer to farmers' movements, strikes, and radical political parties. . . . Greenfield Village distorted the past, mystified the way the present emerged, and thus helped to inhibit effective political action in the future.[19]

While Ford's open-air museum resembles Skansen in the selection process and layout of displayed buildings, Greenfield Village *does* have some first-person programs, and this is where it leans more heavily toward the model of programming preferred in American museums. On the day I visited Greenfield Village, there were many opportunities to hear presentations by first-person characters. One costumed presenter near the front entrance, for instance, barked the benefits of the soybean and its newly developed food and household products, and Orville and Wilbur Wright were scheduled for later in the afternoon. According to tourist literature, sometimes Henry Ford himself may be found in his restored workshop, perhaps talking to visitors about his first car, the "quadricycle."[20] An actor portraying George Washington Carver also appears from time to time, demonstrating, for instance, how to make peanut butter from scratch.[21] Attempts at naturalistic performance at Greenfield Village, however, are thwarted by crowd sizes and theme-park nature of the place. Like those at Colonial Williamsburg, many of the interpretive programs are backed up by microphone and loudspeaker system for audibility, and thus have a rather anachronistic feel.

To further separate Skansen from American models, the Skansen of today is more than just Hazelius' ethnographic museum. It is also skirted by a large zoo displaying Sweden's animals (bears, seals, moose, wolverines, lynx, and wild boars). It features an amusement park, a picnic destination, and (See fig. 8) a major concert venue: Solliden Stage was added in 1938-39 (Paul Simon was scheduled to appear later in the month I visited Skansen).[22] Given the ethnographic bent, the unique selection process, the tone of tourist literature and signage, and the supplementary (non-historic) attractions at Skansen, it becomes quite clear that we are dealing with two very different models of museum performance, especially when going as far as to compare the third-person programming of Skansen to a fully-first-person living environment like that of Plimoth Plantation. But even museums like Colonial Williamsburg, Greenfield Village, Old Sturbridge Village, Conner Prairie, Mystic Seaport, and Living History Farms, that consist mostly of costumed interpretation in the third person, and feature role playing in special areas or for scheduled events, are for this reason much closer in style, tourist literature, and performance practices to Plimoth than they are to Skansen.

I am not the first to weigh the pros and cons of first- and third-person interpretation. Previous work, though, has tended to concentrate on the logistical and practical side of the debate—that is, the difficulty in training first-person interpreters, or the gaps in historical information that prevent role-players from holding forth with the same confidence on matters of planting and harvesting (which are fairly well known) and domestic issues (much of which needs to rely on conjecture). Warren Leon and Margaret Piatt ask "to role-play or not to role-play?" in their 1989 essay on living history museums. As food for thought, they present sticky situations like Plimoth

Figure 8. Solliden Stage, Skansen. June 2002.

interpreters needing to pretend they don't know what a camera is, yet still being willing to pose appropriately for a tourist snapshot.[23] Third-person interpreters are able to draw comparisons between the past and the present, say the authors, but third-person is limited as well. Not only does it fail to draw visitors into the past as effectively as first-person interpretation, but it can become a "pointless gimmick to make a site seem quaint" and "may only serve to give uninformed staff members and undeserved symbol of knowledge and authority." Leon and Piatt conclude that the choice of interpretive mode depends on the goals and mission of the museum. "[O]ne style may do a better job of teaching visitors an understanding of historical change and historians' methods, while the more theatrical approach probably is more successful at stimulating interest in the past."[24]

Jay Anderson posited in his 1984 *Time Machines: The World of Living History*, that Skansen was the "prototype of all open-air museums,"[25] suggesting that this museum, at its inception, contained the kernel of potential museum performance that would later blossom at museums like Plimoth Plantation. While Skansen, in Anderson's account, was the inspiration for many other open-air museums in Europe, he feels that the "children of Skansen" are not quite what visitors come to expect at living history museums in the United States. "Visiting most European open-air museums is akin to time-traveling through the past, only to find vacant and silent homes and shops,"[26] he concluded. Such a picture is admittedly bleak compared to contemporary living history museums like Plimoth that people their sites with costumed interpreters who encourage a willing suspension of disbelief in their visitors.

***

Whether the origins of the living museum movement can be pinpointed so precisely to Skansen in 1881 seems doubtful to me. First, events that Anderson and others choose as the links in such an evolutionary development of living history become authoritative moments which limit the way these institutions and their recent shifts in programming may be thought about and discussed. By restricting the events only to those which fit into a model of linear evolution of museum display, scholars not only engage in a selection process informed by political and intellectual ideologies, but they also construct the identity of these events as links in a cause-and-effect chain, rather than autonomous moments. J.D. Rockefeller, JR's twentieth-century restoration of Williamsburg, Virginia, to its eighteenth century-appearance, for instance, is often cited as one of the steps in the narrative of evolution. Rockefeller's reasons for restoring Williamsburg, though, had less to do with being inspired by Skansen, and more to do with a combination of philanthropy, his attention to his own "impression management," and the good timing of Williamsburg resident W.A.R. Goodwin in appealing to Rockefeller as a patron when the latter was in a giving vein.[27] Second, by subscribing to the evolutionary model of museum development, other events in the past that lie outside of a linear time line (and most especially events that occur chronologically prior to what has been established as the "origin" of living history development—Skansen), are neglected. Disparate events, such as medieval English Cycles, restaging the Fall of the Bastille in France (1790), or restaging the Storming of the Winter Palace in Russia (1920), are instances which are spatially or temporally distant from the canonized dates and places of the living history time line. Each of these moments, like living history museums today, were intersections of memory, monumentalization, and performance, and likewise may be discussed in terms of restagings of history through performative or paratheatrical acts. Yet, because of their assigned places in western history, they cannot be easily reconciled with a model of living history development. Finally, the evolutionary model tempts the museum visitor, interpreter, and curator, as well as the reader and scholar, to favor the present as more advanced, and indeed the pinnacle of evolutionary development. This favoritism produces a bias against the past. Thus, discussion of early history museums as well as the subject of their exhibition, the past, is marked by implicit or explicit labels of "primitive" or "naïve."

Nevertheless, Skansen's legacy on the time line of museum-display has been secured by Anderson, Kirshenblatt-Gimblett, Alexander, Wallace and others, as has its place on the performance continuum of traditional museum display and total living interpretation—it being on the far side of the old-fashioned end of the spectrum. Such categorization establishes a narrative of Darwinian progression from simple to complex, with Skansen at the earliest, most primitive stage, followed by successive links in the chain that attempt to explain how museums got from the Skansen model to Plimoth Plantation. The problem is that this kind of historiography, in order to find the links, seeks out and chooses similar or related events so that they appear as a cause-and-effect chain, or a survival-of-the-fittest evolution. In this case, according to Anderson, the model starts in Sweden with Hazelius' early experiments in three-dimensional ethnographic displays, and makes the jump over the Atlantic when Hazelius ships his half-dozen wax *tableaux* ("folk-life pictures") to the 1876 Centennial Exhibition in Philadelphia. There, the idea is picked up by wealthy philanthropists like Rockefeller, Ford, and George Francis Dow, all of whom funded major American outdoor museums in the coming decades, many of which developed into living museums with role-playing interpreters.[28] These are convenient markers that allow historians to construct a successive chain, but they disallow consideration of other events that do not easily fit into that chain. And, upon closer examination, the narrative of step-by-step evolution may not be as easy to reconcile with other accounts.

For example, both Kirshenblatt-Gimblett and Alexander, more conservatively than Anderson, assign Hazelius only *partial* credit for the creation of three-dimensional ethnographic museum displays. While Hazelius was not the first to explore the "character group" in "waxwork tableaux," since he borrowed this already popular European form, he can be credited with blending the three-dimensional scene with authentic costumes to produce a new kind of ethnographic display.[29] Bjarne Stoklund, however, holds that the birth of ethnographic dioramas has been wrongly assigned to Hazelius, perpetuating what he terms "The Hazelius Myth." Ethnographic *tableaux*, Stoklund writes, had appeared at World's Fairs as early as 1873 "quite independently of Hazelius."[30] According to Stoklund, Hazelius did present Söderman's Lapp scene in Paris 1878, but there is no evidence that he was connected to the scene when it appeared in Philadelphia two years earlier.[31]

Furthermore, there appears to be little evidence that suggests that Ford, Rockefeller, or Dow actually visited Hazelius' exhibits in 1876 or the Philadelphia World's Fair in general. The link between Hazelius' ideas and American museums in Anderson's history is already a bit tenuous: Anderson bases his history largely on that of Charles B. Hosmer. According to Hosmer, Dow "was familiar with . . . new types of museum installation in use in Europe," and opened the Essex Institute's Ward House "as a true outdoor museum in the Skansen tradition."[32] Hosmer, however, either assumes the connection between Skansen and Dow without evidence, or holds that Dow's familiarity with the Swedish museum or with Hazelius' exhibits is general knowledge.

The connection between Dow and Ford is a little more easily traced, albeit through some degrees of separation. After his early work with the Essex Institute, Dow joined the administration of the newly created Society for the Preservation of New England Antiquities in 1919. The secretary of this group was William Sumner Appleton. Appleton admired the Swedish museum model, and corresponded back and forth with Skansen curators regarding preservation techniques, restoration laws and other issues.[33] That same year, Appleton wrote an article entitled "Destruction and Preservation," which appeared in *Art and Archaeology*, and advocated for the model to be adopted by American museums. "One form of preservation work has yet to be even begun in America, namely the Outdoor Museum, formed by the removal to one large site of old buildings condemned where standing," he wrote. "Something of the kind has been done with notable success at Skansen in Sweden, at Arnhem in Holland, at Hamar, at Elverum, at Bygdö, and particularly at Lillehammer in Norway."[34] Appleton despaired at the relative absence of such museums in America, and issued a call for help: "That the future of . . . such houses should be in jeopardy is a sad commentary on the public neglect of antiquities. Surely there must be somewhere, someone able and willing to make secure the future of each of them."[35] According to Anderson, then, Ford took up Appleton's call and went to New England to approach Appleton and Dow on this subject in 1923.[36]

However, in the history published by Ford's own Greenfield Village, the authors do not mention any connection between Ford and Dow or Ford and Appleton. According to this source, Ford learned about the open-air museums by sending his son Edsel to scout east coast museums. Edsel told his father about Mercer Museum in Doylestown, Pennsylvania, which greatly interested him.[37] Edsel also set up a meeting between Ford's advisor, Harold Cordell, and the curators of Chicago's Rosenwald Museum (now Museum of Science and Industry), and "perhaps Cordell even mentioned Skansen" when he was telling Ford about The Deutsches Museum in Munich (11).

Even without complicating the evolutionary links in discourse on museum development, the question remains: if this has been a progressive movement, then why has Skansen not developed like its North American "children?" We can begin to answer the question by reexamining the practices of American museums—not as ideal culminations of museum evolution, but a current set of practices delimited not only by current historiographic methodology, but by the very conservative agendas that were established by their founders.

Living museums that incorporate first-person costumed interpretation into their programming have to create a sense of the "real" for visitors in order to make good on their promise of a place where history "comes alive." Their emphasis on scientific accuracy limits the legitimate material for presentation to that which may be corroborated by archaeological digs and written documents, which means that the stories of the disenfranchised, women, children, and racial and ethnic minorities are pushed to the margins. In their desire to show how the values espoused by the founding fathers are what made America a great nation today, the historical events are forced into Procrustean themes—narratives of "Becoming Americans" at Williamsburg,[38] for example, or "Democracy strengthened by conflict" in Sturbridge Village.[39] And first-person costumed interpretation, while fun for visitors, disallows discussion of events that happened *after* the time period represented, since interpreters do not acknowledge that which has taken place thereafter. Because of this, some programs within the larger structures of living history museums, such as the African-American Interpretation Program at Williamsburg and the Native American interpretive staff at Plimoth (comprised of members of the Wampanoag and other Native Nations) have broken from this strict performance mode. These groups often refuse to speak in first person unless there is a space for breaking character—such as a follow-up question and answer period—or stay out of first-person completely.

Because Skansen and other European open-air museums have not developed their performance programming with the same itinerary as their North American counterparts, they retain much more potential for responsible historical interpretation. While Plimoth Plantation, Colonial Williamsburg, Old Sturbridge Village, Old Fort William in Thunder Bay, Louisbourg on Canada's Cape Breton, and Connor Prairie are billed in tourist literature as places where history "comes alive," or that transport visitors "back in time," maybe Skansen curators and interpreters are more pragmatic in recognizing the disparity in truth between the way an event originally transpired and a representation of it.

As opposed to American museums, there is no indication that what the visitor is seeing at Skansen is an "authentic village" as it would have appeared in Sweden's past. Instead, it is a set of *tableaux* on the order of a traditional in-situ museum exhibit. Literature is devoid of phrases suggesting that as you walk down Skansen's paths you'll be stepping back in time (the closest it comes, from the material I've seen, is a somewhat awkwardly-worded "Skansen is a setting for encounters in space and time" in one English translation Skansen brochure [40]). And by using third-person interpretation, costumed hosts at Skansen can field questions both about the historical buildings they interpret, as well as those having to do with modern issues. A host in the farm building at Ekshärads-Gården from Värmland County in western Sweden told me, "We're not really acting here. It's difficult because Skansen is so much more than just houses. We have entertainment and stage programs. And people come in here and ask about cars and parking and things. And we can't really say 'I don't know what a car is because I'm a nineteenth century kind of person.'"[41] Assistant Director Johansson agrees:

> [O]ur hosts working in the buildings, they're not *actors* in that way. They are interpreters—historical interpreters. . . . And if a visitor comes in the house and wonders where is the [stage] where I can see Paul Simon, it doesn't work if the host says, "I don't know what you're talking about."[42]

Where it becomes essential to be able to speak to visitors about the present is in those situations when the interpreter can use a discussion of the past to teach visitors about complex issues in the twenty-first century. In America, for example, a Native Wampanoag interpreter at Plimoth Plantation's third-person venue, Hobbamock's Homesite, can discuss the massacres of Native people by English settlers *after* 1627, along with treaty violations and current issues in museums surrounding the repatriation of native remains.[43]

Visitors to Old Sturbridge Village, too, will often have their experience of "stepping back in time" tempered with reminders that the past cannot be too quickly understood from a twenty-first century standpoint. At a short program called "Traditions, Customs and Raising the American Flag" in June 2003, the costumed third-person interpreter invited children to help him attach and hoist the period stars-and-stripes up the flagpole at the center of the Village Common. (See fig. 9) He pointedly explained to the children and the rest of the crowd that we always have to be careful about the word "tradition," lest we take it for granted that the practices associated with our national flag have always existed. In the 1830s, the time of Old Sturbridge Village's portrayal, the United States is only fifty years old, he continued, and the "current" flag has been in existence for about one generation, after having its final color and arrangement stabilized with two Flag Acts passed through Congress. "All the traditions we associate with the flag—folding it in a triangle, not letting it touch the ground—were all invented in the twentieth century." Likewise, "all the scholars in the classroom today," referring to the Summershop daycamp program at Sturbridge, "won't be reciting the Pledge of Allegiance because it's not around yet."[44]

Elsewhere in the village, interpreters seemed to point out historical inaccuracies in their areas almost as if it were a staple of their programming: The 1830s Sawmill presenters told us that the sawdust would have normally been dumped in the river, below, but that current environmental standards require that sawdust from demonstrations be collected in bins and more properly disposed. The tinker in the Tin Shop indicated the anachronistic soldering tool he was using. The female interpreters demonstrating a toy hot-air balloon activity admitted that this would have only been practiced by boys. The Shoemaker told us he lacked authentic tacks for his craft. One gets the sense that these reminders were actually geared toward inculcating *more* visitor trust in the legitimacy and authenticity in the museum's exhibit. The sign at Sturbridge's front entrance promises the following:

> Old Sturbridge Village is an authentic re-creation of a rural 1830s New England community. Every detail of early American life has been painstakingly researched to provide a unique experience for you and your family. Each historic building has been carefully restored. The furniture, tools, implements—even the farm animals and gardens—are all true to the period. And our historically-costumed staff demonstrate the daily life, work, and celebrations of early 19th-century New England.

The sign spells out what visitors have the right to expect from the museum. So, by having any inaccuracies like those above made visible to them, visitors can trust that what *isn't* mentioned must otherwise be authentic.

At Greenfield Village, too, the staff could articulate reasons for using a combination of first and third-person, especially in making connections between the

Figure 9. A third-person costumed interpreter demonstrates an 1830s flag-raising, with the help of some children, at Old Sturbridge Village. The costumed children in the background are daycampers with the SummerShops program. June 2003.

past and the present. At the Firestone Farmstead, from the estate of the tire baron and Ford's colleague, I asked a group of interpreters sitting down to their midday dinner if anyone played character in the village: "We're in third-person here" a young woman answered, "which means we can make comparisons between [the late nineteenth century] and 2003. Some places use first-person, so they can't do that. But there are advantages to both."[45]

Skansen, likewise, with its third-person performative interpretation has a lot of potential for engaging discussion about the past that might not be immediately apparent in the visible *milieu.* Because Skansen hosts can speak in twenty-first century voice, everything, theoretically, is legitimate for discussion, thereby creating opportunities for dynamic and changeable portrayals of the past. To be realistic, though, not all hosts can be expected to cover such a range of history in detail, nor is this necessarily the mission of the museum. I asked Johansson about the backgrounds of Skansen's costumed hosts. She explained that they have range of backgrounds, education, and ages:

> Most of them have studied at the university. Some also have, in addition to that, different handicraft—or maybe some person can sing Swedish Folk songs or folk music. . . . What they do have in common is some kind of education: culture, sciences. But from the beginning, as you might know . . . if you go back to 1891 when Skansen was founded, it was very common that people who came to Skansen and worked as hosts if they were from that region that the house represents. And that is a tradition that has been going on in the history of Skansen for a long time. So, today, it's not really like that anymore. It has changed all sort of naturally because a lot of people that used to be based in the countryside and living in this kind of environment, they don't exist anymore (she laughs).[46]

Like Plimoth, though, Skansen reserves the costumed interpretation of its indigenous people, the Sami, for members of that ethnic group: "It's a little bit special, that Sami house, because the people working they are always Sami people. So they are always representatives of that culture."[47]

It is also important to recognize that the way the subject matter and agenda of history is communicated to the visitor is shaped by the way the host perceives his or her role and the goals of Skansen. I asked a hostess at 1860s Oktorps-Gården from Halland in southern Sweden, if she thought there were aspects of the past that would be uncomfortable or inappropriate to show to family audiences: "No. I don't think so," she answered. "We can show most of the houses and the surroundings. . . . That's the good idea about Skansen. It's from the south to the north in Sweden. We have different houses from different places."[48] It is apparent that this hostess saw the mission of Skansen to be a representative collection of buildings and artifacts from all over the country, and in this regard it was excelling. I asked the hostess at Ekshärads-Gården, who studies museology at university in Upsala, the same question about whether there were elements of the past that would be difficult to portray. Her response: "Yes, probably, lots of things. . . . Of course there are always sensitive things that I think they should show anyway because it's important to show all sides." She added that the reputation of the museum as a utopian celebration of the past may limit it from treating the darker aspects of Swedish history. "Skansen is a very nice place—no bad things happen here—ever," she remarked with some cynicism. "People come here to have a nice time.[49]

For both the interpreter and myself, the irony was apparent. The time period depicted in the museum was relatively grim. Hundreds of thousands of Swedes were emigrating in the second half of the nineteenth-century, most of whom came to America. As the museum guide book reminds visitors, "[c]rop failures at the end of the 1860s caused more than 100,000 Swedes to emigrate to America." This figure consistently increased, and in the 1880s "325,000 Swedes left for America and a further 52,000 emigrated to other countries."[50] The waves of emigration, and the consequent threat to Swedish life and culture, in fact, was one of the major reasons Hazelius built his museum. It's hard to imagine that those who stayed had much reason to celebrate, especially those contented themselves with meals of long-milk and hard tack supplemented with birch bark.

The historiographic discrepancy between conditions of the lived past, and the celebratory attitude of the exhibits and some of the hosts hearkens back to Michael Wallace's description of Henry Ford's open air museum as a "static utopia." Wallace's critique mainly concerned the way Greenfield Village perpetuated overly romantic and nostalgic depictions of a past free of worker's movements and strikes, and which struck from its record any evidence of radical politics. But the tendency to push programming toward utopic depictions of the past, heavily prompted by visitor expectations according to the interpreter, above, is a problem on both sides of the Atlantic.[51]

***

Such limitations necessarily disallow any conclusions that Skansen's current interpretive programming is more responsible in mediating between past and present for museum visitors, much less that Skansen's programming is qualitatively better than that of Plimoth Plantation (which has been strongly fixed in discourse as the best, most advanced living museum since Jay Anderson's 1984 book, *Time Machines*). It would be difficult in any sense to uphold a European open-air museum model over a North American living history model or vice-versa. Nor is it so easy anymore to distinguish the open-air performance practices at Skansen as particularly Swedish or even European. Recently opened in Östersund, in the northern part of Sweden, is Jamtli, an open-air museum that follows the living history model of immersion into the past, inhabited by costumed performers playing characters from the region.

What is the practical use of this discussion for museum performance? Skansen has been assigned the status of the fountainhead of the living history movement, but as that which has been subsequently left far behind. I proposed that Skansen be taken out of this discursive positioning and reinserted into present discussion about living history programming. Should U.S. and Canadian museums hold to Skansen's third-person mode of costumed performance? Not necessarily. But, to continue to regard Skansen's interpretation as primitive or naïve is tantamount to disregarding those American programs that use third person as a political choice in the present. In these cases, the interpreters do not resist being "in character" in order to tell visitors where to park for the Paul Simon concert, but to allow for topics of discussion outside of those surrounding a single historical event, and to allow for some amount of visitor agency in determining the trajectory of the discussion. Furthermore, our museums over here can learn from Skansen to make the procedures of the curatorial decisions visible. Markers for visitors as simple as Hazelius' bust can signal to them that these museums are *not* photographic likenesses of the authentic past, but are the product of a series of choices made by influential people about what aspects of the past to privilege over the rest of it. That, indeed, this is one of *several* possible histories they could have encountered on their family vacation.

NOTES

[1] Jay Anderson, *Time Machines: The World of Living History* (Nashville: American Association for State and Local History, 1984), 17.
[2] Ibid., 19.
[3] Edward P. Alexander, *Museums in Motion: An introduction to the History and Functions of Museums* (Walnut Creek: Alta Mira, 1996) 10.
[4] Ibid., 10.
[5] Ibid., 10-11. See also Alexander, "Artur Hazelius and Skansen: The Open Air Museum" in *Museum Masters, Their Museums, and Their Influence* (Nashville: American Association for State and Local History, 1983), 239-275.
[6] Barbara Kirshenblatt-Gimblett, *Destination Culture: Tourism, Museums, and Heritage* (Berkeley: U of CA P, 1998), 39-40.
[7] Ibid., 40.
[8] James D. McCabe, *The Illustrated History of the Centennial Exhibition* (Philadelphia: National Publishing Company, 1876) 405. The depiction of the Lapland scene in *Frank Leslie's Historical Register of the Centennial Exposition 1876* (Reprint, New York: Paddington Press, Ltd., 1974) shows a crowd gathering around the scene in attentive admiration.
[9] "Centennial Curiosities . . . Quaint and Expressive Character Groups from Sweden," *Frank Leslie's Illustrated Newspaper*, 26 August, 1876, 411.
[10] Cited in Alexander 1983 p. 246 from "Exposition Ethnografique du Musée d'Ethnographie Scandinave à Stockholm, Representé par le Docteur Artur Hazelius, Fondeur et Director du Musée" in *Exposition Universelle de Paris, 1878* (Stockholm: Impremerie Centrale, 1878) Alexander's trans.
[11] Kirshenblatt-Gimblett, 40.
[12] Ibid., 41.
[13] *Skansen,* ed. Karin Belent, Anna Dahlén, Mona Larsson and Marita Wikander (Stockholm: Sandvikens Tryckeri AB, 2002), 6.
[14] Annika Johannson, personal interview, 8 July 2002.
[15] *Skansen,* 8.
[16] Ibid., 113.
[17] *An American Invention: The Story of Henry Ford Museum & Greenfield Village*, eds. Wes Hardin, William S. Pretzer and Susan Steele (Ann Arbor: Henry Ford Museum & Greenfield Village, 1999), 46. It should also be noted that Ford did not initially

intend his Greenfield Village as a museum open to the general public. His original goal was educational: to create an immense outdoor curriculum where hand-selected students of his "Edison Institute" would "learn by doing." Only after public interest became too overwhelming did Ford open the doors to the general public in 1933.

[18] Ibid., 14.

[19] Michael Wallace, "Visiting the Past: History Museums in the United States," *Radical History Review* 25 (1981): 72-73. Like Anderson, Wallace also credits Skansen as the beginning of the open-air museum movement, which snowballed in other European countries, disseminating, like Ford's Greenfield Village, incomplete, depoliticized, and largely unhelpful narratives of the past: "The Skansen movement blended romantic nostalgia with dismay at the emergence of capitalist social relations. As the new order had introduced mechanized mass production, a burgeoning working class and class conflict, these museums, often organized by aristocrats and professionals, set out to preserve and celebrate fast disappearing craft and rural traditions. What they commemorated, and in some degree fabricated, was the life of 'the folk,' visualized as a harmonious population of peasants and craft workers" (72).

[20] *Henry Ford Museum & Greenfield Village: A Pictorial Souvenir* (Deerborn: Edison Institute, no date given), 22.

[21] Ibid., 29.

[22] Greenfield village, incidentally, also has a concert venue, the testing for which, on the afternoon I visited, drowned out the calliope music of the nearby historic carousel.

[23] Warren Leon and Margaret Piatt, "Living-History Museums" in *History Museums in the United States: A Critical Assessment,* ed. Warren Leon and Roy Rosenzweig (Urbana: U of IL P, 1989), 88.

[24] Ibid., 90.

[25] Anderson, 17.

[26] Ibid., 22.

[27] See Richard Handler and Eric Gable, *The New History in an Old Museum: Creating the Past at Colonial Williamsburg* (Durham: Duke U P, 1997), 31-34.

[28] Starting in 1907, Dow amassed and restored sixteenth- and seventeenth-century structures, peopled with costumed staff, for the Essex Institute in Salem, Massachusetts (Anderson, 27).

[29] Edward P. Alexander, "Artur Hazelius and Skansen: The Open Air Museum" in *Museum Masters: Their Museums and Their Influence* (Nashville: American Association for State and Local History, 1983), 245.

[30] Bjarne Stoklund, "International Exhibitions and the New Museum Concept in the Latter Half of the Nineteenth Century," *Ethnologia Scandinavica* 23, 1993: 91.

[31] Ibid., 91.

[32] Charles B. Hosmer, *Presence of the Past* (New York: Putnam 1965), 214, 215.

[33] Hosmer, 255.

[34] William Sumner Appleton, "Destruction and Preservation of Old Buildings in New England," *Art and Archaeology* 8 (May 1919) 176, 177.

[35] Ibid., 175.
[36] Anderson, 28.
[37] *An American Invention: The Story of Henry Ford Museum and Greenfield Village*, 10.
[38] "Becoming Americans: Our Struggle to Be Both Free and Equal: A Plan of Thematic Interpretation" (January 1996 Training Edition). Williamsburg: Colonial Williamsburg Foundation, 1996.
[39] See Andrew Baker and Leon Warren, "Old Sturbridge Village introduces Social Conflict into its Interpretive Story," *History News* (March, 1986).
[40] "Skansen: Catch a Glimpse of Swedish History" (Summer 2001).
[41] Costumed host, personal interview, 8 July 2002.
[42] Annika Johannson, personal interview, 8 July 2002.
[43] Third-person, costumed Native interpreter at Hobbamock's Homesite, personal interview, 17 June 2000.
[44] Costumed Interpreter, Old Sturbridge Village, 24 June 2003. That same morning, an interpreter in the Center Meeting House, adjoining the village common, shared with visitors how excited he was about the Summershops Program running that week. The daycampers, all in period costume, go to school, do chores, and learn about history in an experiential environment. This interpreter liked the groups of children around in costume because it made the village look "more representational" than usual.
[45] Third person interpreter, Greenfield Village, 2 July 2003.
[46] Annika Johannson, Personal interview, 8 July 2002.
[47] Ibid.
[48] Host at Oktorps-Gården, personal interview, 8 July 2002.
[49] Host at Ekshärads-Gården, 8 July, 2002.
[50] Ibid., 4.
[51] I have not yet been able to track down helpful comparative information between museum audiences in European and North American museums. By analyzing similarities or contrasts in terms of values, tastes, economic status, class, or education levels of museum visitors throughout the twentieth century, one might begin to tease out some of the ways audience expectations were instrumental in the development of first person interpretation in America. That is, if indeed this development did not transpire due to some natural tendency on the part of American museums to evolve in a progressive manner. Any conclusions at this point would be speculative, but these questions warrant further investigation.

Scott Magelssen teaches theatre history and dramaturgy at Augustana College, Rock Island, Illinois. He received his M.A. and Ph.D. in theatre history from the University of Minnesota. His most recent articles on living history performance have been published in *Journal of Dramatic Theory and Criticism*, *TDR: The Drama Review*, and *Theatre Survey*.

Book Reviews

"That Furious Lesbian": The Story of Mercedes de Acosta. By Robert A. Schanke. Carbondale and Edwardsville: Southern Illinois University Press, 2003; pp. xi + 210. $45.00 cloth, $25 paper.

The author took his title from Cecil Beaton, who referred in his diary to Mercedes de Acosta as "that furious lesbian," a judgmental put-down of one he found so boldly honest about her sexuality that he was embarrassed to be seen in her company. Of course, Beaton, who spent a bitchy lifetime putting others down to raise himself up, could with justice be called "that furious queen," and I herewith dub Sir Cecil with that moniker.

By 1919, when de Acosta produced her first full length play, *Sandro Botticelli*, starring Eva LeGallienne, and her first book of poetry (*Moods),* the American arts scene, especially in theatre, poetry, and literature, had begun breaking away from traditional forms of expression, directly influenced by the European "art theatre" movement, which had its origins in the innovative works of Ibsen, Chekhov, Strindberg, and others. The new American drama of Eugene O'Neill, Susan Glaspell, Rachel Crothers, and other artists of the early decades of the twentieth century, reflected growing concerns for aesthetic, social, and political themes, and a remarkable indifference to conventional Broadway commercial appeals.

Would-be writers, such as Mercedes de Acosta and her generation of young, articulate, intellectuals, excited and inspired by the avant garde movements of the day, found markets for their esoteric works, markets that did not exist prior to the advent of the art theatre movement. Not only did "non-commercial" literary and theatrical pieces receive attention and respect from a new wave of producers, but, too, female playwrights and poets were breaking up the dominant ranks of the traditional male role models.

Tracing the life and works of de Acosta within the context of America's fertile, experimental arts movements (on stage and in film), and through her relationship with many of the leading arts practitioners of the era (Nazimova, LeGallienne, Duncan, Dietrich, Garbo, and others), the author contributes a significant and insightful chapter to American theatre history. Impressively and exhaustively researched as well as skillfully written, Schanke's work avoids academic jargon or scholarly pretension. He has an uncanny ability to take his readers into his confidence, encouraging us to share his exhilarating research journey of joyful discoveries, and, sometimes, painful disappointments.

Between 1919 and 1928 (from the age of 26 to 35) de Acosta was remarkably productive; she wrote three books of poetry, two novels, and four produced plays, including *Sandro Botticelli* (1919) and *Jehanne d'Arc* (1925), with Eva LeGallienne in the title roles; *Jacob Slovak,* which appeared in New York in 1927, and, under the title of *Prejudice,* in London in 1928, featuring John Gielgud and Ralph Richardson. Except for her autobiography, *Here Lies the Heart* (1960), after 1928 and until her death in 1968, de Acosta did not publish another work. Schanke especially sought throughout his research to discover why de Acosta's early promise as a writer never became more fully realized.

Mercedes de Acosta's early literary ambitions, her incessant struggle for artistic relevance and recognition, and her fierce determination to find fulfillment in her personal life as well as in her art, led her by the age of 35 to focus more and more upon personal achievement and satisfaction, that is, upon the sexual pursuit of her famous lovers. "Her love for other women" and her struggle for personal and artistic acceptance "were sources of her originality and fueled her writing." But her undisciplined desire to find her ideal woman, "along with the cloying emotionalism with which she suffocated her lovers, turned to fanaticism, clouding her vision, taste, and artistic decisions. She was blinded by sexual passion" (Schanke, 173).

"That Furious Lesbian" and a companion volume, *Women in Turmoil,* containing six plays by de Acosta, edited and introduced by Professor Schanke, have both been selected as finalists for the LAMBDA Literary Award.

Billy J. Harbin
Louisiana State University

A History of African American Theatre. By Errol G. Hill and James V. Hatch. Cambridge: Cambridge University Press, 2003; pp. xxiv + 608. 43 b/wh illustrations. $110 cloth.

Impressive in scope, this magisterial history of the hardships and achievements of black creators of theatre in America takes the reader from the early-1400s origins of the African slave trade to events-in-progress at certain theatres in the spring of 2001, includes theatrical forms like minstrelsy and vaudeville, and looks at African American theatre in cities all across the United States as well as in the Caribbean. Breadth of coverage does not mean shallow overview, for the writing is rich in anecdotal detail, recently unearthed evidence, and pertinent statistics, all anchored by copious endnotes (488-546).

The late distinguished scholar Errol Hill wrote most of the early history, beginning with a chapter on slavery as a background to black theatre. While theatrical activity was not an option for blacks under slavery, Hill skillfully weaves theatre into the narrative through references to modern plays like Amiri Baraka's *Slaveship,* William B. Branch's *In Splendid Error* (on the meeting between Frederick Douglass and abolitionist John Brown), and others. William Alexander Brown's African Grove and African Theatre get close attention, drawing upon George A. Thompson, Jr.'s recent findings, to support the claim that we may consider Brown to be "the true father of African American theatre" (40). Chapter 2 also treats Ira Aldridge, William Wells Brown, developments in antebellum New Orleans and Baltimore, and culminates in a thoughtful analysis of our evolving views of *Uncle Tom's Cabin* from the Civil War era through the "Jim Crow" years to George Abbott's 1936 version *Sweet River.* The opening of the floodgates of theatrical activity after the Civil War is evident in Chapter 3's profusion of names of playwrights and performers, notably the Hyers sisters and Henrietta Vinton Davis. William Edgar Easton, the playwright associated with Miss Davis, is treated in Chapter 5, along with theatrical forms ranging from coon songs to opera.

The chapter on minstrelsy by James V. Hatch overlaps a bit with its preceding chapter in that both have material on Sam Lucas and Ernest Hogan. Overlapping of black and Irish culture fed the complex development of minstrel shows. Black performers appear in the narrative of white minstrelsy, but most of this chapter is devoted to the black minstrel shows, many of which found success abroad.

If African American theatre from 1900 to 1920 tends to be overlooked in favor of the great ragtime musicals of the 1890s and the Harlem Renaissance of the 1920s, Errol Hill and James Hatch find much to write into the record of the intermediate decades. The remarkable story of Chicago's Pekin Theatre and the contributions of journalist-manager Lester A. Walton are of particular interest. This jointly written chapter further examines anti-lynching plays (also treated in the subsequent chapter), pageants, the Lafayette Players, TOBA, Ethel Waters, and some leading blacks in vaudeville.

Following Chapter 7's coverage of the frenetic, multifaceted activities of the Harlem Renaissance comes a change of pace with two chapters devoted to specific topics: educational theatre and the Caribbean connection. Howard University is appropriately central to Chapter 8, but we learn that three other black colleges and universities were presenting plays even before the 1911 appearance of Howard's drama club. From the Caribbean come not only Derek Walcott and Geoffrey Holder, but dozens of other playwrights and performers. Indeed, the latter third of the historical narrative, Chapters 10 to 13, from the Great Depression to the millennium, is crammed with hundreds of artists in all facets of theatre (although dramatists tend to predominate) as well as large and small black theatre companies and their founders.

A History of African American Theatre surely takes its place as our definitive work on the subject. As such, it will have subsequent editions, and thus its occasional errors must be noted so that they can be corrected: The trailblazing entrepreneur of minstrelsy was Edwin P. Christy, not Edward (94). The infamous New York law of 1927 was the Wales (not Wade) Padlock Law (238). Strictly speaking, "Paul Robeson's stage career began" not with his succeeding Gilpin in *The Emperor Jones* (346), but when he played in *Simon the Cyrenian* at the Lafayette Theatre in 1921, followed by *Taboo* in 1922. The correct name of the Washington D.C. company is Arena Stage, not Arena Theatre (409). On page 460, one is directed to "see chapter 11" for the history of AEA's Non-Traditional Casting Project, but no such information appears in that chapter.

Other infelicities that might be reconsidered for future editions are not necessarily errors of fact, but tendentious phrasings that may have the cumulative effect of cheapening the work for some readers. A couple of examples of these are: "...the interpretations of Paul Robeson ...[et al] would force Whites to relinquish Othello. Blacks were able to capture these roles because their portrayals were equal or superior" (229); "Fascism had been defeated in Germany but not in America" (347); "President Nixon and his staff manipulated the war in Vietnam to linger on and on" (375); "soiled by the malice of the Un-American Activities Committee" (incomplete title for HUAC, 409); and "the reign of Ronald Reagan" (430).

There is good news in response to a comment in the book about Robeson's death in 1976: "Three decades later, the United States still denied Robeson's genius by refusing to issue a postage stamp with his image." A 37-cent stamp with a photographic portrait of Paul Robeson was issued by the United States Postal Service in January 2004.

Felicia Hardison Londré
University of Missouri-Kansas City

The Federal Theatre Project: A Case Study. By Barry B. Witham. Cambridge: Cambridge University Press, 2003; pp. xiv + 190. $60 cloth.

Since the demise of the Federal Theatre Project in June 1939, studies of the arts-oriented projects of the New Deal's Works Progress Administration have often focused on lively retellings of controversy. The discourse has been dominated by stories about blocked productions (*Ethiopia*, the first Living Newspaper), censorship (Marc Blitzstein's *The Cradle Will Rock*), and red-baiting politicians hoping to undermine President Roosevelt. These stories often center on the New York units of the Federal Theatre Project, whose proximity to Broadway undoubtedly helped to magnify their activities — and it probably did not hurt that boy-genius and publicity-hound Orson Welles was involved.

In recent years, though, scholarly essays by James Wilson, John R. Poole, Ron West, Tina Redd, Barry B. Witham, and others have helped to reclaim the FTP's larger, national legacy. With the publication of Witham's book, *The Federal Theatre Project: A Case Study*, we now have a serious, in-depth examination of how a government-funded theatre can influence the life of a community in a region far beyond the Great White Way. During the fifteen years that Witham pored over FTP reports, memoranda, and other correspondence — an advantage of researching the government is the amount of paper it tends to generate — he constructed a narrative that examines discrete parts of the Federal Theatre Project in Seattle and Washington State. Witham's art is in the way individual chapters, which often focus on felicitously paired topics ("Typists and models," "*Power* and control," "*Dunbar* and the children," "Slums and syphilis"), combine to create a historiographic matrix that draws both the Pacific Northwest's project and the national FTP into sharper focus.

A member of the drama faculty at the University of Washington in Seattle since 1979, Witham writes, "I was fortunate enough to turn up a great deal of information in Seattle, as well as to interview people who had worked on the project there. Seattle was important because [its project] survived to the final days and thus illuminated all of the tensions and contradictions that were played out across the country." (5) What were those tensions? Beyond the banner stories of censorship and fiscal crisis, which affected projects in many locales, were the quotidian indignities that burden government bureaucracies. These are the tales of power and pride that found WPA administrators attempting to control artistic output, haggling over who might be eligible to work for the FTP and who would not, and generally asserting petty authority in ways one tends to associate with officious clerks for the postal service or the Department of Motor Vehicles.

In one particularly egregious case, Washington State WPA administrator Don Abel ordered the closure of the so-called "Negro" unit's 1936 adaptation of *Lysistrata* following a successful opening performance. Although Abel had not seen the performance, "he had heard that it was 'indecent and bawdy.' . . . [M]ost accounts suggest that it was his wife and secretary who had probably been offended by the sight of black people performing the sexually suggestive comedy" (72). The closure caused considerable consternation in the ranks of the local and national FTP — particularly after it was suggested that Abel wanted to preview all future scripts. As a result, Harry Hopkins, head of the WPA in Washington, D.C., sent an emissary of his own along with an FTP representative to help untangle the mess.

Although Hopkins had authorized the reopening of the production, J. Howard Miller, the FTP representative assigned to the case by Federal Theatre Project administrator Hallie Flanagan, found the production to be unsuitable for aesthetic reasons of casting, direction, etc. As for the work's ribaldry, Miller thought it "adolescent" and imagined that the WPA administrator "probably has a dirty mind" (73). In a compromise negotiated by Miller, Abel agreed to leave FTP programming decisions to FTP personnel but the production of *Lysistrata* remained closed.

Despite the truncated run of *Lysistrata*, the Negro Company was perhaps the most effective producing arm of the FTP in Seattle. In one of two appendices to the book (the other is a helpful glossary of persons associated with the Northwest project), Witham lists the productions of the Seattle FTP that occurred in a theatre — as distinct from those done on tour in the camps of the Civilian Conservation Corps, for example. The lone exception on the appendix list is the pageant *Flotilla of Faith*, which played on the banks of the Columbia River in May 1939. The first and the final productions noted in the appendix (*Noah* and *Taming of the Shrew*) were both created by the Negro Company, demonstrating more than three years of continuity within the group. Discussing a production from the spring of 1939, Witham notes, "Many of the same names [from the beginning] are still there. They were a company" (62).

For Witham, the Negro Company is clearly central to an understanding of Seattle's FTP history — which is ironic, he points out, because the African-American population probably never exceeded 5,000 in those days. One of the paradoxes of African-American participation in Federal Theatre Projects was the paternalism of its oversight by white people. In Seattle, the Negro Company was overseen by Florence and Burton James, whose commitment to progressive issues caused them later to be hounded by the Washington State legislature's Canwell Committee on Un-American Activities in 1948. But even Florence James, by all accounts a talented teacher and director, participated in unconscious reifications of what passed for "Negro authenticity":

> So widespread were accepted attitudes about what constituted *Negroes* in the 1930s, that other representations were not perceived as authentic or valid. Most members of this Northwest US company had no notion of the kind of "southern" dialect or folk music knowledge that directors assumed they knew. Sara Oliver [a company member] remembered that Florence James, "was so surprised that here we had this Negro dialect in plays that we were supposed to do, but Seattle people didn't speak Negro dialect. [. . .] So she says 'Well, just speak like yourself. Don't try any dialect. Speak the lines.'" (76)

Besides Witham's compelling stories about the Negro Company — and its productions of *Stevedore, It Can't Happen Here,* and *An Evening With Dunbar* — his study also examines the impact of Living Newspapers on the Seattle community.

Of particular interest in Seattle were productions of *Power, One-Third of a Nation,* and *Spirochete.* Each of these Living Newspapers was researched and created in major cities — *Power* and *One-Third of a Nation* in New York, *Spirochete* in Chicago — but the urgency of their stories (and their politics) influenced local Seattle culture. In the case of *Power,* the late 1930s in Seattle found two companies competing as electric utilities — one public (City Light), one private (Puget Power). In partnership with City Light, which purchased blocks of tickets to shows and helped in other material ways, the Seattle FTP brought to public consciousness the ways in which private utilities tend to enrich investors at the expense of subscribers.

City Light argued vociferously in the media that it could reduce rates per kilowatt hour. Quoting a City Light-sponsored radio broadcast, Witham notes that an announcer "stressed that there were more than 43,000 customers paying over five million dollars for Puget Power services that essentially were the same as the public utility" (81). What's unclear from the statement is how much the typical subscriber's bill might have decreased under public ownership because no comparative numbers are offered, but Witham indicates that *Power* and City Light's campaign helped swing public opinion in favor of public ownership by the end of 1937 (87).

Another fascinating tale about *Power* turns on its postponement due to 1937 budgetary cuts at WPA. *Power*'s postponement came at the same moment that "dozens of other productions all across the country" had been stopped for the same reason (84). Blitzstein's *The Cradle Will Rock* was one of those shows, which leads Witham to caution against "accepting the romanticized accounts that have circulated" regarding censorship of the famed Orson Welles and John Houseman production (84).

As with *Power, One-Third of a Nation* helped raise local awareness — in its case of those who were homeless or poorly housed. Between 1933 and 1937, only four permits were issued for apartment housing in Seattle (107-08). After *One-Third of a Nation*'s record long-run in 1938, the housing-reform lobby was able to push legislation in 1939 that created the Seattle Housing Authority, which became "one of the most active in the country" (113). With the successful production of *Spirochete,* the Seattle FTP managed to engage a public-health discourse on venereal disease. Coming at a time when syphilis often was believed to be punishment for immoral behavior, guardians of "morality" resisted open discussion of the topic. At the same time, doctors' groups were nervous about proposals aimed at "socializing" medicine, and were legitimately concerned about disease-reporting requirements and the possible disruption of doctor-patient confidentiality. But the tide had turned in favor of better syphilis testing and reporting not long before the show opened (115). The production's emphasis on inverting the moral issue — arguing that it was immoral *not* to test and report — may have helped to gain approval for legislation passed shortly after *Spirochete* opened (120).

Witham also points to other ways that the Seattle Federal Theatre Project made material contributions to local culture. These days, Seattle has a cherished children's theatre company that opened a $10 million new home in the mid-1990s. But Witham argues that the FTP's Children's Theatre helped to develop the taste for, and support of, children's theatre that continues today (156). Another major resource developed by a wing of the FTP was a research project that created a theatrical history for the region:

> Their goal was to examine newspapers, magazines, journals and other printed material to uncover references to theatrical activity and then pass that material along to a team of typists who would synopsize the information and compile lists for future research. They also proposed to conduct interviews with "old-timers" and made an appeal for photographs, diaries, theatre programs, letters and other ephemera. (51)

Witham discovered that, by December 1936, "52,570 sheets of material" had been examined and collated into "a typed manuscript of some 2,010 pages" (52).

The final significant contribution of the Seattle Federal Theatre Project that we will consider here was the brainchild of Glenn Hughes, who led the drama program at the University of Washington and also headed the Seattle FTP in its early days. Hughes envisioned the building of theatre models that would assist in teaching theatre history. "A list of sixteen historical theatres was prepared," Witham writes, "and work began on the initial project: the Theatre of Dionysus from classical Greek history" (55). Hughes had planned for the theatres to reside permanently at the University of Washington and a battle ensued for "ownership" of the massive models: "the stunning Acropolis is eight feet long and the Elizabethan Fortune Theatre is nearly four feet high" (54).

Hughes ultimately won the battle only because the FTP was defunded before the issue was resolved. The university stills owns them, but they are now tucked away in a warehouse because, as Witham reports one dean saying: "Nobody cares about them but you, Barry" (53). Witham quotes a 1937 letter by Hallie Flanagan, written after she first viewed the models, "They are absolutely accurate, and marvelous as to workmanship. Each detail is worked out exquisitely . . . In my opinion they should be in the Smithsonian or the Folger" (53). If the University of Washington cannot find a place to display these national treasures, perhaps they should take Flanagan's advice and move the models to the Smithsonian where they can be viewed and enjoyed.

Witham's scrupulous care in burrowing through the minutiae of the Federal Theatre Project's archives and the substantial literature created since it ended in the summer of 1939 pays large dividends to those who seek a deeper understanding of this period in US theatre history. Although it was plagued by bureaucratic inefficiencies, beset by critics who found the project wasteful or subversive, and was never well funded, the Federal Theatre Project in Seattle rose above its straitened circumstances. The project offered a bit of hope to audiences and theatre people, brought diverse communities together, and built a theatrical legacy that continues to evolve today.

Jeffrey Eric Jenkins
New York University

Staging America: Cornerstone and Community-Based Theater. By Sonja Kuftinec. Carbondale, IL: Southern Illinois University Press, 2003. pp. xv + 259. $45 cloth.

This book will challenge any reader who questions what it means to create American theater. Sonja Kuftinec's account of the company Cornerstone is a dense work about American community theater written from an historical, enthnographic and critical perspective. The book effectively recounts how over 16 years, Cornerstone's formation of America "transformed from a collage of geographically bounded areas to a matrix of diverse cultures, to a rethinking of how community and identity could be defined and bridged" (188-9).

To scholars interested in the European perspective toward community arts, this is quite different source than Ian Watson's *Towards a Third Theatre: Eugenio and the Odin Teatret* or Tony Coult's and Baz Kershaw's *Engineers of the Imagination: The Welfare State Handbook.* These latter sources delve more in the recording of the process and the artists involved. In contrast, Kuftinec's concerns delve into critical and historical perspectives that make community theater American.

The Preface includes a telling comment on an early draft of Kuftinec's works. She recalls how Cornerstone Artistic Director Bill Rauch reading an early draft comments, "I was really struck by how densely intellectual the writing is. I had trouble keeping up sometimes, and I know this stuff better than many" (xvi). However Kuftinec is honest and begins by writing, "I begin a work based on many years of participation and reflection in the theater with the confession of a guilty secret: I often don't like going" (1). Perhaps because of this position, the author is bold and passionate about asking provocative questions throughout her text; perhaps her position about theater creates a different objectivity.

In the first chapter entitled "Introduction: Surveying the Terrain," Kuftinec acknowledges utilizing multiple approaches and perspectives within the methodology for *Staging America.* The methodology includes chapter headings which serve as "various sites for the reader to engage with community-based theater, depending on interests in practice, historiography, or performance and identity" (19). As a consistent approach to explore community-based theater and scholarship, each chapter asks the question how do I talk about this theater; she writes that she with each chapter she responds in a slightly different way (19).

Chapter two is entitled, "Identity Traces: Historiographic Perspectives on Cornerstone and Community-Based Theater." This chapter walks the reader between the semantic and historical differences within the use of the term community theater. Kuftinec cites how scholars and practitioners shifted away from pejorative or dismissive attitudes toward community theater, once the hyphenated base was "borrowed from public funding language and popularized in the 1980s" (23). But Kuftinec is clear that she is more concerned "with notions of staging American than with archiving community-based theater as a whole" (24). To the scholar interested in this movement of theater, this chapter contains helpful information because of the synthesis during the search for a "definition and negotiation of American identity" (24). This search draws upon works that range from Percy Mackaye's *New Citizenship* (1915), John Anderson's *American Theatre* (1938) approach to Americanization pageantry, plus the socialism, identity politics and community specific theaters. Some of the latter companies span decades and include the Group Theater, El Teatro Campesino, El Teatro de las Esperanza and the Free Southern Theater. Kuftinec concludes that "Alongside these theatrical developments, a paradox emerges: In the quest for group identity, performance is seen as both a manifestation and formation of culture. Identity then is not pre-formed but performed, essential but not essentialist" (37). Kuftinec continues observations that another community-based theatrical trace emerges that forge "links across a variety of communities" and this is the American Festival Project and "radical coalition building" (37). It is at this point that the creation story of Cornerstone emerges with a description of a community that "embodies several shifting identities," ensemble and organization (41). The conclusion of the chapter is how during the formation of the company the founding members had discussions as to what theater should and should not be "shaped Cornerstone as idea and organization" and that negotiations "between individuals and ideology, structure and chaos, continuity and change, remain at the crux of Cornerstone's identity" (57). The remaining chapters try to record how these ongoing discussions and negotiations work toward artistic process, development of the company, and current critical thought toward community-based theater.

In chapter 3, "Perfor(m)ations: Cornerstone and Transactions of Community," assistance is given to this chapter through "Clifford Geertz's image of the webs of signification-creating culture" (61). The intention is that this more "explicitly theoretical chapter details the social and aesthetic interactions" where the search for a definition of the company's work begins the recording of interactions "that both animate and disrupt community in an ongoing process of reweaving" (61).

Cornerstone formed in 1986, from a group of recent graduates from Harvard that questioned "what they believed to be a limited idea of national identity, as defined by the American Repertory Theater in Cambridge." From the discussions cofounders Alison Carey and Bill Rauch with other founding members desired to travel to "engage a truly diverse American theater audience" and travel beyond the "geographic and economic confines of East Coast regional theaters" (61). This moved the Cornerstone members to redefine culture by geography and economics. The artists process addressed and artistically incorporated symbolic systems that directly speak or communicate to respective communities. Some of the most interesting information in the book about the process used by Cornerstone is here.

Kuftinec suggests by numerous examples how the cultural translations were created by Cornerstone. One adaptation discussed includes that in Schurz, Nevada, with a production of *The House on Walker River* derived from *The Oresteia.* Other diversified communities who produced adaptations include: Norcatur, Kansas, with a production of *Tartoof,* in Long Creek, Oregon, a production staging of *The Good Person of Long Creek,* and in Eastport, Maine, *Pier Gynt.* The pictures, such as an actress clogging in *Three Sisters from West Virginia,* expand an understanding of the process utilized by the company.

Kuftinec's discussion of the manipulation of language with Shakespearean text fills in much about the company and their exchanges with the community to create relevant culture from archaic language. While at Marmarth, North Dakota, cofounder Bill Rauch recalled "we actually said that to rewrite Shakespeare is blasphemous, but what the hell?" while working with the text of *Hamlet* for a Wild West production (73). The few snippets of lines from production texts are quite useful in understanding how the company worked.

Chapter 4, "Rural Routes," further describes the evolution of the company as it struggles as to how to define Americanism culturally. The choice of icons for posters demonstrates how various group dynamics worked amidst Cornerstone's travels and touring. Larry Tasker, the tour bus driver, might summarize many of the tales from this chapter best: "You can't solve every problem with forty people" (85). Eventually after years traveling, it became clear that there was little or no consensus about consensus. In attempts toward equity for the communities with artistic decisions, the company discovered, "Rather than solving problems by giving everyone a voice in making decisions, consensus increased the stress of the project by pressuring attendance on people who felt as though the process wasted their valuable time" (102). The conclusion of the chapter is a considers what created the conditions to make the 1991 national tour of *The Winter's Tale* the last production of the rural community-based productions.

In Chapter 5, "Urban Revisions", Kuftinec shifts the focus of the research in this chapter from archival interpretation to ethnography. And because of the move to Los Angeles residencies, Cornerstone began to rethink how they defined community: they selected "three distinct methods — by culture, age and geography" (115). Additionally since the Cornerstone ensemble members no longer experienced a residency within the community there was "decreased awareness and a sense of collaboration" and lack of awareness of potential audience members (114). As Cornerstone evolved "the politics of payment, volunteerism, and institutional diversity continued to challenge the company's restructuring" (117). But Cornerstone further developed relationships between guest artists, resident, residents, Latinos and African Americans. As within most community organizations, Cornerstone members experienced the difficult lesson that "Work time for professionals is free time for nonprofessionals" (120).

The end of the chapter considers at length aesthetic revisions within the company. Kuftinec asks a pertinent critical question: "who defines appropriate representational politics in collaborative productions: the community, Cornerstone artists, or some temporary critic/participant-observer?" (129) Scholars interested in aesthetics, and specifically current criticism toward theater in the United States, have much to consider from this chapter.

Chapter 6, "Regional Returns: A Tale of Two Collaborations," recounts Cornerstone's collaborations with Doug Wager and the Arena Stage in Washington, D.C., and the Long Wharf Theatre in New Haven, Connecticut. Drawing upon descriptions of the process from earlier productions, there is a synthesis of earlier discussions that adds an additional layer of questions about professional practices and aesthetics. Again the critical importance and audience reception of the productions are considered. Kuftinec writes "Future community-based collaborations with regional theaters may need to think further about orienting audience members to the experience" (174). And even more difficult is the critical challenge by the author to consider what is or should be an American company: "For if the nature of goodness and community is never addressed, we all stagnate as artists and citizens" (182).

Within Chapter 7, "Conclusion: Curtain Calls," the author positions focus upon two specific questions: "How does Cornerstone and, more broadly, community-based theater stage America? And what is the role of the scholar in framing this and other questions about the work?" (185) Peter Sellars responds, "To my mind, Cornerstone is on the forefront of cultural democracy. We always hear from artists telling us what America is about, but we've seldom seen artists such as these who go out and meet America. They just go out and do it" (185).

By the end of Kuftinec's writing, the reader gains a cursory understanding of how Cornerstone co-produces American theater by the community, for the community and within the community.

Kuftinec includes hundreds of names and references within the body of the work. There is a helpful five page appendix entitled "Cornerstone Production History 1986-2001." This is followed by 33 pages of truly interesting notes, 15 pages of works cited on this subject, and an index. Since there are few lines of production texts included or available in any supplemental text or appendix, the few photographs are key in the reading and understanding of the company's production elements.

Mary Jo Sodd
Central College

American Theatre and the Culture of the Cold War: Producing and Contesting Containment, 1947-1962. By Bruce McConachie. Iowa City: University of Iowa Press, 2003; pp. vii-364; $49.95 cloth.

In his landmark study *Melodramatic Formations: American Theatre and Society, 1820-1870* (University of Iowa Press, 1992), noted theatre historian Bruce McConachie offered a sophisticated and original reading of what had been (and too frequently still is) an oft maligned and ignored area of study: nineteenth century, American melodrama. Unlike many previous studies, wherein this subject was considered strictly in formalist terms as literary genre, McConachie instead charted the ever-evolving shape and scope of American melodrama as a phenomena on the theatrical stage, offered convincing arguments as to how these scripts in production were received by various audiences, and in turn, deftly demonstrated how these performed plays included discursive traces that were drawn from and concurrent with the equally dynamic major social, political and metaphysical developments in the United States during the middle years of the nineteenth century. Melodrama was thus situated as both product and producer of culture and ideology. The force of McConachie's erudite materialist reading of theatre and society in the nineteenth century was swift and profound, as is evidenced by the appearance of a number of studies on the same and related topics in the years immediately following the publication of *Melodramatic Formations.* Indeed, it does not seem an exaggeration to suggest that many able scholars, both of the nineteenth century popular theatre—e.g., Jeffrey Mason, Lisa Merrill, Rosemarie Bank, John Frick and Elizabeth Reitz Mullenix—as well as melodrama as a more largely construed cultural trope—e.g., Ben Singer and Lawrence Levine—owe a great deal to McConachie, in that their insightful reconsiderations are most surely indebted, either directly or indirectly, to the context rich mode of analysis practiced most skillfully by McConachie.

After reading McConachie's most recently published work *American Theatre and the Culture of the Cold War: Producing and Contesting Containment, 1947-1962,* I cannot help but think it likely that in three or four years time, he will again be positioned as an avatar of American theatre history and historiography. Assuming this occurs (and I am quite certain it will), I imagine one discernable dissimilarity between the quality and profile of McConachie's authority and scholarly stature circa the early 1990s, as based on *Melodramatic Formations*, and now in the first years of the new millennium, as based on *American Theatre and the Culture of the Cold War*, will be that the focus of those discussions will be less on the relative worth of the study as a critical history of cold war theatre—although, I would certainly argue that there is considerable worth on this front—and more on the sophisticated, interdisciplinary, historical methodology theorized by the author. That is to say, I project that the more far-reaching value of *American Theatre and the Culture of the Cold War* is the potential use, principally by other cultural and theatre historians, of the historiographic approach forged by McConachie, rather than the ways in which he skillfully employs it in his interpretation of the theatre in the New York in the decades immediately following World War II.

Broadly speaking, in *American Theatre and the Culture of the Cold War* McConachie is still concerned with the materiality of theatre, specifically the ways it engenders and in turn is engendered by culture. As such, he continues to rightly include in his analysis a nuanced consideration of the connectivity of economics, class, politics, and the practice of theatre. Nonetheless, by drawing on the analytical power of cognitive psychology and linguistics, principally from the work of George Lakoff and Mark Johnson, McConachie has considerably reinforced this now widely emulated materialist methodology. Near the beginning of the study, McConachie speaks to the possibilities of this approach when he suggests, "cognitive psychology holds particular promise for historians because it encourages them to discover [the] historical patterns in embodied actions centered on primary metaphors"(10). He continues, "Merging Lakoff and Johnson's cognitive psychology with [cultural theories such as] hegemony theory theoretically opens up a significant possibility for change in historical cultures. The reserve of concepts and metaphors beyond the constellations of the dominant culture constitutes a potentially enormous reservoir for different cultural constellations . . ."(15). In terms of cold war theatre, McConachie persuasively argues that the cognitive primary metaphor/ organizational schema of "containment" served to nurture and maintain the ideology of "containment liberalism" in postwar America (9). "In short," McConachie writes, "containment was the hub of a vast network of cold war conceptions that structured much of the dominant culture of the era" (12).

Following this summation of cognitive psychology, encapsulation of its potential application for the cultural historian, and overview of the "containment" metaphor, McConachie utilizes the balance of the first chapter (all told, over fifty pages of rather dense but accessible prose) to characterize more fully the terms and procedures requisite for the cultural historian interested in joining theories of culture to cognitive psychology. Correspondingly, he effectively models the process by explicating and applying the metaphor of containment in a fascinating reading of the initial productions of Clifford Odet's *Awake and Sing* and Arthur Miller's *Death of a Salesman.* As entry into this discussion, McConachie offers an absorbing and lucid discussion of the ontological shift that occurred when photographic culture gave way to radio culture, and the corresponding shift in the definition of the "real." In charting and theorizing this shift from vision to sound, McConachie not only demonstrates the fluidity of the dominant cognitive culture, but also portrays powerfully the extent to which the aesthetics and rhetoric of "containment liberalism" branded cold war culture in general, and the theatre specifically. Hence, it is in this section that the reader is offered the first glimpse in a specific sense of the stunning capacity of McConachie's method.

The bulk of the study that follows (i.e., Chapters 2, 3 and 4) is comprised of McConachie's cogent examination of three chief kinds of containment figures populating the theatrical boards on Broadway during the cold war—"the Empty Boy," "the Family Circle," and "the Fragmented Hero"—and his convincing theorization and explication of the cognitive conceptions that likely made them appealing to audiences. Each of these chapters opens with a useful and rigorous summation of the historical context that buttressed the creation and maintenance of the cognitive mechanism under consideration. So for example, in the case of the Empty Boy, McConachie argues that "the linkage between the militarization and the 'psychologization' of the nation" fashioned the Empty Boy, an "identity container that was "fundamentally empty; it had not yet been filled with an adult personality" (57). The initial Broadway productions of Michael Gazzo's *A Hatful of Rain* and George Axelrod's *The Seven Year Itch* serve as McConachie's primary examples in his reading of the hegemonic culture of the 1950s, which "praised adult males who preserved their boyishness" (57). Significantly, in the second half of each chapter McConachie offers a reading of a production and figure that in some respects served as counterpoint and antithesis to these hegemonic constructions. In his introduction McConachie explains, "The image of the homosexual shadowed the character of the Empty Boy, the black Family Circle stood behind its white counterpart, and the threat of the fecund female shaped the Fragmented Hero" (54). Hence, the initial production of Tennessee Williams's *Cat on a Hot Tin Roof*, specifically the character Brick as played by Ben Gazzara, is positioned by McConachie as an "abject Other," contesting the hegemonic containment figure of the Empty Boy.

Throughout *American Theatre and the Culture of the Cold War*, McConachie cites a truly impressive cross-section of sources, from fields as diverse as cultural history, history of aesthetics, political philosophy, rhetoric, and media studies. His cogent epilogue, which rounds out the study, offers a brief overview of the continued presence of containment in the American theatre in the years 1962-1992. While there is without question great value in McConachie's documenting of the presence of containment as a metaphor that held considerable force in structuring much of commercial theatre in the United States in the cold war era, it is nonetheless his convincing argument for, as well as the modeling of, the use of cognitive psychology as a tool available to the cultural historian that makes this study a most valuable addition to the field of theatre history. As such, all who are interested in the procedures and practices of theatre history will find McConachie's study an important, if not essential, addition to their libraries.

Jonathan Chambers
Bowling Green State University

Staging the War: American Drama and World War II. By Albert Wertheim. Bloomington & Indianapolis: Indiana University Press; 2004; pp.xviii+328. $35 cloth.

Although World War II seems familiar to us from television screenings of movies old and new, the plays of the period, which reveal something rather different about the war then in progress, are not often seen or even heard of. Even plays like *Idiot's Delight*, *Cry Havoc*, *Tomorrow the World*, and *Command Decision* which were made into movies often were re-written with important changes. Albert Wertheim's Staging the War reminds us of the way we were in the period of the war in his analysis of how playwrights dealt with the changing views of that war from the period just before to the ten years after. His is the first book that I know of that deals with the dramas presented on Broadway, on the radio and in the military camps before, during, and after the war. From curtain raisers to the war like *The Wookey* (1934) to post-war nostalgia like *No Time for Sergeants* (1955), Wertheim presents a thorough and informative work of social history as well as of drama criticism. He includes the impact of radio on a listening nation. Although he says that radio deserves a book in itself, his own account of the cooperation of writers, networks, and government to produce dramas that developed public opinion about the war and its purpose is extensive. He also examines the government's efforts to provide plays and instructions for putting on plays for the entertainment of soldiers as well as the plays provided for schoolchildren by the Treasury Department. These plays had as their propaganda mission the increasing of patriotism through the purchase of War Bonds and War Stamps. Wertheim's view is, indeed, comprehensive.

Looking not only at plays that were popular successes but also at those whose runs were short, Wertheim shows the preoccupation of the wartime playwrights and audiences with life on the home front. Indeed, the evidence reinforces the idea that the strategies of war and the reality of the battlefield become subjects for dramatic or any other kind of literature only after the battle is done. The action may be taking place on the battlefield, but the drama shows that on the home front, attitudes toward the war are seen through home front dilemmas. The housing shortage, changing relationships between the sexes when the men, and then the women, went off to war, the changing attitudes toward women and sex, and fears of what would happen if the enemy turned up in our midst provide motives for the drama.

Wertheim examines the well-known plays of the Broadway theatre (*The Voice of the Turtle*, *Watch on the Rhine*, *Tomorrow the World*, and *Winged Victory*, among many others), but he also treats the plays that are not well remembered but that he sees are, all the same, worthy of investigation and in some cases of praise. He finds neglected excellence in such plays as Dan James's *Winter Soldiers*, Rose Franken's *Soldier's Wife*, Maxine Woods's *On Whitman Avenue*, Robert Ardrey's *Jeb* and Harry Brown's *A Sound of Hunting*; and neglected authors like Edward Chodorov, even unknown musicals by Frank Loesser.

Wertheim goes beyond the obvious choices of plays that have to do with some aspect of the wartime experience to point out that national preoccupations turned up in plays not usually thought of as relevant to the war. He has interesting points to make about *Our Town* and *The Time of Your Life* as well as the historical dramas *Abe Lincoln in Illinois* and *Harriet*. Even *A Streetcar Named Desire* (1947) comes under his careful gaze as a depiction of the effect the war had on post-war America.

Taking the plays chronologically, Wertheim shows the movement from pre-war isolationism and pacifism to wartime patriotism, sometimes in the work of one author. The pacifism of Robert Sherwood's *Idiot's Delight*, for example, gives way to the more patriotic *Abe Lincoln in Illinois* and *There Shall Be No Night*. He shows that the plays reveal what Americans thought, or, in certain cases, were encouraged by the government to think, about the war, the nature of the enemy, the meaning of the conflict. Attitudes were changing, too, about social issues, and sexual and even racial stereotypes were being challenged. Still, old prejudices died hard and, not noticing that the world was changing, the Army recommended plays for production by soldiers for their own entertainment that maintain sexual and racial stereotypes.

Wertheim suggests in his introduction that his own childhood, growing up in the United States with German refugee parents, has given him reason to explore the accuracy of his memories. He shows in the course of his narrative that the World War II we have come to know, the war that has as one of its most memorable feature the horrors of the Holocaust, is not the war that Americans experienced from the works on their stage. In the immediate post-war period , playwrights showed interest in the topics of anti-Semitism in America and racial inequality, but moved on to plays that suggest the need to forget the difficulties of wartime. Even Anne Frank, he argues, is presented as an American teenager.

Wertheim's history includes not only the plays but the actors, directors, and writers whose careers were well-established before the war as well as those who were beginning their careers during the war years (e.g., Gregory Peck in *Sons and Soldiers*, Burt Lancaster in *A Sound of Hunting*, Elia Kazan directing *The Skin of Our Teeth*, Arthur Laurents, and Arthur Miller showing talented beginnings.)

This thorough survey of the Broadway stage, radio programs, and government-sponsored theatre is much needed. There are already fine studies of the films of the period and of the connections and disconnections between the government and the film makers. Wertheim's study fills us in on the importance of theatre in wartime.

Joe Kissane
Columbia University

From Traveling Show to Vaudeville: Theatrical Spectacle in America, 1830-1910. Edited by Robert M. Lewis. Baltimore, MD: The Johns Hopkins University Press, 2003; pp. xii + 384. $45 cloth.

Over the years, I've collected a number of documentary studies. Hence, from my relatively remote corner of Northwest Pennsylvania, I can easily page a diverse range of materials that were once available solely to the scholar in an archive or the myopic researcher after years of accumulation. For example, the bookshelf behind my desk allows me to read through the first casts of Otway's *Venice Preserved* (Van Lennep et. al., *The London Stage, 1660-1800)*, Barnum's business and personal correspondence (A.H. Saxon's *Selected Letters of P.T. Barnum)*, diatribes against the *Commedia dell'Arte* (Richards and Richards' *Commedia dell'Arte: A Documentary History)*, and the nature of seventeenth century French stage machinery (A.M. Nagler's *A Sourcebook in Theatrical History).* While in no way comprehensive, each of these works reflect their editors' perspectives on what the most useful, insightful, and critical documents are in understanding their respective fields. Robert M. Lewis's *From Traveling Show to Vaudeville: Theatrical Spectacle in America, 1830 – 1910* is no exception. While many might quibble with documents that were omitted from Lewis's compiled trove of sources, few could argue the book's value to the scholar or student of popular entertainments.

Lewis argues that by 1910 (the year that he halts his study), vaudeville reached its heyday, with film's surge in popularity on the immediate horizon. Yet, the reasons for why he begins his study in 1830 are a bit fuzzier and never fully articulated. The book contains marvelously detailed sections devoted to the dime museum, minstrelsy, the circus, melodrama, "leg show" burlesque extravaganzas, the Wild West show, and summer amusement parks. Lewis argues that these genres evolved into vaudeville, the subject of *From Traveling Show to Vaudeville's* last chapter. Lewis introduces each form, discussing its significance, typical presentation style, and principal personalities. His brief essays serve as illustrative prefaces, synthesizing the work of numerous historians rather than offering new scholarship or insight. Each section is comprised of audience accounts, prejudices that were levied against the forms, typical gags and jokes, essays from the period's popular press, and several extended scripts. Further, each individual selection is contextualized by the author.

Yet, the documents Lewis asks us to consider are this book's resounding strength. In a work chock-full of gems, some highlights (at least for this reviewer!) includeCharles White's long-lived minstrel olio *Oh, Hush! or, The Virginny Cupids;* the outlandish sum circus manager W.C. Coup expected to pay for a hippopotamus ($5,000); the transmogrification of William English's *Rosina Meadows, The Village Maid: or, Temptations Unveiled* from lachrymose novel to Charles H. Saunders' long-lived stage vehicle; the doggerel published by toy makers McGloughlin Brothers' celebrating the Wild West; the printed notes disseminated to vaudeville patrons daring to carry unlit cigars in their mouths. Scattered throughout the book, some of the era's leading literary figures weigh-in with their impressions of these forms, including Mark Twain, Emily Dickinson, Nathaniel Hawthorne, and Louisa May Alcott. Rescued from older periodicals and newspapers, the pieces are insightful, inspiring, and wonderfully detailed. Even Maxim Gorky details his visit to Coney Island, likening the joyous screams of an amusement rider to the "merry yelp of a puppy let to the floor after he has been held up in the air by the scruff of his neck."

While the majority of material Lewis collects is quite rare, some is readily available, including Barnum's letters, the texts of the *Mulligan Guard Ball* and *The Black Crook,* Nate Salsbury's reminiscences, and scripts that are featured on the Library of Congress's American Memory website. Still, to review this material alongside the more obscure and rare artifacts is quite valuable. Of course, specialists of popular entertainments will browse the book wondering how certain figures and pieces were omitted from this wide-ranging collection. For example, Adah Isaacs Menken makes just fleeting appearances; luminaries like the Hanlon Brothers and the Kiralfys are not to be found; the importance of the circuits and the wheels are largely ignored. In addition, Lewis tends to favor the inclusion of descriptive accounts of these genres over extant business materials. Still, perceived omissions are the nature of these sorts of compilations, and truth be told one of the pleasures of reading such works. For in the process of reading through what one scholar deems of import, we are introduced to materials that might have eluded us otherwise.

Presenting primary sources surrounding the growth of a quintessentially American form of popular entertainment, Robert M. Lewis's *From Traveling Show to Vaudeville: Theatrical Spectacle in America, 1830-1910* is a most welcome addition to our field. Indeed, my copy already has a treasured spot on my research shelf, and I'm eager to assign sections to pupils enrolled in my nineteenth century American theatre courses. The book is supplemented by a most useful and resoundingly complete annotated bibliography. In addition, numerous photographs and prints—many of which are presented in print for the first time—admirably illustrate this work.

Mark Cosdon
Allegheny College

Theatre, Culture and Temperance Reform in Nineteenth-Century America. By John W. Frick. New York: Cambridge University Press, 2003; pp. xiii + 256. $60.00 cloth.

In his groundbreaking work *Melodramatic Formations*, Bruce McConachie enumerates a plurality of dramatic inventions in his typology of plays that fall under the genre of melodrama from sensational and apocalyptic melodramas to fairy-tale, domestic, gothic and moral reform melodramas. With regard to the latter, John W. Frick's discerning study builds upon and extends the work of McConachie, David Grimsted, Peter Brooks, Rosemarie Banks et. al. by exploring the arc of the theatrical expressions of the temperance movement of the 19th century. In this carefully laid out, and well researched project, Frick wrests from oblivion the issue of temperance reform—even as other historians have largely regarded it "a near-marginal movement" (2)—and its concomitant theatrical manifestations. Such plays as *The Drunkard* and *Ten Nights in a Bar-room* (if not the issue of temperance reform) are worthy of scrutiny if for no other reason than such plays were second in popularity only to that other towering, behemoth of mid 19th century melodrama, *Uncle Tom's Cabin.* Frick successfully erases the facile binary argument that temperance plays (and melodrama in general) represent an inferior theatrical venture "while Americans waited for O'Neill" (6).

Always mindful of the drama's social origins, Frick's exegeses of these plays resonate with the rhetoric and goals of the temperance movement. One of the many strengths of this study is the researcher's recursive use of various texts to make clear the ever changing cultural influences working upon the temperance movement as expressed through the theatre. In the opening chapter Frick lays the foundation for temperance melodrama by examining the roots of the reform movement in the opening decades of the 19th century. One of the book's more engrossing chapters, the author successfully renders an American culture steeped in the use of spirits as a medicinal palliative as well as being integral to social functions such as town and business meetings, church gatherings and, ironically enough, at early intemperance meetings! Subsequent incarnations of temperance meetings (here I am thinking of the

Washingtonians) utilized a device called the "experience speech" in which reformed drinkers "narrate their own sufferings and . . . publicly embody the possibility of becoming temperate" (34).

Such narratives represented a rich source for theatrical exploitation. Frick carefully develops, in the second chapter, the social and cultural forces that served as a major influence on the temperance literature of the day in the form of gazettes, pamphlets, speeches, and pulpit sermons. He effectively argues that print media and sermons alone failed to reach the illiterate, working class masses and forwards the notion that theatre stands in bold relief to temperance literature as an oft-overlooked yet highly successful vehicle that appealed to the emotions rather than the intellect of the hoped for reformed drinker.

This idea of visually representing the various stages and consequences of alcoholism is developed further in an otherwise pedantic third chapter by the author as he explores British temperance drama in comparison to its American counterpart. The chapter is ultimately saved by Frick's analysis of caricaturist George Cruikshank's serial illustrations entitled *The Bottle* (illustrations amply and illuminatingly provided both here and throughout the book) of the "course and effects of alcoholism" (92). Cruikshank's narrative images were "directed principally at the senses; they appealed to the emotions rather than to reason" (60) and thus served as a visual reminder as to the evils that await those who take that first drink.

The fourth and perhaps most engaging chapter, is a somewhat lively read of the success of *The Drunkard* as popularized by P. T. Barnum—reformed drinker, pledge signer and teetotaler—who exhibited (and exploited) temperance dramas at his famed American Museum. Recognizing that "entertainment and morality are highly compatible" he adopted the same zeal and showmanship that he brought to his other more well-known entrepreneurial endeavors, unabashedly promoting "his moral views through artistic means" (120). Frick vividly examines other similarly successful temperance plays in this chapter such as *Ten Nights in a Bar-room* and *Hot Corn* all of which are accompanied by a parade of stock characters that leap from the page: the fallen husband, the faithful yet long-suffering wife, martyred children, the disreputable barkeeper/tavern owner and finally, the ubiquitous bottle as prop, a symbol that embodies the evils of alcohol consumption. Chapter 5 continues to explore the popularity of plays that carried a message of intemperate drinking beyond the theatres of New York to the hinterlands in the form of touring combination companies. These professional companies and other "controlled" leisure-time activities produced for regional circuit theatres or local Temperance Halls included popular songs such as "Father's a drunkard, and Mother is dead," skits, short musicals, and even, in one case, a "pro-prohibition musical for children" (164).

In the sixth and final chapter Frick briefly reviews the decline of the temperance movement as theatre is inexorably eclipsed by the rise of cinema. Hastily, he guides the reader through the shift in the temperance movement away from moral imperative to that of imposing laws of prohibition via the body politic. The anti-temperance movement is also briefly explored here and exemplified in the stereotype of the "lovable lush" made popular by Joseph Jefferson's Rip Van Winkle, and expressed in another century by Jimmy Stewart's Elwood P. Dowd in *Harvey* and the comedy of Foster Brooks in the 1970s and 80s, all of whom mined humor out of the benign, if liberal, use of alcohol.

Although not the type of work that might be embraced by the general reader, John Frick's work offers a trove of material directed to the serious scholar interested in the temperance movement and its dissemination practices in the 19th century. This study should also be of significant interest and value to the student of melodrama in general.

John R. Poole
Illinois State University

The Temptation of Innocence in the Dramas of Arthur Miller. By Terry Otten. Columbia, MO: University of Missouri Press, 2002. pp. xvi + 280; $39.95 cloth.

The single best word to describe *The Temptation of Innocence* is "comprehensive," for in both its survey of Arthur Miller's entire corpus of plays (including works for television and film) and in its incorporation of scholarly and critical commentary, this book is full and ample. In these two valuable ways, Terry Otten's study stands alongside and in some ways supercedes such standard critical works on Miller as *The Cambridge Companion to Arthur Miller* (edited by Christopher Bigsby in 1997), *Arthur Miller* by June Schlueter and James K. Flanagan (1987), and the still valuable *Critical Essays on Arthur Miller* (edited by James Martine in 1979).

In choosing to focus on Miller's career-long depiction of man's craving for innocence — a craving that to Miller is always morally self-destructive — Otten is bringing to bear a perspective that he began to define two decades earlier. *After Innocence: Visions of the Fall in Modern Literature* (1982) was a broad exposé of modern writers' attack on moral idealism. Not surprisingly, Miller was one of fifteen writers treated. *The Temptation of Innocence* has been twenty years in the making.

But first Otten sought to delve more deeply into the idea by narrowing his focus to a single writer. The result was *The Crime of Innocence in the Fiction of Toni Morrison* (1989). Thus, this book on Miller, which develops the same central themes and uses the same methods, stands as a companion volume to the one on Morrison, the book on the novelist establishing the paradigm that the one on the dramatist follows. In truth, countless passages in the former are echoed in the ideas and phrases in the latter and could be used interchangeably: "[I]nnocence is itself a sign of guilt, because it signals a degenerate acquiescence. Not to fall becomes more destructive than to fall. [Hence, t]he tragic drama of a fortunate fall is played out in a setting . . . wrought with destruction but one that is still morally superior to prolonged self-ignorance. . . ." (*Crime of Innocence*, 4-5). Lest I be misunderstood, I note this mirroring with respect, for the view that "Innocence kills." (to use Miller's own phrase from *Timebends*, 1995) rightly places both of these major writers squarely within a dominant American literary tradition that also includes authors like Hawthorne and Melville, O'Neill, Steinbeck and Faulkner. Otten emphasizes this connection in both of these volumes, and he has right to do so.

Taking his three studies together, one must concede that Otten has done all one scholar-critic can do to eradicate man's desperate penchant to plead innocent. And I mean "man's," not "humanity's," when it comes to Miller, for in play after play it is Miller's men (and often in their father-son relationship) who resist responsibility and guilt. As Otten observes, in doing so they are following their mythic ancestor in Eden who, after the fall, blamed both God and Eve. Eve on the other hand said simply, "The serpent beguiled me, and I did eat." In this regard, Otten is gracious when he deals with critics of Miller's women, for in truth they neglect the mythic when they fail to see Miller's emphasis on what seems to be a distinctly male tendency.

Our best moral hope, then, lies with Eve and with the idea of a "fortunate" fall based on her. The trope is of course old, old; nor is Otten the first to apply to Miller its accompanying idea — that innocence, though tempting, is evil. His titular phrase "the temptation of innocence," as he points out, comes from June Schlueter in her 1987 discussion of Quentin's moral maturation in *After the Fall.* Otten's contribution, then, is to show that this is "an integral theme in virtually every Miller text" (186). Accordingly, he examines the full breadth of Miller's dramatic production, from *No Villain* (1936), his first play written as a 21-year old undergraduate at the University of Michigan, to *Mr. Peters' Connections* (1998). Otten comments to some extent or other on 33 plays in all (whether or not they were produced), including one-acts and full-length dramas. Supplementing his study of the play texts, Otten interweaves references to Miller's prose works — his novel *Focus* (1947), his book of reportage *Situation Normal* (1947), a number of short stories, and most of all his numerous essays and interviews on theatre and drama. All this is undergirded by a staggering display of scholarship, reflected by an average of over five citations per page (Bigsby's work is relied upon especially heavily). The result is a text loaded with citations, summaries and documentation. It's true that Otten's prose matches the heavy weight of his topic, but the very comprehensiveness of these elements is what makes his book worth the heavy pull.

This is essentially a literary study, with only occasional considerations of production matters and Miller's role in them. Although the focus is on a theme, the chronological (or, more accurately, biographical) arrangement generally succeeds, despite Otten's inconsistency when it comes to specifying dates for the plays (amazingly, the book does not include a Chronology, either, so that the reader must keep the *Cambridge Companion* or one of the other standard works handy). The success of this approach is because Otten seeks to demonstrate the thematic continuity of Miller's plays.

Then if the "temptation of innocence" theme has remained so constant, the question naturally arises: Has Miller remained static over these many years (he was 87 and had been a playwright for more than 60 years when Otten's book appeared), and are his plays, therefore, only variations on that theme? Otten's answer is emphatically No, and he often repeats his insistence that in response to postmodernism and absurdism Miller "evolved" both thematically and dramaturgically. This seems to say that Miller both changed and remained the same, and it is not clear what Otten is truly convinced of. Every time he points to a step in Miller's evolution, he elaborately explains how the new event is at the same time a continuity of the old. One passage among many is illustrative: "Miller's confrontation with the present coexists with his continuing vision as he engages the cynicism of the postmodern era with a residue of hope long apparent in the range of his plays, forming an arc extending back to the forties when Miller's first play reached Broadway" (246). In *The Temptation of Innocence,* all things merge and "coexist" — past and present, cynicism and hope, evolution and continuity. There is a need for greater discrimination and more nuanced judgment.

This is the downside of comprehensiveness, and compounding it is an eagerness to include a multitude of other themes, all of which seem equally important as the temptation of innocence one. Otten lists the "big themes" — personal responsibility, guilt, the relation between the microcosm of the family and the macrocosm of modern society, the effect of the passing in time on memory and on perspective, and the moral stance and value of protest, [and] public and private integrity — as undeniable signature themes for Miller (179-180). It's too much, and at that it is not complete for it omits the "theme" of tragedy — whether tragedy is still possible in a world after Nietzsche and Ibsen, in which God is dead and where realism, not myth, reigns in drama. Not unlike Miller himself, Otten takes no definite position on this, though he seems to think, with dismay, that tragedy is dead.

No doubt, this overlong list of "signature themes" is owing to Miller's long and productive life. What he witnessed was enormous, and it affected his art: the Depression, the New Deal, the Second World War and the horrors of the Holocaust, the Cold War, McCarthyism, the assassinations of John F. Kennedy and Martin Luther King, Jr., the Civil Rights movement, Watergate, the Vietnam War, the collapse of Communism in Europe, and more (246-247). Otten points to these events one by one as they relate to Miller's plays (although, unaccountably, he seriously downplays Miller's deep involvement in the McCarthy hearings from 1954-1958, particularly important with regard to *The Crucible*, 1953).

The greatest strength of Otten's *Temptation of Innocence* is in demonstrating the pervasiveness of the "innocence kills" theme in Miller's works, and he is at his best when he concentrates on it alone. Surprisingly, his discussion of *Death of a Salesman* (1949) is least satisfying in this regard, with scant reference to this theme; Otten seems intimidated by the play and by the vast amount of criticism on it, and his writing is choked with citations, footnotes and attributions. But many discussions are superior and loaded with information: *All My Sons* (1947) establishes the theme; *The Crucible* is shown to continue it by way of an original and richly illuminating comparison with Robert Bolt's *A Man for All Seasons* of the same period; *A View from the Bridge* (1955-56) solidifies it. *After the Fall* (1964), though denigrated by most other critics, is the highpoint for Otten, where his theme is most fully developed and displayed. In this play, "Miller shows us that, after the Fall, the supreme temptation is innocence itself." (132). Otten's discussion is aided by another original and insightful comparison, this time to Camus' novel *La Chute* (*The Fall*, 1956). Later plays, like *Broken Glass* (1994), reiterate the theme in varying contexts; and according to Otten, Miller's last play, *Mr. Peters' Connections*, containing virtually every aspect of his theme and reverberating with nearly all the plays, is a "looking back" by Miller and an assessment "of the vast scope of his distinguished career" (246).

Such a retrospective is only appropriate. After a period when they were called passé, Arthur Miller's dramas have been staging a comeback, with revivals and festivals. Terry Otten's book contributes to that renaissance, and lends credence to the proposition that it will last.

Terry Oggel
Virginia Commonwealth University

Early American Theatre from the Revolution to Thomas Jefferson: Into the hands of the People. By Heather S. Nathans. Cambridge: Cambridge University Press, 2003. pp. xi + 246. $70.00

Heather S. Nathans is interested in the interplay between cultural and political developments as the American Revolution unfolded, and in its aftermath the conflicting ideas of "nation" as viewed by the Republicans and the Federalists. She believes that the "American theater emerged as a cultural product of conflicting ideas of nationalism--shaped by 'the hands of the people' into a uniquely American mold"(1). She seems to have read everything from William Dunlap's *History of the American Theatre* to the most recent monograph dealing with American history which she references in her introduction and in an extensive bibliography. Perhaps the most unique aspect of her book is that she has limited the scope of her study to three cities: Boston, New York and Philadelphia. While this seems to be going against the grain of much of contemporary scholarship that includes French, Spanish and Native American dramatic activity in studies of eighteenth-century America theater, Nathans has limited her study to cities that she believes were "the most economically powerful, and, one might contend, the most intellectually and culturally advanced cities in the new nation"(2). Anticipating cries of anguish from defenders of Charleston and other southern cities, she makes a strong case that different economic and political structures separated the southern colonies, later states, from those in the north.

Nathans begins her first chapter by examining pre-war attitudes towards the theater in the three cities surveyed. Groups that opposed the theater usually did so with either a religious or anti-British bias. Elites who supported the theater identified it with civilization and, specifically, with British culture. Religious leaders sought an ideal society that excluded the theater, and elites a cultivated society with theater a necessary and important status symbol. But motives became more complicated as the century progressed when attitudes towards the theater began to be identified with local political factions. It becomes more difficult to identify specific causes of anti-theatrical legislation without understanding local politics and the infighting that occurred in local assemblies.

In Chapter two, Nathans explores the post-war efforts to re-establish the theater after the Continental Congress had forbid the production of plays, and the British occupying New York and Philadelphia had spent much of their time staging plays. Scholars disagree whether the British efforts encouraged or discouraged theater after the war. The Anglican elites who had supported the theater were identified with the Tories. With loyalists fleeing the country to Canada and back to England, the pro-theater crowd faced a stiff challenge in re-gaining acceptance of theater as an honorable activity. Nathans notes that 'by the end of the war for many citizens anti-theatricalism had become identified with patriotism, and by extension, republican virtue"(39). For theater to regain some measure of its former authority after the Revolution, it became necessary for it to preach "republican" virtues. Fortunately, after the war there was a shift in power from the "Old Revolutionaries" to a younger generation of elites focussed on establishing "banks, corporations, and cultural institutions to place them on the world stage"(48). This shift in power took several years and the "movers and shakers" of commercial development were many of the same men who attempted to re-established the theater. Nathans identifies many of these men in the three cities under investigation.

In Chapter three, the author reviews the success of Boston and Philadelphia in building new theaters and attracting audiences in the early national period. Business elites established the Federal Street Theatre in Boston and the Chestnut in Philadelphia to challenge comparison with the best houses of Europe. While they wanted a theater that would improve manners and educate the public about their views of nationalism, political events in France turned the theaters into a forum over the merits of the Revolution. As Federalists tended to support Britain and the anti-Federalists the French, tensions arose during performances if any part of the evening offended one side or the other. Also class differences became an issue over division of the audience into box, pit, and gallery. Surely in a republican form of government, there should be no recognition of any kind of class distinction. Managers were torn between offering audiences the latest dramatic fare from Europe(edited, of course, to remove aristocratic references) and producing inferior but nationalistic plays written by Americans. Meanwhile economic conditions in the 1790s bankrupted many of the new post-war "movers and shakers" and together with the yellow fever epidemic, threatened the existence of these new status symbols of wealth and power.

In chapter four, Nathans relates how the working classes developed their own theaters in opposition to elitest Federal and Chestnut theaters. The growing strength of the Democratic-Republican party parallels the attempts by the mechanics to establish their own playhouses with their own plays and entertainment. While the Haymarket Theatre in Boston did not succeed, the success of Ricketts's Circus in Philadelphia when compared with the financial woes of the Chestnut Theatre suggests that the elites were losing ground. The same comparison can be made in politics with the decline of the Federalists under attack by the urban underclass and the new populations of the west. The flow of power was away from the post-war elites to the common people and this trend would be played out in the early nineteenth century theaters.

In her next chapter, Nathans explains that the New York theater differed because it lacked a republican ideology. The merchant elites who financed the building of the Park Theatre wanted it as a means to social, political and financial advancement. Like the founders of the Boston and Philadelphia theaters, they were the "movers and shakers" who established banks, businesses, and supported the passage of the Federal Constitution. But they differed in that they seemed to have no "overt political or ideological motives for the creation of their theater"(128). The financial depression of the 1790s destroyed many of the backers and made the building of the Park Theatre difficult. In examining financial records of the time, Nathans makes sense of the relationship between commerce and the theater.

In her last chapter, the author suggests that the rise to power of Thomas Jefferson and the election of 1800 marks "a turning point in the development of America's national drama"(150). With republican simplicity came a wave of sentimental drama that seemed to follow the Romantic revolution in Europe. The author reviews the failure of Dunlap's *Andre*, the death of Washington and the theater's response, and the attempts by theaters in Boston, Philadelphia and New York to broaden their appeal to include a wider spectrum of the population. The transfer of power from the founding fathers to the next generation of leaders was a painful process for the nation and for the theater, but necessary if both were to survive. In her Epilogue, the author notes how the theater provided a forum for the people to debate differing views of nationhood. This was a time when the theater mattered in the life of the nation, and Nathans makes the case clearly and concisely. At the end of the book she includes Tables that provide the names of the founders of the Boston, Philadelphia and New York theaters and their connection to banking, commercial and political allegiances.

This is an important book because it goes beyond the generalities of earlier histories and provides specific evidence to link theaters in the early national period with financial and political institutions. Nathans claims that while the immediate post-war theater reflected Enlightenment ideals, after Jefferson's election, the "Revolutionary Center" shifted away from enlightenment to one of sentiment and feeling. In other words the Romantic Revolution had arrived in America. The subtitle of this book is: "Into the Hands of the People." This means that after the Jefferson election, control of the theater began to pass from elites to the people. And in the early years of the nineteenth-century, we will find increasing evidence of what a democratic theater means. Tocqueville explains it vividly in his *Democracy in America* written after his visit of 1831.

Nathans writes well and her research is impressive. She explains her points clearly although her summaries are a bit redundant. Also she is too content at times to use secondary sources without analysis. For example, she quotes Jeffrey H. Richards' opinion on Washington's execution of Major John Andre' without comment (159). But these are minor faults. Nathans has written the most thorough cultural analysis of the theater in Boston, Philadelphia and New York for the last two decades of the eighteenth-century. Her book should remind us all that a thorough knowledge of American history is necessary to connect the dots and make sense of the American theater, that most public of the arts.

Tice L. Miller
University of Nebraska-Lincoln

Books Received

The listing of a book in this section does not preclude subsequent review.

Albright, Daniel. *Beckett and Aesthetics*. New York, NY: Cambridge University Press, 2003. pp. vii + 179. $60 cloth.

Allain, Paul. *The Art of Stillness: The Theater Practice of Tadashi Suzuki*. New York, NY: Palgrave/Macmillan, 2003. pp. x + 214. $18.95 paper.

Barbour, Richmond. Before *Orientalism: London's Theatre of the East, 1576-1626*. New York, NY: Cambridge University Press, 2003. pp. xii + 238. $60 cloth.

Blackadder, Neil. *Performing Opposition: Modern Theater and the Scandalized Audience*. Westport, CT: Praeger, 2003. $69.95 cloth.

Bower, Martha Gilman. *"Color Struck" — Under the Gaze: Ethnicity and the Pathology of Being in the Plays of Johnson, Hurston, Childress, Hansberry, and Kennedy*. Westport, CT: Praeger, 2003. pp. xii + 158. $49.95 cloth.

Bratton, Jacky. *New Readings in Theatre History*. New York, NY: Cambridge University Press, 2003. pp. xi + 238. $55 cloth.

Charlton, David, ed. *The Cambridge Guide to Grand Opera*. New York, NY: Cambridge University Press, 2003. pp. xxi + 496. $70 cloth, $26 paper.

Chen, Xiaomei, ed. *Reading the Right Text: An Anthology of Contemporary Chinese Drama*. Honolulu, HI: University of Hawaii Press, 2003. pp. x + 457. $65 cloth, $29.95 paper.

Crespy, David A. *Off-Off Broadway Explosion: How Provocative Playwrights of the 1960s Ignited a New American Theater*. New York, NY: Back Stage Books, 2003. pp. 192. $19.95 paper.

Davis, Tracy C. and Thomas Postlewait, eds. *Theatricality*. New York, NY: Cambridge University Press, 2004. pp. xi + 243. $55 cloth, $20 paper.

Erne, Lukas. *Shakespeare as Literary Dramatist*. New York, NY: Cambridge University Press, 2003. pp. xii + 287. $65 cloth.

Foulkes, Richard. *Performing Shakespeare in the Age of Empire*. New York, NY: Cambridge University Press, 2003. pp. x + 235. $70 cloth.

Frank, Marcie. *Gender, Theatre, and the Origins of Criticism.* New York, NY: Cambridge University Press, 2003. pp. ix + 175. $60 cloth.

Frick, John W. *Theatre, Culture, and Temperance Reform in Nineteenth Century America.* New York, NY: Cambridge University Press, 2003. pp. 270. $70 cloth.

Gewirtz, Arthur and James J. Kolb, eds. *Experimenters, Rebels, and Disparate Voices: The Theatre of the 1920s Celebrates American Diversity.* Westport, CT: Praeger, 2003. pp. xvii + 196. $59.85 cloth.

Grantley, Darryll. *English Dramatic Interludes, 1300-1580: A Reference Guide.* New York, NY: Cambridge University Press, 2004. pp. xvi + 427. $95 cloth.

Griffin, Gabriele. *Contemporary Black and Asian Women Playwrights in Britain.* New York, NY: Cambridge University Press, 2003. pp. x + 291. $65 cloth.

Harris, Jonathan Gil and Natasha Korda, eds. *Staged Properties in Early Modern English Drama.* New York, NY: Cambridge University Press, 2002. pp. x + 347. $70 cloth.

Harvell, Tony A. *Latin American Dramatists Since 1945: A Bio-Bibliographical Guide.* Westport, CT: Praeger, 2003. pp. vii + 504. $90 cloth.

Hauser, Frank and Russell Reich. *Notes on Directing.* New York, NY: RCR Creative Press, 2003. pp.xxvii + 126. $19.95 cloth.

Herr, Christopher J. *Clifford Odets and American Political Theatre.* Westport, CT: Praeger, 2003. pp. xii + 177. $49.95 cloth.

Hill, Errol G. and James V. Hatch. *A History of African American Theatre.* New York, NY: Cambridge University Press, 2003. pp. 632. $110 cloth.

Hirsh, James. *Shakespeare and the History of Soliloquies.* Cranbury, NJ: Associated University Presses, 2003. pp. 470. $75 cloth.

Horn, Barbara Lee. *Edward Albee: A Research and Production Sourcebook.* Westport, CT: Praeger, 2003. pp. ix + 325. $79.95 cloth.

Houchin, John. *Censorship of the American Theatre in the Twentieth Century.* New York, NY: Cambridge University Press, 2003. pp. ix + 332. $70 cloth.

Innes, Christoper, ed. *A Routledge Literary Sourcebook on Ibsen's* Hedda Gabler. New York, NY: Routledge, 2003. pp. xiv + 184.

Jeyifo, Biodun. *Wole Soyinka.* New York, NY: Cambridge University Press, 2003. pp. xxxiii + 322. $70 cloth.

Kattwinkel, Susan, ed. *Audience Participation: Essays on Inclusion in Performance.* Westport, CT: Praeger, 2003. pp. xviii + 221. $69.95 cloth.

Kuftinec, Sonja. *Staging America: Cornerstone and Community-Based Theater.* Carbondale, IL: Southern Illinois University Press, 2003. pp. 272. $45 cloth.

Lewis, Robert M. *From Traveling Show to Vaudeville: Theatrical Spectacle in America, 1830-1910.* Baltimore, MD: Johns Hopkins University Press. pp. 400. $45 cloth.

Malarcher, Jay. *The Classically American Comedy of Larry Gelbart.* Lanham, MD: Scarecrow Press, 2003. pp. xvi + 294. $44.95 cloth.

Marker, Frederick J. and Lise-Lone Marker. *Strindberg and Modernist Theatre: Post-Inferno Drama on the Stage.* New York, NY: Cambridge University Press, 2002. pp. xi + 176. $65 cloth.

Mordden, Ethan. *One More Kiss: The Broadway Musical in the 1970s.* New York, NY: Palgrave, 2003. vi + 264. $27.95 cloth.

Nathans, Heather S. *Early American Theatre from the Revolution to Thomas Jefferson.* New York, NY: Cambridge University Press, 2003. pp. 258. $70 cloth.-

Nivelon, François. *The Rudiments of Genteel Behavior: Facsimile Reprint of the First Edition of 1737.* Seattle, WA: University of Washington Press, 2003. pp. 72. $16.95 paper.

O'Higgins, Laurie. *Women and Humor in Classical Greece.* New York, NY: Cambridge University Press, 2003. pp. x + 262. $60 cloth.

Otten, Terry. *The Temptation of Innocence in the Dramas of Arthur Miller.* Columbia, MO: University of Missouri Press, 2002. pp. xvi + 280. $39.95 cloth.

Patterson, Michael. *Strategies of Political Theatre: Post-War British Playwrights.* New York, NY: Cambridge University Press, 2003. pp. xviii + 232. $70 cloth.

Sauer, David K. and Janice A. Sauer. *David Mamet: A Research and Production Sourcebook.* Westport, CT: Praeger, 2003. pp. xi + 382. $75 cloth.

Schafer, Elizabeth and Susan Bradley Smith, eds., *Playing Australia: Australian Theatre and the International Stage.* Amsterdam, The Netherlands: Rodopi B.V., 2003. pp. ix + 230. $60 paper.

Schanke, Robert A. *That Furious Lesbian: The Story of Mercedes de Acosta.* Carbondale, IL: Southern Illinois University Press, 2003. pp. xxv + 210. $45 cloth, $25 paper.

Schanke, Robert A., ed. and with an Introduction. *Women in Turmoil: Six Plays by Mercedes de Acosta.* Carbondale, IL: Southern Illinois University Press, 2003. pp. xxviii + 252. $40 cloth.

Schiesaro, Alessandro. *The Passions in Play:* Thyestes *and the Dynamics of Senecan Drama.* New York, NY: Cambridge University Press, 2003. pp. xii + 284. $65 cloth.

Smith, Grady, trans. and with an Introduction. *Travel Abroad: Frulovisi's* Peregrinatio. Tempe, AZ: Arizona Center for Medieval and Renaissance Studies, 2003. pp. vii + 166. $30 cloth.

Taylor, Diana. *The Archive and the Repertoire: Performing Cultural Memory in the Americas.* Durham, NC: Duke University Press, 2003. pp. xx + 326. $79.95 cloth, $22.95 paper.

Turra, Elisabetta Caminer, trans. and ed. *Selected Writings of an Eighteenth-Century Venetian Woman of Letters.* Chicago, IL: University of Chicago Press, 2004. pp. xxxv + 234. $21 paper.

Walsh, David and Len Platt. *Musical Theatre and American Culture.* Westport, CT: Praeger, 2003. xiii + 200. $64.95 cloth.

Wertheim, Albert. *Staging War: American Drama and World War II.* Bloomington, IN: Indiana University Press, 2004. pp. 304. $35 cloth.

Wiles, David. *A Short History of Western Performance Space.* New York, NY: Cambridge University Press, 2003. pp. ix + 316. $60 cloth.

Witham, Barry B. *The Federal Theatre Project: A Case Study.* New York, NY: Cambridge University Press, 2003. pp. xiii + 190. $60 cloth.

Worthen, W.B. *Shakespeare and the Force of Modern Performance.* New York, NY: Cambridge University Press, 2003. pp. vii + 274. $60 cloth, $22 paper.

Ziter, Edward. *The Orient on the Victorian Stage.* New York, NY: Cambridge University Press, 2003. pp. ix + 235. $65 cloth.